# SHAPING THE NORTH STAR STATE

## A HISTORY OF MINNESOTA'S BOUNDARIES

## Minnesota: Bordering States and Provinces

Ontario

Manitoba

Lake of the Woods

North Dakota

Lake Superior

Minnesota

Michigan

South Dakota

Wisconsin

Iowa

N
W E
S

0    50   100        200
Miles

By: Matthew S. Lassonde

# SHAPING THE NORTH STAR STATE

## A HISTORY OF MINNESOTA'S BOUNDARIES

## William E. Lass

## NORTH STAR PRESS OF ST. CLOUD, INC.
### Saint Cloud, Minnesota

# DEDICATION

*To Barbara and Bill, one-time boundary tourists.*

Copyright © 2014 William E. Lass

ISBN 978-0-87839-700-6

Much of chapter three was previously published in *Minnesota History* (Winter 1987) and is reproduced here with the permission of the Minnesota Historical Society

First Edition: May 2014

Printed in the United States of America

Published by
North Star Press of St. Cloud, Inc.
P.O. Box 451
St. Cloud, Minnesota 56302

# ACKNOWLEDGMENTS

The English poet John Donne probably was not thinking about book acknowledgments when he wrote "no man is an island" about four centuries ago. Nonetheless, his timeless words seem appropriate for this occasion. My research and writing experience has been enhanced by the gracious assistance and support of some individuals and organizations. My initial study of the Minnesota-Canada boundary was facilitated by research grants from the Minnesota Historical Society and Minnesota State University, Mankato.

Peter Jarnstrom, interlibrary loan librarian of Memorial Library at Minnesota State University, Mankato, helped locate and obtain sometimes elusive source materials. Patricia Maus, university archivist and special collections curator, University of Minnesota Duluth, promptly and cordially responded to my requests for information and illustrations. Anne R. Kaplan, editor of *Minnesota History*, encouraged me to undertake various studies that have contributed to my gaining a better understanding of the broad milieu of Minnesota history. Deborah L. Miller, research specialist, Minnesota Historical Society, was of invaluable assistance in locating materials, including photographs.

Additionally, I am obligated to David G. Malaher of Kenora, Ontario, who has a long-standing interest in the history of the Canada-United States boundary. Visiting and corresponding with him has helped shape my perspectives on the Ontario-Minnesota boundary section. Furthermore, he and his wife, Rosemary, graciously hosted me during my last trip to Lake of the Woods.

For help with the technical aspects of boundary determination, I am indebted to Kyle K. Hipsley, acting commissioner, United States Section, International Boundary Commission and Trevor Wolf, assistant engineer, Winnebago County, Iowa.

I thank Matthew S. Lassonde and James Zierdt for preparing the maps and Martin D. Mitchell, professor of geography, Minnesota State University, Mankato, for his interest and advice during that process.

I appreciate the assistance of Daardi Sizemore, Anne Stenzel and Harry Perkins of Memorial Library, Minnesota State University, Mankato, and Charles Scott of the State Historical Society of Iowa for facilitating my search for photographs and other illustrations.

Lastly, I thank my children, Barbara and Bill, for their continuing encouragement and moral support.

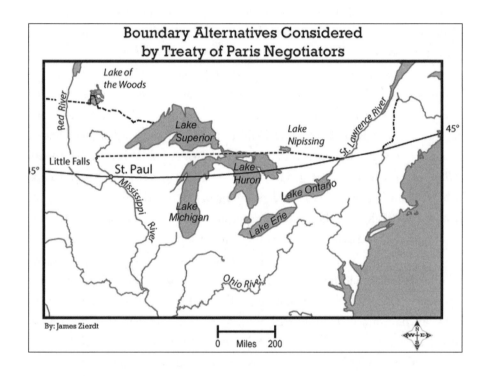

Boundary Alternatives Considered
by Treaty of Paris Negotiators

Lake of
the Woods

Red River

Lake
Superior

Lake
Nipissing

St. Lawrence River

45°

Little Falls

St. Paul

Lake
Huron

15°

Mississippi River

Lake
Michigan

Lake Ontario

Lake Erie

Ohio River

By: James Zierdt

0    Miles    200

N
W   E
S

# PREFACE

INNESOTA IS BOUNDED BY THE Canadian provinces of Manitoba and Ontario on the north, Michigan (in Lake Superior) and Wisconsin on the east, Iowa on the south and North Dakota and South Dakota on the west. The international boundary was determined first followed in chronological order by the southern, eastern and western boundaries.

In the 1857 congressional act that authorized the creation of the Minnesota statehood process, these boundaries were specified as:

> Beginning at the point in the centre of the main channel of the Red River of the North, where the boundary line between the United States and the British possessions crosses the same; thence up the main channel of said river to that of the Boix [i. e. Bois] des Sioux River; thence [up] the main channel of said river to Lake Travers [sic]; thence up the centre of said lake to the southern extremity thereof; thence in a direct line to the head of Big Stone Lake; thence through its centre to its outlet; thence by a due south line to the north line of the State of Iowa; thence east along the northern boundary of said State to the main channel of the Mississippi River; thence up the main channel of said river, and following the boundary line of the State of Wisconsin, until the same intersects the Saint Louis River; thence down said river to and through Lake Superior, on the boundary line of Wisconsin and Michigan, until it intersects the dividing line between the United States and the British possessions; thence up Pigeon River, and following said dividing line to the place of beginning.[1]

A casual look at Minnesota's boundaries suggests a rigidity that belies past contentions, quarrels and uncertainties. With respect to history, some observers use the cliché that there are no ifs in the past. Such a view leaves the impression that history is a mere recording of accomplished facts. Anyone who studies the past should consider that every generation lived in its own present, which in turn had to deal with the ifs of its time. Thus, people of any time had alternative paths to their destiny. This aspect is certainly evident in Minnesota's boundary history. At various times, all of Minnesota's boundaries were in flux. The story of their development helps explain an important dimension of Minnesota's past.

Minnesota's limits, like those of the other forty-nine states, are political boundaries. With the exception of Hawaii, all American states share at least one boundary with neighboring states and provinces. Thus, boundaries are usually dividing lines separating political entities. This feature means that state boundaries were oftentimes created by external forces before the state was formed. Minnesota's northern, southern and eastern boundaries pre-date the formation of Minnesota Territory in 1849.

The international boundary resulted from treaties between the United States and Great Britain. The southern boundary was an outcome of Iowa's campaign to become a state. Minnesota's eastern boundary was defined by the achievement of statehood for Michigan and Wisconsin. However, the western boundary was an offspring of Minnesota territorial politics, when there was a dispute between advocates of a north-south state (the present shape) and an east-west state stretching from the Mississippi and St. Croix rivers to the Missouri River.

My interest in Minnesota's boundaries dates to the fall of 1960, when I began teaching Minnesota history at what was then Mankato State College. Like virtually everyone who has contemplated the origins of Minnesota's boundaries, I was first intrigued by the Northwest Angle in Lake of the Woods. In attempting to explain this oddity and other boundary features to students I soon determined that secondary accounts, such as those published in general histories, were incomplete and sometimes erroneous. Doing research for classroom purposes caused me to consider writing a history of Minnesota's boundaries. I discussed the possibility with June D. Holmquist, the Minnesota Historical Society's assistant director, for publication and research. As a result of these meetings I decided to devote my study to the Minnesota-Canada boundary. The result was my book *Minnesota's Boundary with Canada: Its Evolution since 1783*, published by the Minnesota Historical Society Press in 1980.

Among other things, I was pleased that I had proven that the Northwest Angle was the logical result of Anglo-American diplomacy and surveying. I must confess that over the years I have been disappointed by the persistence of the urban myth that the angle was caused by a surveyor's error.

As part of my research on Minnesota's political origins, I later studied the formation of the Minnesota-Wisconsin boundary. This led to the publication of my article "Minnesota's Separation from Wisconsin: Boundary Making on the Upper Mississippi Frontier" in the Winter 1987 issue of *Minnesota History*.

While writing about Minnesota's boundaries with Canada and Wisconsin, I continued to be interested in doing a history of all of the state's boundaries. In this history I have drawn on my previous publications. The coverage of Minnesota's boundary with Canada in this book is mainly derived from my 1980 book. However, I have updated the scholarship and made the story of the international boundary current. Much of the chapter on the Minnesota-Wisconsin boundary is from my 1987 article but I have added information from the *Congressional Globe* and other sources, and described the surveying of the boundary's meridian line portion from the St. Louis River to the St. Croix River.

Minnesota's boundary with Wisconsin is well-recognized. Traditionally, Minnesota maps have clearly shown the boundary following the Mississippi and St. Croix rivers, the short meridian line and the St. Louis River. But until very recent times, Minnesota's 54.43-mile boundary with Michigan in Lake Superior has not been depicted on maps. This boundary section dates to the creation of the states of Michigan and Minnesota, but it was not formally determined until 1947, as part of a tri-state agreement by Minnesota, Michigan and

Wisconsin. The Lake Superior areas of the three states were not added to the state areas until the United States Census Bureau acted in 1990. The addition of part of Lake Superior to the state's area has resulted in a changed perception of the shape of northeastern Minnesota.

The coverage of Minnesota's southern and western boundaries is derived entirely from new research. This is the first history to explain the reason for the determination of the Minnesota-Iowa boundary as a latitudinal line. In some ways, researching and writing the chapter about Minnesota's western boundary was the most trying. As I progressed with the research, I found that the boundary question had to be considered in a political context that included territorial contention over proposed capital removal and railroad construction.

This is the first history to systematically describe the shaping of Minnesota. I hope it will enable Minnesotans and others to better understand the development of the North Star State.

NOTE:

1. *U. S. Statutes at Large,* 11: 166.

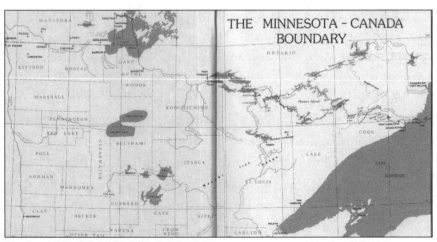

Courtesy of the Minnesota Historical Society.

# CHAPTER ONE

## ESTABLISHING THE NORTHERN BOUNDARY

INNESOTA'S NORTHERN BOUNDARY was created by three treaties between the United States and Great Britain. That portion starting in Lake Superior to the northwest point of Lake of the Woods resulted from the Paris Peace Treaty of 1783, which ended the Revolutionary War, and the Webster-Ashburton Treaty of 1842. The remainder of the northern boundary was delineated by the Convention of 1818.

In 1779, when the government of the Second Continental Congress first considered a peace treaty with Great Britain, its boundary preferences were influenced by recent history. During their long North American struggle, France and Great Britain had never agreed on boundaries separating their rival claims. But the situation was changed dramatically in 1763, at the end of the fourth colonial war between the two powers. Britain won the French and Indian War (called the Seven Years' War in Europe) so decisively that France was forced to relinquish Canada and all land claims south of the Great Lakes between the Appalachian Mountains and the Mississippi River. Presuming that the British would take over all French claims in North America, France had transferred Louisiana Territory to Spain in 1762.[1]

With France out and the Mississippi separating its new acquisitions from Spanish Louisiana, Great Britain was free to propose a grand colonial design. Part of the Royal Proclamation of 1763 drew a formal boundary between French-speaking Quebec and the English colonies to its south. Quebec's southern boundary, which extended from the Atlantic to the southeast corner of Lake Nipissing, included two direct courses. The demarcation from the Connecticut River to the St. Lawrence River was the forty-fifth parallel. From the point where that line touched the St. Lawrence, the boundary ran due northwest

1

to the southeast corner of Lake Nipissing, about fifty miles northeast of Lake Huron.[2]

The congress was well aware of the Lake Nipissing and forty-fifth parallel lines when it contemplated the future northern boundary of the United States. Its first preference was the Lake Nipissing line, which, congressmen proposed, be extended due west to the Mississippi. If that was unattainable, a forty-fifth parallel boundary to the Mississippi was acceptable.[3]

From the start of its boundary considerations, American policy makers wanted a northern boundary based on Quebec's southern limits under the Royal Proclamation and a Mississippi River western boundary. Desirous of their new nation reaching the Mississippi, congressmen implicitly rejected any notion of dealing with Britain on the principle of *uti possidetis* (literally, "as you possess") because Americans occupied only a portion of the land west of the Appalachians. Instead, they based their Mississippi claims on America's legal right to the land under the sea-to-sea colonial charters of six states and New York's protectorate of the Iroquois Indians.[4]

The Articles of Confederation government, which succeeded the Second Continental Congress, did not require the American negotiating team at Paris in 1782 to strictly follow its boundary desires. Nonetheless, the peacemakers, dominated by John Jay and Benjamin Franklin, proposed both the Lake Nipissing and forty-fifth parallel boundaries to the Mississippi. Such dividing lines would have had profound effects on the shaping of Minnesota. A Lake Nipissing line would have struck the Mississippi slightly upstream from present-day Little Falls and a forty-fifth parallel boundary would have run through the later site of St. Paul.[5]

The British government, while inclined to be generous to the United States with the aim of negotiating peace without involving America's allies, France and Spain, had reservations about both direct line boundaries. The lines, which would run through the Great Lakes, not only would have severed the trade route of British fur traders but would also have added land north of the lakes to the United States.

Partially to mollify British concerns, the American negotiators proposed a water line boundary from the point where the forty-fifth parallel struck the St. Lawrence to the northwest point of Lake of the Woods. Such a natural boundary, the diplomats reasoned, would have the advantage of being visible on the ground, or so it would seem to people on opposite shores.

Once they agreed that the United States would be bounded on the north by the Great Lakes and on the west by the Mississippi River, American and British diplomats reached a boundary agreement. From the western end of the forty-fifth parallel boundary, the line was to run through the middle of all rivers, lakes and connecting waterways to Lake Superior. In Lake Superior, the boundary deviated from the middle course. The treaty, ratified by both countries in 1783, prescribed that the boundary was to be drawn "through Lake Superior Northward of the Isles Royal & Phelipeaux to the Long Lake, thence through the middle of said Long Lake and the water communication between it and the Lake of the Woods, to the said Lake of the Woods, thence through the said Lake to the Northwestern Point thereof." At the end of this water line the boundary was to be "on a due West Course to the River Mississippi. . . ."[6]

Unwittingly, the treaty specified a geographic impossibility. The negotiators believed that a due west line from the northwesternmost point of Lake of the Woods would intersect the Mississippi, because they relied primarily on John Mitchell's *Map of the British and French Dominions in North America with the Roads, Distances, Limits and Extent of Settlement.* Mitchell, a Virginia-born medical doctor who spent most of his life in Great Britain, first published the map in 1755. By the Paris negotiations of 1782, the map, which had gone through many editions, was reputed to be the best depiction of North American geography. But it had some serious flaws. Although he used firsthand travel accounts for many of the map's features, Mitchell also simply copied some details from other maps. His illustration of Lake Superior and the region westward was a composite derived from several other maps.[7]

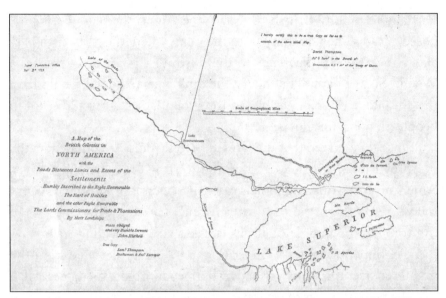

Copy of the northwest portion of John Mitchell's map of North America drawn by David Thompson. (Source: U.S. Congress. House. Report on Boundary between the United States and Great Britain, 25th Cong., 2d sess., H. Doc. 451, Appendix D, Serial Set 331)

In and west of Lake Superior, only five places on the Mitchell Map—Isle Royale, Isle Phelipeaux, Long Lake, Lake of the Woods and the Mississippi River—were mentioned in the treaty. Isle Phelipeaux proved to be non-existent. Long Lake, in the Pigeon River location, was shown as the estuary of a large river emanating from Lake of the Woods. British fur traders, who had been trading through Grand Portage for years before the treaty, never identified the Pigeon River as Long Lake. Lake of the Woods was elliptically shaped with a southeast-northwest axis, so it had a discernible northwest point. The source of the Mississippi was obscured by an inset of the Hudson Bay region. To explain the river which emerged from under the inset, Mitchell inscribed, "The Head of the Missisipi [sic] is not yet known: It is supposed to arise about the 50th degree of Latitude, and Western bounds of this Map."[8]

Anyone who accepted the map could only conclude that Lake of the Woods was the source of the Great Lakes watershed and that the northern and western boundaries of the United States would intersect due west of the lake's northwest point.

Why did the American and British negotiators rely so heavily on a map that contained major errors? They were unaware of its deficiencies and there was no better map. If they had done systematic research, they would certainly have found the correct nature of the Great Lakes drainage system. But their purpose was to conclude a peace treaty, not to complete a scholarly research project. If they had had the inclination and time they could have sought the advice of fur traders, who were very familiar with the Lake Superior-Lake of the Woods region. But both sides were anxious to reach an agreement without French and Spanish participation. The Americans, especially, realized that their former enemy was much more receptive to their territorial demands than their wartime allies. Like diplomats of any time, they knew they could not solve all potential problems. Furthermore, none of them saw any great value in the wilderness region west of Lake Superior.

Any land-minded American should never regret the geographical errors incorporated in the peace treaty. If the diplomats had used a map that properly showed the St. Louis River as the source of the Great Lakes and Lake Itasca as the Mississippi's source, they undoubtedly would have agreed on a boundary from the source of the St. Louis River to Lake Itasca. Such a line would have altered drastically the course of Minnesota's development.

The Anglo-American goodwill during the peace negotiations soon lapsed. A change of British ministries, disputes over American payments to Loyalists for appropriated property and complaints from fur traders about the boundary that evidently left their important Grand Portage post in the United States hardened attitudes. The British refused to order their traders to evacuate American soil and the United States did not have the power to evict them.[9]

The northwest boundary question languished until February 1792, when George Hammond, the British minister to the United States, came into possession of a map showing the Mississippi's source south of Lake of the Woods. If accurate, the map would prove that there was a northwest boundary gap between the northern and western limits of the United States. Since any gap closure would probably reduce America's land claims, Thomas Jefferson, secretary of state in the George Washington administration, refused to acknowledge that the map sent to Hammond positively proved there was a northwest boundary gap.[10]

But the United States soon had to recognize there was a gap. In 1797-1798, the British trader-astronomer-cartographer David Thompson completed a wide-ranging reconnaissance that carried him from Grand Portage, to Lake of the Woods, to the Missouri River back to the upper Mississippi. In April 1798, Thompson reached Turtle Lake, about ten miles north of present Bemidji. Proclaiming it to be the Mississippi's northern source, he determined its latitude was well south of Lake of the Woods.[11]

Thompson's determination was widely circulated with the 1801 publication of Alexander Mackenzie's *Voyages from Montreal on the St. Laurence, Through the Continent of North America, to the Frozen and Pacific Oceans; In the years 1789 and 1793*. James Madison, secretary of state in Thomas Jefferson's administration, accepted Thompson's conclusion that the Mississippi started south of Lake of the Woods. Therefore, Madison authorized Rufus King, American minister to Great Britain, to add the northwest boundary gap to the agenda for negotiations on all outstanding boundary matters with Lord Hawkesbury, Britain's secretary of state for foreign affairs.[12]

King and Hawkesbury concluded their Convention of 1803 on May 12, 1803. Most of it pertained to northeastern boundary issues, but Article Five stipulated that in the northwest a direct line would be drawn from the northwest point of Lake of the Woods to the nearest source of the Mississippi.[13]

The desirability of that provision was soon called into question. Two days after signing the convention, King learned that on April 30, the United States had agreed to buy Louisiana Territory from France. Since Louisiana did not have specified boundaries, Article Five of the Convention of 1803 might enable Britain to propose that the northeast corner of the territory be shifted south from the northwest point of Lake of the Woods to the Mississippi's nearest source.[14]

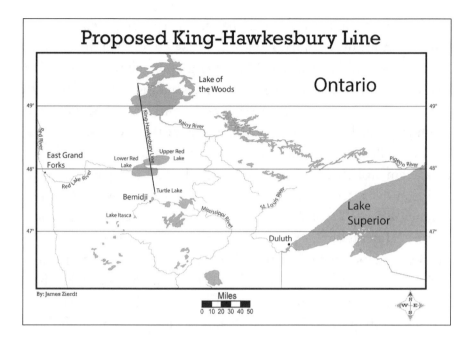

When he received the Louisiana Purchase Treaty and the Convention of 1803, President Thomas Jefferson worried that the convention's Article Five threatened to limit America's Louisiana claims . Louisiana's extent was known only generally. Jefferson's Paris negotiators, Robert R. Livingston and James Monroe, had agreed to buy the territory "with all its rights and appurtenances as fully and in the same manner as they have been acquired by the French Republic" under the Treaty of San Ildefonso. In 1800, when Spain retroceded Louisiana to France at San Ildefonso, the territory was described as having the same extent that it had when France possessed it before 1762.[15]

When Congress reconvened in October 1803, Jefferson made sure that the Senate considered the Louisiana Purchase treaty without reference to the Convention of 1803. He withheld the King-Hawkesbury agreement until the Senate approved the treaty with France. Believing that Article Five of the Convention of 1803 threatened to reduce Louisiana's extent, the Senate approved the treaty with the deletion of the troublesome article. Great Britain scuttled the entire convention by refusing to accept the change.[16]

Anxious to determine Louisiana's northern extent, Jefferson did research in his own library. He learned that France had first defined Louisiana's boundaries in a 1712 charter granted by King Louis XIV to Sieur Anthony Crozat. Crozat was given trading rights as far north as the natural boundary that ran eastward from the continental divide "round the heads of the Missouri & Misipi & their waters."[17]

But, Jefferson concluded, this boundary was soon superseded by an agreement between France and Great Britain to separate Canada and Louisiana. Citing *An Historical Narrative and Topographical Description of Louisiana and West-Florida* (1784) by American geographer Thomas Hutchins as his principal source, Jefferson believed that commissioners appointed under the 1713 Treaty of Utrecht had agreed to divide British and French claims by the forty-ninth parallel. Furthermore, he determined that the Mitchell map showed an uneven boundary line north of the Lake of the Woods labeled "Bounds of Hudsons [sic] Bay by the Treaty of Utrecht."[18]

Wanting yet more conclusive proof, Jefferson through Secretary of State James Madison, ordered a search for forty-ninth parallel boundary information in British sources. Without access to official British records, James Monroe, the American minister to Great Britain, had an agent search London bookstores in 1804. This effort yielded a 1755 map by English cartographer Ellis Huske showing a forty-ninth parallel boundary line starting east of the Lake of the Woods and running west "indefinitely."[19]

Because the Huske map seemed to substantiate Jefferson's sources, Monroe reported that he had no reservations about using it and Hutchins's narrative as proof of a forty-ninth parallel boundary precedent. The very best evidence, he thought, would be the report of the commissioners appointed under the Treaty of Utrecht. He assumed that the British government had the report and could produce it if they wanted to contradict America's forty-ninth parallel quest.

The Louisiana boundary question was temporarily shunted aside when Great Britain and the United States turned to such critical issues as alleged British impressment of sailors from American ships and the negotiation of a commercial treaty. In 1806, Monroe and special envoy William Pinkney concluded a commercial agreement with Great Britain. Contrary to their specific instructions, it did not include a British agreement to cease impressment. This omission caused Madison and Jefferson to reject it summarily.[20]

With trans-Atlantic mail service that usually took at least several months for round-trip exchanges, Monroe and Pinkney were unaware of the administration's decision. Consequently, in 1807, they opened talks about outstanding boundary issues with their British counterparts, Lord Auckland and Lord Holland. On northeastern boundary issues they essentially restated the provisions of the abortive Convention of 1803. But in the northwest, both sides recognized the new reality of America's acquisition of Louisiana. Thus, their major task was to agree on the territory's northern boundary and its reconciliation with the line prescribed in the 1783 treaty.[21]

Knowing that the American diplomats would work for a forty-ninth parallel demarcation, Auckland and Holland asked Hudson's Bay Company officials if the firm's southern limits had ever been agreed to with France. Although the company could not produce any documents, its executives reported that they believed there had been a forty-ninth parallel boundary agreement. While hardly proof, the response was good enough for the British diplomats, who apparently thought such a boundary was as reasonable as any other.[22]

Although the Monroe-Pinkney and Auckland-Holland teams agreed in principle on the forty-ninth parallel as Louisiana's northern boundary, they initially disagreed about how it should be connected to the water line of the Paris Peace Treaty boundary. The British negotiators proposed that the forty-ninth parallel be followed westward from the point in Lake of the Woods where the water boundary first touched it. Monroe and Pinkney countered that the 1783 line had to run all the way to the most northwestern point of Lake of the Woods. From there, they insisted, a due north-south line should be followed to the forty-ninth parallel. These stances presaged subsequent British and American attitudes about the evolution of Northwest Angle Inlet.

The British rather casually assumed that the simplest solution was to follow the 1783 line to the forty-ninth parallel and then proceed westward. The more legalistic Americans insisted that no part of the treaty under which the United States had gained its independence was negotiable. Thus, the most northwestern point of Lake of the Woods had to remain as the inviolable terminus of the 1783 boundary.[23]

After Auckland and Holland acceded to Monroe and Pinkney's rigidity on the most northwestern point, the negotiators were able to conclude the Convention of 1807. From a due north-south line running through the most northwestern point, the forty-ninth parallel was to be followed westward as far as the respective claims of both countries extended.[24]

The convention was doomed by further deterioration of Anglo-American relations. In 1807, the Jefferson administration simply refused to consider any agreement with Great Britain unless the British renounced impressment. Nonetheless, the convention was an important step in establishing the forty-ninth parallel boundary tradition.

Although the 1807 negotiators had no way of knowing otherwise, their belief that the forty-ninth parallel boundary had been established by commissioners appointed under the Treaty of Utrecht was fictitious. However, there was an element of truth imbedded in the myth. The Treaty of Utrecht, under which Great Britain acquired the Hudson Bay drainage area from France, did specify that the countries would create a joint boundary commission. Furthermore, in 1714, the Hudson's Bay Company requested the establishment of a boundary between British and French realms. The company evidently believed the Hudson Bay drainage could be separated from those of the Great Lakes and the Mississippi by two straight-line courses. The first section it proposed was a northeast-southwest line starting at Grimington Island on the Atlantic coast slightly south of the fifty-eighth parallel and running through Lake Mistassini to its intersection with the forty-ninth parallel in present-day western Quebec province. From this point westward the forty-ninth parallel would separate British and French lands indefinitely.[25]

Somehow, the Hudson's Bay Company's desire got contorted into a reputed historical fact. The boundary commission called for in the Utrecht treaty never reached an agreement. Nonetheless, various British cartographers and historians reported the commissioners had created a forty-ninth parallel boundary. Like some other historical myths, the forty-ninth parallel boundary story gained an undeserved veracity by being repeated in undocumented secondary sources.

After the failed Convention of 1807, Great Britain and the United States did not revisit boundary issues for seven years. Open animosity over the impressment issue and British support for Indians in the Northwest stimulated calls for war in the United States. When America declared war on June 18, 1812, the War Hawks, the most belligerent congressmen, wanted the United States to solve its frontier problems by conquering Canada.[26]

Not only did the invasions of Canada fail, but the United States was humiliated in the Northwest. With strong support from its numerous Indian allies, British forces seized such key outposts as Prairie du Chien, Green Bay and the island fortress of Michilimackinac and even forced the evacuation of Fort Dearborn at present-day Chicago. These victories led British fur traders, still seething about the 1783 boundary, to think a radical boundary rectification was possible. In the spring of 1814, a major London agent of the traders asked the British Foreign Office to work for the Ohio River as the northwestern boundary of the United States.[27]

Although it did not endorse a specific boundary, the British government presumed that it should gain land from the United States in any peace settlement. But when the two countries opened peace negotiations at Ghent (in present-day Belgium) on August 8, 1814, the American diplomats were determined that *status quo ante bellum* had to be the basis of any territorial settlement.[28]

During their intermittent four and a half months of deliberations, the Anglo-American diplomats considered wide-ranging boundary matters. The British, initially assuming they had a military advantage, sought the creation of an Indian buffer state in the Northwest and the

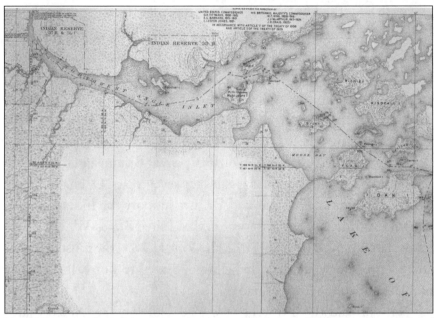

Map of Northwest Angle Inlet. (International Boundary from the Northwesternmost Point of Lake of the Woods to Lake Superior, sheet 1. International Boundary Commission: United States and Canada, 1928)

northwestern boundary line specified in the Convention of 1803. The Americans, naturally, rejected both proposals and called for the northwestern boundary closure agreed to in 1807.

Fortunately for the United States, as the negotiations proceeded, its military position improved dramatically. The decisive American naval victory on Lake Erie combined with the British failures to seize Fort Erie and Baltimore made the British diplomats realize that the war had to be resolved on the *status quo* principle. Anxious to conclude their negotiations and with the realization that they could not resolve outstanding boundary issues, the Anglo-American diplomats signed the Treaty of Ghent on Christmas Eve, 1814.

In the agreement, the negotiators deferred decisions on all boundary matters by agreeing to four articles calling for joint boundary commissions. Articles Four through Seven authorized commissions to survey the Canada-United States boundary specified in 1783, with the exception of the established St. Croix River line in New England. Article Six provided that a commissioner from each country was to supervise the boundary survey from the point where the forty-fifth parallel struck, to St. Lawrence, to the northwestern end of Lake Huron. Once they had completed this section, the same two commissioners were to lead the Article Seven survey from "the water communication between Lake Huron and Lake Superior to the most North Western point of the Lake of the Woods." Mindful of the significance of the most northwest point, the peacemakers agreed that the Article Seven commissioners were to "particularize the Latitude and Longitude of the most North Western point of the Lake of the Woods, and of such other parts of the said boundary as they may deem proper."[29]

Because there were no territorial cessions as a result of the War of 1812, the conflict seemed to end as a virtual tie. That assumption is quite apt relative to Great Britain and the United States. But there were really three components involved in the war—Great Britain, the United States and the natives. The indigenous peoples of the Northwest had traditionally allied with the British and opposed Americans primarily because British traders were much less disruptive to their traditional hunting lifestyle than American farmers. Without specifically stating so in the Ghent treaty, Great Britain and the United States recognized the 1783 boundaries as firm dividing lines. British fur traders could no longer pretend that they had a right to operate south of the Great Lakes. In the new reality they were only foreign trespassers and their Indian allies were left to the mercy of the United States. The removal of Great Britain as an Indian ally in the Great Lakes and Upper Mississippi regions ushered in an era of unprecedented American expansion with an accompanying precipitous decline in the fortunes of the Native American populace.

After the war the presidential administrations of James Madison and James Monroe pursued domestic and foreign policies to bolster America's position in its northern borderlands area. Domestically, they wanted British traders replaced by Americans and wanted to establish control over its Indian residents. The United States moved to oust British traders by the Foreign Intercourse Act of 1816, which mandated that they either remove to Canada or become American citizens. Congressional approval of the law was greatly influenced by John Jacob Astor's American Fur Company, which established its own Upper Mississippi posts soon after the Ghent peace.[30]

To wean the Indians from Great Britain and bind them to the United States, the Madison and Monroe administrations extended the military frontier. In the summer of 1816, when James Monroe was serving as both secretary of state and secretary of war in the Madison administration, he ordered the establishment of an army post at the village of Prairie du Chien on the Mississippi four miles above the mouth of the Wisconsin River. In 1817, army topographical engineer Stephen Harriman Long reconnoitered sites for another post farther up the Mississippi.[31]

Long was specifically assigned to assess likely fort locations on two tracts of land acquired under the 1805 treaty which Army Lieutenant Zebulon M. Pike made with some Dakota Indian chiefs. After ruling out a fort site on the lower cession at the juncture of the Mississippi and St. Croix rivers, Long recommended a post be built on high ground above the point where the Minnesota River (then called the St. Peter's) joined the Mississippi.

Two years later Colonel Henry Leavenworth, who led the first sizable American army force to the Upper Mississippi, established a temporary camp on river bottom land near the site chosen by Long. In 1820, he started constructing a permanent post at the Long site. Initially called Fort St. Anthony, the bastion was renamed Fort Snelling in 1825. Symbolically, the fort was the most important indication to the indigenous Dakota and Ojibwe that the United States, about four decades after it had gained the area from Great Britain, had finally taken control.[32]

The surge of northwestern frontier expansion, which included the creation of the states of Indiana (1816) and Illinois (1818), was accompanied by foreign policy changes vis-à-vis Great Britain. Although their postwar relations were strained, the United States and Great Britain saw mutual advantages in resolving some potential problems. In 1815, they agreed on a four-year commercial agreement and by the Rush-Bagot Agreement two years later demilitarized the Great Lakes.[33]

This newfound willingness to cooperate was carried into negotiations to renew the commercial agreement. In late 1817, Richard Rush, the American minister to Great Britain, was instructed by Secretary of State John Quincy Adams to seek a commercial treaty extension. Lord Castlereagh, the British foreign minister, not only indicated a willingness to consider the extension, but also proposed negotiating the northwest boundary gap closure. As an opening bargaining gambit, Castlereagh suggested the line of the Convention of 1803. While not rejecting the notion out-of-hand, Rush reminded him that the closure article had been expunged by the United States.[34]

After Rush sought advice from the Monroe Administration, Adams named Albert Gallatin, America's minister to France, to assist him in the London negotiations. Castlereagh agreed to consider a broad agenda including a commercial treaty extension, the northern boundary, conflicting claims to the Columbia River area and even impressment. He then named Henry Goulburn, a Ghent treaty commissioner, and cabinet member Frederick John Robinson, secretary of the Board of Trade, to deal with Rush and Gallatin.

Under strict instructions from Adams to accept no boundary south of the forty-ninth parallel, Rush and Gallatin firmly rejected British desires to gain access to the Mississippi. Hampered by their belief that there was a legal precedent for the forty-ninth parallel boundary, Goulburn and Robinson agreed to use the Convention of 1807 as the boundary settlement basis.[35]

In Article Two of the treaty they signed on October 20, 1818, after nearly two months of negotiating, the diplomats specified:

> It is agreed that a Line drawn from the most North Western Point of the Lake of the Woods, along the forty Ninth Parallel of North Latitude, or, if the said Point shall not be in the Forty Ninth Parallel of North Latitude, then that a Line drawn from the said Point North or South as the Case may be, until the said Line shall intersect the said Parallel of North Latitude , and from the Point of such Intersection due West along and with the said Parallel shall be the Line of Demarcation . . . to the Stony Mountains.[36]

Combined with the Paris Peace Treaty of 1783, the Convention of 1818 not only laid the legal basis for Minnesota's northern boundary, but created a Canadian-American demarcation from the Atlantic to the continental divide. The convention was the most significant agreement between Great Britain and the United States since the 1783 treaty. Other than closing the northwest boundary gap and extending the forty-ninth parallel boundary, it included an agreement on the Columbia River country, a commercial agreement and an extension of American fishing rights in Canadian waters. During their negotiations, Rush and Gallatin suggested that the forty-ninth parallel boundary be extended all the way to the Pacific Ocean. However, Goulburn and Robinson objected because Great Britain still entertained hopes of gaining a Columbia River boundary in the Oregon region west of the Rocky Mountains. The best the diplomats could do was agree that the Oregon area, with unspecified boundaries, would be free and open to the citizens, subjects and vessels of both countries for ten years.[37]

While the Convention of 1818 was being negotiated, the joint survey commission appointed under Article Six of the Ghent treaty was conducting field work on its assigned section from St. Regis, New York, the western end of the forty-fifth parallel line, to the point where the 1783 boundary reached the connecting waterway between Lake Huron and Lake Superior. Once this survey was completed, the same commission was to undertake the Article Seven survey from the northwestern end of Lake Huron to the northwest point of Lake of the Woods. Slow progress on the Article Six work delayed planning the Article Seven survey until early 1822.[38]

In forming the Article Seven joint commission, Great Britain and the United States adhered to provisions in the Treaty of Ghent and precedents established by previous boundary commissions. Each side was to be staffed by a commissioner, agent, secretary, surveyor and assistant surveyor. Once in the field the commissions were to add boatmen, guides and other laborers, which would bring their total complement to ten to twelve men each. Administratively, the American commission was under the State Department and the British commission was reportable to the Foreign Office.

The selection of the American and British commissioners demonstrated that the United States and Great Britain wanted strong representatives of their national interests. Peter B. Porter, the American commissioner, was well-known as one of the most belligerent congressmen before the War of 1812. When he was serving his second term in the House of Representatives from the district of western New York state, Porter was a leader of the "War Hawks," a small group of young congressmen who urged American conquest and annexation of Canada. Porter was re-elected to Congress in 1814, but resigned so he could be named American commissioner under the Article Six and Seven surveys.[39]

At a time when Anglophobia was raging in the United States and Canadians generally disliked America, the British Foreign Office named Anthony Barclay as its commissioner to complete the Article Six work and conduct the Article Seven survey. Barclay was the son of the prominent Loyalist Thomas Barclay. The elder Barclay had fled to Halifax, Nova Scotia, from New York City during the Revolutionary War. After the war, the British Foreign Office named him to head the St. Croix River survey in the 1790s and to lead the Article Four and Article Five surveys under the Treaty of Ghent. Anthony Barclay had served as the secretary for his father's Treaty of Ghent commissions.[40]

Although Barclay and Porter were the joint commission leaders and the principal liaisons with their governments, they were not expected to supervise field operations. Theoretically, their main task was to act as impartial judges when the board met to consider presentations of survey data and claims from both sides. But neither man could rise above nationalistic stances. At board meetings they usually acted as antagonistic diplomats rather than neutral judges.[41]

Agents, who planned field work, maintained financial accounts and ultimately made recommendations to the commissioners, were the survey's main administrators. Joseph Delafield of New York City was the American agent and John Hale, a prominent politician in the province of Lower Canada, was the British agent. Like the commissioners, Delafield and Hale had much discretion about how they carried out their duties. Delafield, although he did not supervise the surveyors in their daily tasks, spent much time reconnoitering the area west of Lake Superior. Hale, on the other hand, usually stayed home and depended on reports from the British surveyor.

The actual field work was led by the American surveyor James Ferguson and the British surveyor David Thompson. Ferguson was assisted by George W. Whistler and Thompson by his son Samuel. Surveyors were required to have training in astronomy and their assistants worked principally as draftsmen. Ferguson and Thompson were usually assigned a season-long mission by their agents and then left on their own. Normally, when they were working west of Lake Superior, they had only irregular mail contacts with their agents and commissioners. Ferguson and Thompson were not expected to coordinate their activities. Consequently, they worked independently on their assigned tasks of surveying in a designated area and reporting their findings to their superiors.[42]

In February-March 1822, when Barclay and Porter were concluding their Article Six survey at a Utica, New York, meeting they started planning the Article Seven work. Porter especially was under some compulsion to complete the survey rapidly. The Article Six work, much to the distress of a budget-minded Congress, had proceeded very slowly. Porter and Barclay attributed this laggardly pace to their use of a detailed triangular survey on the rivers and lakes. Barclay, who enjoyed the freedom of being distant from the Foreign Office and Parliament, was never as concerned as Porter about hurrying. Nonetheless, he initially agreed with Porter that the wilderness area west of Lake Superior was of no especial importance to either country and its survey should be routine. Partially on the basis of his meetings with Barclay, Porter reported to Secretary of State John Quincy Adams that he was confident the Article Seven survey could be completed in 1823, after only two seasons of field work.[43]

As events transpired, this was a colossal misjudgment. Starting in 1822, there was field work during four successive navigation seasons.

Beforehand, the commissioners were in no position to anticipate the complicated problems they would encounter nor their lack of a mutual willingness to compromise them.

At least several months before their surveyors entered the area west of Lake Superior, Barclay and Porter realized they would not find the country to be as described in the Paris Peace Treaty of 1783. West of Lake Huron, the treaty mentioned only five specific places in the Article Seven range—Isle Royale, Isle Phelipeaux, Long Lake, Lake of the Woods and its most northwest point. With information from American and British fur traders, they knew the location and approximate size of Isle Royale and that there was no island known as Phelipeaux. However, they had to be open to the possibility that their surveyors would find an island near Isle Royale that they would decide should be designated Phelipeaux. Fur traders had long known that a boundary north of Isle Royale s taying on a northwestern path would come to the end of Lake Superior near the Pigeon River. The North West Company recognized soon after the Paris Treaty that its important depot of Grand Portage, south of the Pigeon, was on American soil. Consequently, the company abandoned it in 1803, and in its stead opened Fort William (present-day Thunder Bay, Ontario).[44]

As the meeting point of the 1783 and 1818 treaties, the most northwest point of Lake of the Woods was especially critical. But because of David Thompson's earlier work, Porter and Barclay tended to underestimate the difficulty in determining it,. During his 1797 reconnaissance, Thompson assumed that Rat Portage (present-day Kenora, Ontario), the lake's outlet, was the most northwest point. If this proved to be true, that issue would be resolved easily.[45]

Much of the reason Barclay and Porter assumed the Article Seven survey would move expeditiously was that they were quite certain the Pigeon River route would best conform to the treaty makers's intention that the boundary should be in the middle of the water communication from Lake Superior to the most northwest point of Lake of the Woods. Consequently, in 1822, they intended to survey only the Pigeon River route.[46]

However, as the surveyors gathered information about the area west of Lake Superior, complications arose about three fundamental issues—the Long Lake location, the nature of the most continuous water route and the northwest point of Lake of the Woods.

Because the Paris Treaty had specified that Long Lake was the outlet of the most continuous water route, an agreement on its location was critical. The Pigeon River, due to its proximity to Isle Royale, was the most likely Long Lake location. But if Long Lake had to be connected to the most continuous water route, did this mean there were other possibilities? By the end of 1822, David Thompson thought so. When he talked over the season's work with Ferguson, he opined that a St. Louis River route was the best water communication to Lake of the Woods. Ferguson, knowing there was no stream of note between the Pigeon and the St. Louis, immediately realized that a compromise line between the two was impossible.[47]

As Barclay was gradually converted to Thompson's insistence on a St. Louis River line, the Americans thought they had to make an extreme demand to force a Pigeon River compromise. After Delafield personally explored parts of the region, he advanced a claim to the Kaministikwia waterway, the passage west of Fort William. In his private communications with Porter and Secretary of State Adams, Delafield admitted that he did not really believe the mouth of the Kaministikwia could be construed to be Long Lake, but that the United States had to insist it was to force the British to relinquish a St. Louis River line.[48]

During their first surveying season, Ferguson and Thompson confirmed what fur traders had known for at least two generations—there was no continuous water route from Lake Superior to Lake of the Woods. Such a feature was geographically impossible because any boundary starting at the mouths of the Pigeon, St. Louis and Kaministikwia would cross the continental divide separating the St. Lawrence and Hudson Bay drainages. The divide, which was much closer to Lake Superior than to Lake of the Woods, was not shown on the Mitchell Map. Other than the continental divide, any boundary line from the mouths of the Pigeon, St. Louis and Kaminitikwia would have crossed numerous portages. Thus, all three could be best described as part-water, part-land lines.[49]

To complicate matters, Ferguson discovered that the old voyageur route from the site of Fort Charlotte at the northwest end of the nine-mile long Grand Portage Trail did not even follow the most continuous water route to Lake of the Woods. Beginning at the juncture of the Pigeon and Arrow rivers, the most continuous water line followed the Arrow northwesterly to Arrow Lake and rejoined the old route at present-day Rose Lake. The land between this line and the traditional route to its south came to be known as Hunter Island.

Establishing the most northwest point of Lake of the Woods proved to be arduous. Prior to the survey there was no accurate map of the lake. But when both Thompson's and Ferguson's parties reconnoitered it in 1823, they found several deep long narrow bays on the lake's west side. Without making a final judgment, both surveyors were inclined to believe that the most northwest point would be in the vicinity of Rat Portage, the lake's outlet. However, these opinions, which were not based on actual calculations, could not determine the point.[50]

The Americans and British had sharply different views on the northwest point. The Americans, who emphasized strict adherence to the 1783 treaty, insisted it had to be located precisely. But the main British interest in Lake of the Woods was economic. Influenced by Hudson's Bay Company officials, the Foreign Office was convinced that it had to safeguard the important Rat Portage post from the United States. If the determination of the point placed it in America, the company would lose one of its most important assets and have its trade disrupted.

Barclay ordered Thompson to conduct a detailed survey of Lake of the Woods in 1824, with the specific aim of determining the most northwest point. Before undertaking the trip, Thompson had explained that the point would be at the intersection of the highest latitude and the greatest longitude, both of which would have to be calculated astronomically.[51]

But for some inexplicable reason, he failed to apply this principle to his observations. As he carefully investigated bay ends on the deeply indented west side of Lake of the Woods, Thompson constructed three large monuments. At the northwesternmost point of Northwest Angle Inlet he erected a massive wooden monument seven feet square and twelve feet high. Recognizing that wood was very prone to decay, he wanted to use stone, but the closest source was several miles away. After designating his wooden monument "The North West corner of the Lake of the Woods No. 1" he proceeded north to a small island near the western end of Monument Bay. There he erected a pyramidal stone monument, seven feet high with a base four feet square. On a pierced tin plate, he identified the site at "The North Western corner of the Lake of the Woods No. 2." On a steep rocky bank at the west end of Portage Bay, the first deeply indented bay north of Monument Bay, Thompson built another stone pyramid, which he labeled "The North Western corner of the Lake of the Woods No. 3." He did not revisit Rat Portage, but still believed that it was a fourth possible most northwest point.

Remnants of David Thompson's Monument No. 2 near west end of Monument Bay, Lake of the Woods. (Photo by William E. Lass, 2010)

Barclay and Foreign Minister George Canning were displeased with Thompson's failure to establish the most northwest point. Barclay's first idea was to simply finesse the matter by closing the 1783 and 1818 boundary lines at the point where the water line first touched the forty-ninth parallel. This would be sensible, he reasoned, because it would avoid the creation of a northwest angle with American land north of the lake. Canning endorsed the notion but felt obligated to get a legal opinion from Advocate General Christopher Robinson. Robinson responded that the most northwest point, because it was specifically prescribed in the 1783 treaty, could not be modified by the 1818 agreement. The only way to change it, he ruled, was to make a treaty to that effect with the United States.[52]

Well aware of American determination to fix the most northwest point, Canning took another tack. In a departure from his usual conduct of giving Barclay great latitude, Canning became personally involved in the northwest point question. Despite Barclay's reservations, Canning interviewed and then hired Johann Ludwig Tiarks to determine the most northwest point.[53]

Tiarks, a German émigré who held a doctorate degree in mathematics, had served as Thomas Barclay's astronomer on the Article Five survey and later on the British government's Board of Longitude. Canning was convinced that Tiarks had the necessary background in theoretical mathematics to ascertain the most northwest point. While interviewing Tiarks, Canning showed him Thompson's charts of Lake of the Woods and then asked how its northwest point could be determined. Tiarks responded that "The most N.W. Point of this lake (or of any other object) is that spot which a due North East line first touches, when approached to the lake from a N.W. direction."[54]

When Canning asked Tiarks how that principle could be applied to Lake of the Woods, the astronomer first stated that they should not assume Thompson's chart was perfect. It would be necessary to resurvey the area. In this work the ends of all bays on the lake's west side, starting with the southernmost, would be measured astronomically. At each bay terminus a due northeast-southwest line would be determined and drawn toward the lake. If the subsequent survey to the north showed that the line touched water, the point could not be the most northwest. For Canning's edification, Tiarks drew a sketch illustrating the process for five points designated A through E. Point E, he concluded, had to be the most northwest point if only the northeast line from it did not touch water.

Canning was intrigued enough to authorize Tiarks to prove his theory on the ground in a private 1825 reconnaissance. Barclay, who had to plan the expedition, decided not to inform the Americans about Tiarks's official mission. He advised Canning that Tiarks should land in New York City as a private tourist. Barclay would pretend to meet him by chance and invite him to go on a western jaunt. If the secret mission failed to find the most northwest point, Barclay probably never would have told Porter. But if Tiarks was successful, Barclay was willing to face Porter's criticism of the connivance.[55]

After he and Barclay reached Lake of the Woods in late July 1825, Tiarks devoted most of his time to studying the two most likely most

End of Northwest Angle Inlet. (Photo by William E. Lass, 2010)

northwest points—Thompson's Monument No. 1 in Northwest Angle Inlet and Rat Portage. Over the course of eight days he made dozens of latitudinal and longitudinal determinations at both places. Finally, he decided that Monument No. 1 was farther northwest than Rat Portage. Well aware of the British desire to retain the portage, he worried the Americans would challenge his finding that a due northeast line from Angle Inlet passed less than a mile west of Rat Portage. To remove any argument of margin of error, he decided to shift the most northwest point from Thompson's monument. In exploring the area he found the bay ended in a small pond about a mile northwest of the marker. He decreed that the pond's northwest end was the true most northwest point of Lake of the Woods. Conveniently, a due northeast line from it cleared Rat Portage sufficiently to eliminate any possibility of a mathematical error.[56]

Although Porter was not informed about the real purpose of Tiarks's mission until the next year, he and Barclay assumed at the end of the 1825 navigation season they had the necessary data to determine the Article Seven boundary. But their formal meeting of the joint commission was delayed until October 1826, to allow Ferguson and Thompson time to compile a detailed set of maps in quadruplicate.[57]

During the map preparation Delafield and Hale became aware of a serious problem in the St. Mary's River, which connected Lake Huron and Lake Superior. In the Neebish Channels area there were three possible water routes. Both the westernmost one, which hugged the United States shore, and the middle one were unnavigable by Great Lakes schooners. Consequently, the United States wanted the boundary to run through the Eastern Neebish Channel so schooners could supply Fort Brady, its upstream army post. Placement of the boundary affected the ownership of forty-square mile Sugar Island, reputed to have good land and timber resources. A line through either the western or middle channel would leave the island to Great Britain, whereas an eastern channel line would give it to the United States.[58]

Hale and Barclay deliberately exaggerated the potential worth of Sugar Island. Their real purpose in making it an issue was to link its ownership to the boundary west of Lake Superior question. They hoped

Porter would be willing to accept a St. Louis River boundary in exchange for American navigation rights in the Eastern Neebish Channel.

When the commission meeting was opened in New York City on October 4, the Sugar Island issue was added to the unresolved problems of Long Lake, the boundary westward from Lake Superior, and the precise location of the most northwest point in Lake of the Woods. As expected, Hale called for a boundary through the Middle Neebish Channel and farther west a line that could run southwestward to the St. Louis River estuary after it cleared Isle Royale. While presenting maps prepared by David Thompson, he insisted the boundary should follow up the St. Louis River to the Embarrass River. It would then go up the Embarrass and across the continental divide before descending the Pike and Vermilion rivers to Sand Point Lake, on the traditional Grand Portage route.[59]

Delafield countered by recommending the boundary be placed through the Eastern Neebish Channel and the Kaminitikwia waterway west of Lake Superior. Although the Americans had never surveyed the Kaministikwia route, Delafield argued that it provided the most continuous water route to Lake of the Woods.

By staking out these extreme positions the agents positioned themselves to compromise on a middle course boundary in the Pigeon River vicinity. Porter offered a line up the Pigeon River that would follow the most continuous water route to the north of Hunter Island. Barclay wanted a boundary from the Grand Portage site over the trail to the Pigeon River. From that point, he proposed, the division would follow the old voyageur route to Lake of the Woods. As an alternative Barclay tendered a line up the Pigeon River and old trade route, provided the United States would agree that the Grand Portage Trail and all other portages would be free and open to both British and Americans. Porter rejected Barclay's proposals because he claimed either one would be a part-water, part-land line, which was contrary to the peace treaty's specification of a water boundary.[60]

Additionally, Barclay complicated matters by offering to grant the United States free navigation to the Eastern Neebish Channel, provided

Great Britain was given reciprocal rights at two points on the Article Six survey. Porter had no choice but to reject these proposals. He insisted the Article Six survey questions had been resolved and should not be linked to anything in Article Seven.[61]

Despite their disagreements, Barclay and Porter were able to agree on the boundary from a point in easternmost Rainy Lake to the northwest point of Lake of the Woods. Despite some bombast from Delafield about the secret Tiarks mission, the Americans accepted the British conclusion that the most northwest point was at 49° 23' 55" north latitude and 95° 14' 38" west longitude, the head of Angle Inlet.

Another important area of agreement was how the middle watercourse specified in the Paris Treaty should be located. Although the commissioners had never accepted them as formal surveying rules, principles used in the Article Six survey were also applied to Article Seven. Whenever possible the middle line by water was interpreted to mean one equidistant from opposite shores. But such a line strictly applied would have divided many islands. To leave entire islands to one country, they agreed to survey each one intersected by an equidistant line and grant it to the country that had the larger share. The other country would be given a credit for the lesser share which would be applied to an island in which it had more acres.[62]

Concern for feasible navigation also caused the commissioners to agree on a deviation from the equidistant line principle. In places where there was only a single navigation channel, its middle would be the boundary regardless of its size or proximity to either shore. Where there were two navigation channels the boundary would follow the middle of the one with the greater amount of water. In sites where there were three of more channels, the boundary would pass through the middlemost one, provided each country was left with a navigable channel. If none of the channels were navigable the boundary would be run to assure a fair division of territory.

These principles established important precedents for the later marking of the boundary. Barclay and Porter, before the end of their New York meeting, used them in having the boundary drawn on the maps of the

Rainy Lake to the most northwest point of the Lake of the Woods line on which they agreed. The marked maps influenced the diplomatic settlement of the boundary in 1842. Several generations later the principles were followed when the boundary was monumented.

Since Barclay and Porter could not agree on the Article Seven boundary, they adjourned their 1826 meeting with the understanding that they would refer the matter to their respective governments. If overall Anglo-American relations had been even moderately cordial, Secretary of State Henry Clay and Foreign Secretary George Canning probably would have easily compromised the Article Seven differences. But both men had larger issues in mind. The Maine-New Brunswick boundary was still unresolved, another Oregon country crisis was looming and commercial relations were contentious.[63]

In light of these problems Clay and Canning chose not to negotiate over what they regarded as an unimportant wilderness tract west of Lake Superior. They had been advised by their boundary commissioners that the area would not attract settlers for years to come. With no possibility of clashes between rival groups in the region, there was really no advantage in continuing negotiations.

Before they convened their final meeting in October 1827, Barclay and Porter had been instructed to terminate the commission. During a routine six-day meeting, the commissioners completed submitting all maps, reconciled their financial accounts and agreed to exchange final reports, which would describe each country's position.

Article Seven boundary issues lay dormant until they were revived during a northeastern boundary dispute which threatened to erupt into war. In the Maine-New Brunswick borderlands, commissioners appointed under the Treaty of Ghent disagreed on the location of the "highlands" specified in the 1783 treaty. The United States held that the word meant the divide of the waters flowing toward the Atlantic and the St. Lawrence. Although this interpretation was logical, it was challenged by the British. The preferred American boundary would have left Canada only a narrow tract of land between northern Maine and the St. Lawrence. Concerned with the need for a connecting road between

Lower Canada and the maritime provinces of New Brunswick and Nova Scotia, the British knew that a portion of the best route lay through land claimed by the United States. Consequently, they insisted the boundary be placed about 100 miles south of one claimed by the United States.[64]

In 1827, the countries agreed to submit their dispute over some 12,000 square miles to a neutral arbiter, King William of the Netherlands. In 1831, William announced that he had decided on a compromise line because it was impossible to determine a natural boundary following a highlands. Although the king's decision would have given Maine and the United States nearly two-thirds of the disputed area, it was sharply criticized by Maine and rejected by the United States. Great Britain, on the other hand, favored the award, because it would have assured a good road route through their lands.[65]

The failure to reach a diplomatic solution exacerbated tensions in the disputed area. By 1838, land disputes between American and Canadian settlers threatened to lead to armed clashes. Maine responded by rushing militiamen to the region, where they were soon faced by British troops. When war seemed imminent, the administration of President Martin Van Buren sent army commander General Winfield S. Scott to Maine's northern frontier. Under a truce arranged by Scott, the armed forces withdrew to opposite sides of a compromise line.[66]

The truce at least brought an uneasy calm. But neither Van Buren, influenced by traditional Democratic Party Anglophobia, or Lord Palmerston, the British foreign secretary who openly talked of war, made serious efforts to negotiate differences.

However, political changes in both countries created a more conciliatory mood. The election of Whig President William Henry Harrison in 1840 enabled the United States to shift its posture. Harrison named the celebrated politician Daniel Webster to be his secretary of state. When Harrison died only a month into his term, Webster was retained in the Cabinet of President John Tyler. In Great Britain, new Prime Minister Sir Robert Peel and his foreign secretary Lord Aberdeen wanted a peaceful resolution of the Maine-New Brunswick boundary dispute.[67]

To underscore their willingness to compromise with the United States, Peel and Aberdeen chose Lord Ashburton to negotiate boundary issues with Webster in Washingon, D.C. The sixty-seven-year old Ashburton, whose common name was Alexander Baring, was well-known for his American sympathies. As a young man he had represented the Baring banking firm in the United States and had married an American woman. During his service in Parliament he had advocated for good relations with the United States. Pleased by Ashburton's appointment, Webster was determined to not only resolve boundary issues, but to usher in a new age of Anglo-American cooperation.

When Ashburton arrived in Washington on April 1, 1842, he carried instructions from Aberdeen. The foreign secretary wanted the negotiations to cover three boundary issues—Maine-New Brunswick, the Article Seven area and the Oregon country. Because Great Britain had accepted the Netherlands award, Ashburton was not expected to deviate greatly from it. Although neither Aberdeen or Ashburton thought the country west of Lake Superior was anything more than a wilderness tract that would remain unsettled for decades to come, they agreed its boundary should be settled to preclude future difficulties. The British statesmen were perfectly willing to start negotiations at the Barclay-Porter-proposed Pigeon River compromise lines rather than return to the St. Louis River boundary claim. Significantly, Aberdeen's most ambitious proposal was for the Oregon country, where he wanted Ashburton to strive for a Columbia River demarcation.[68]

Over the course of their several months of negotiating, Ashburton and Webster never took extreme positions. On the Maine-New Brunswick boundary, they were influenced by the Netherlands award. Finally, they agreed that Great Britain would be granted about 900 square miles more than the award. To make this decision palatable to Maine and Massachusetts, which had a claim based on its colonial charter, Webster and the Tyler administration agreed to compensate the states for the lost land.[69]

Once they had defused the explosive New England crisis, Ashburton and Webster were free to deal with the Article Seven survey boundary. Well aware of the Barclay-Porter near-compromise, they never considered an alternative to a route in the Pigeon River vicinity west of Lake Superior. Initially, Ashburton suggested a boundary demarcation over the Grand Portage trail and the traditional trading route to the northwest point of Lake of the Woods. Webster preferred a water demarcation starting at the Pigeon River's mouth and then following the old voyageur route. They easily compromised on a Pigeon River-old voyageur route line with the stipulation that the

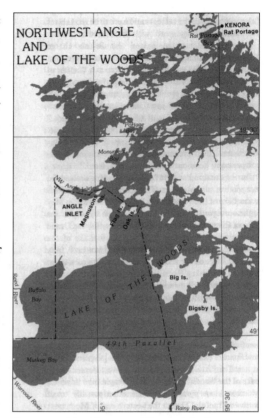

Courtesy of the Minnesota Historical Society.

Grand Portage trail and all portages on the canoe route would be free and open to citizens of both countries. Recognizing the significance of the northwest point of Lake of the Woods, the diplomats placed its precise location—49° 23' 55" north latitude and 95° 14' 38" west longtitude—in their treaty. Furthermore, Ashburton agreed that the United States could have Sugar Island and Webster granted Great Britain navigation rights to an American-controlled passage in the St. Lawrence.[70]

Ashburton and Webster proceeded amicably because they were both realistic enough to recognize the art of the possible. Their New England and Article Seven agreements were in keeping with precedent and acceptable to their respective constituencies. On the other hand, they decided not to deal with the Oregon country boundary, because Webster especially recognized that American expansionists would have regarded a Columbia River boundary as a severe restriction to their ambitions for the Pacific Northwest.

The Webster-Ashburton Treaty, approved by the United States and Great Britain in late 1842, ended the diplomatic phase of Minnesota's northern boundary. By that time, because of settlement in Iowa, there was increasing interest in determining what would come to be Minnesota's southern boundary.

— · — · — · — · — · — · — · — · — · — · — · —

## NOTES:

1. Ray Allen Billington, *Westward Expansion: A History of the American Frontier* (4th ed., New York: Macmillan Publishing Co., 1974), 103-131.
2. Alfred L. Burt, *The Old Province of Quebec* (Reprint ed., New York,: Russell & Russell, 1970), 76-77.
3. *Secret Journals of the Acts and Proceedings of Congress* (Boston: Thomas B. Wait, 1820), 2:138; Samuel Flagg Bemis, *The Diplomacy of the American Revolution* (Rev. ed., Bloomington: Indiana University Press, 1957), 175.
4. Bemis, *Diplomacy of American Revolution*, 95; Paul Chrisler Phillips, *The West in the Diplomacy of the American Revolution* (Reprint ed., New York: Russell & Russell, 1967), 120.
5. Bemis, *Diplomacy of American Revolution*, 189-190, 228, 233. For a detailed history of the Paris negotiations see: Richard B. Morris, *The Peacemakers: The Great Powers and American Independence* (New York: Harper & Row, 1965).
6. Charles I. Bevans, comp., *Treaties and other International Agreements of the United States of America*, vol. 12: *United Kingdom-Zanzibar* (Washington: Government Printing Office, 1974), 10.
7. Hunter Miller, ed., *Treaties and Other International Acts of the United States of America* (Washington: Government Printing Office, 1931), 3:349; On Mitchell's career, see: Edmund Berkeley and Dorothy Smith Berkeley, *Dr. John Mitchell: The Man Who Made the Map of North America* (Chapel Hill: University of North Carolina Press, 1974), "John Mitchell's Map of the British and French Dominions in North America, compiled and edited by Walter W. Ristow from various published works of Lawrence Martin," in Walter W. Ristow, comp., *Ala Carte: Selected Papers on Maps and Atlases* (Washington: Library of Congress, 1972), 102-108, and Edward J. Larson, "Mitchell, John" in *American National* Biography (New York: Oxford University Press, 1999)., 15: 606-607. A list of the various editions and impressions of Mitchell's map is in Ristow, comp., *Ala Carte*, 109-113.

8. Miller, ed., *Treaties*, 3: 330, 333.
9. A[lfred] L. Burt , *The United States Great Britain and British North America: From the Revolution to the Establishment of Peace after the War of 1812* (Reprint ed., New York: Russell & Russell, 1961), 82ff; Billington, *Westward Expansion*, 216-219.
10. Samuel Flagg Bemis, "Jay's Treaty and the Northwest Boundary Gap," *American Historical* Review 27 (April 1922): 468-470.
11. Alexander Mackenzie, *Voyages from Montreal, on the St. Laurence, Through the Continent of North America, to the Frozen and Pacific Oceans; In the Years 1789 and 1793* (London: T. Cadill, Jr. and W. Davis, 1801), lviii; David Thompson Journal, 25 August 1797, photocopy in David Thompson Papers, Minnesota Historical Society. Original in Ontario Department of Public Records and Archives, Toronto.
12. Madison to King, June 2, 1802, in William R. Manning, ed., *Diplomatic Correspondence of the United States: Canadian Relations 1784-1860* (Washington: Carnegie Endowment for International Peace, 1940), 1:158.
13. King to Madison, 13 May 1803, in Manning, ed., *Diplomatic Correspondence*, 1:557.
14. King to Hawkesbury, 14 May 1803, in Manning, ed., *Diplomatic Correspondence*, 1:558.
15. Livingston to Madison, 08 June 1802, in *American State Papers: Foreign Relations* (hereafter cited as ASP, FR), 2: 519; Talleyrand to Duc Denis Decrés, 02 October 1802, in James A. Robertson, *Louisiana under the Rule of Spain, France, and the United States 1785-1807* (Cleveland: Arthur H. Clark, 1911), 2: 141n. For the text of the Louisiana Purchase treaty see Bevans, *Treaties*, vol. 7: *Denmark-France* (1971), 812-815. For the text of the Treaty of San Ildefonso see The Avalon Project, *Documents in Law, History and Diplomacy*, Yale Law School, Accessed 20 July 2012.
16. John Quincy Adams to Madison, 16 December 1803; King to Madison, 09 December 1803, both in ASP, FR, 2:590-591.
17. Thomas Jefferson, "The Limits and Bounds of Louisiana," in *Documents Relating to the Purchase & Exploration of Louisiana* (Boston: Houghton Mifflin 1904), 32.
18. Jefferson, "Limits and Bounds," 41-42. For an English language verbatim text of the Treaty of Utrecht between Great Britain and France see George Chalmers, *A Collection of Treaties Between Great Britain and Other Powers*, vol. 1 (London: J. Stockdale, 1790), 390-424; Copy of Mitchell map, in Ristow, ed., *Ala Carte*, 102.
19. Here and below, see Monroe to Madison, 17 September 1804, in Manning, ed., *Diplomatic Correspondence*, 1:567.
20. Madison to Monroe, 15 May 1806, to Monroe and Pinkney, 17 May 1806, Monroe and Pinkney to Madison, 11 November 1806, 03 January 1807—all in ASP, FR, 3:119-124, 137-140, 142-147.

21. Monroe and Pinkney to Madison, 25 April 1807, and enclosure, ASP, FR, 3: 162-165.

22. William Mainwaring, Hudson's Bay Company, to Holland and Auckland, 24 March 1807, in Great Britain, Foreign Office Records, series 5 (hereafter cited as FO/5), vol. 54, p. 25, microfilm copy in Public Archives of Canada, Ottawa; originals in the Public Record Office, London.

23. Monroe and Pinkney to Madison, 25 April 1807 and Adams to Albert Gallatin and Richard Rush, 28 July 1818, in Manning, ed., *Diplomatic Correspondence*, 1:590, 278.

24. Here and below, see Monroe and Pinkney to Madison, 25 April 1807, in Manning, *Diplomatic Correspondence*, 1:590.

25. Here and below, see: William E. Lass, "How the Forty-Ninth Parallel Became the International Boundary," *Minnesota History* 44 (Summer 1975): 216.

26. On the background of the War of 1812, see: Reginald Horsman, *The Causes of the War of 1812* (New York: Octagon Books, 1975) and Bradford Perkins, *Prologue to War: England and the United States, 1805-1812* (Berkeley: University of California Press, 1961).

27. "Louise Phelps Kellogg, *The British Régime in Wisconsin and the North-west* (Madison: State Historical Society of Wisconsin, 1935), 285-287, 317-320; "Memorial of the Fur Traders in Regard to the American Boundary, 1814," in Gordon Charles Davidson, *The North West Company* (Berkeley: University of California, 1918), 296-301.

28. Here and below, see: Monroe to U.S. Peace Commissioners, 11 August 1814, U.S. Peace Commissioners to Monroe, 12, 19 August 1814, British to U.S. Peace Commissioners, 04 September, 21, 31 October 1814, all in ASP, FR, 3: 705-706, 709, 714, 725-726.; Burt, *United States, Great Britain*, 346; Fred L. Engelman, *The Peace of Christmas Eve* (London: Rupert Hart-Davis, 1962), 132-133, 237.

29. Bevans. *Treaties*, 12:46.

30. Indian Trade Regulation Act, *U.S. Statutes at Large*, 3:332; David Lavender, *The Fist in the Wilderness*, (Garden City, NY: Doubleday & Co., 1964), 233-237.

31. Here and below, see: Lucile M. Kane, June D. Holmquist and Carolyn Gilman, eds, *The Northern Expeditions of Stephen H. Long: The Journals of 1817 and 1823 and Related Documents* (St. Paul: Minnesota Historical Society Press, 1978), 8-9.

32. June Drenning Holmquist and Jean A. Brookins, *Minnesota's Major Historic Sites: A Guide* (2d ed.; St. Paul: Minnesota Historical Society, 1972), 1-3.

33. Billington, *Westward Expansion*, 295; For the text of the 1815 and 1817 treaties see Bevans, *Treaties*, 12:49-56.

34. Here and below, see: Adams to Rush, 06 November 1817, 21 May 1818, to Gallatin, 22 May 1818, Rush to Adams, 25 July, 15, 28 August all in ASP, FR, 4:370-379; Richard Rush, *Memoranda of a Res-*

*idence at the Court of London* (Philadelphia: Crey, Lea & Blanchard, 1833), 93, 97, 307; J[ohn] H. Powell, *Richard Rush, Republican Diplomat 1780-1859* (Philadelphia: University of Pennsylvania Press, 1942), 116-118.

35. Rush, *Memoranda of a Residence,* 371; Gallatin and Rush to Adams, 20 October 1818 and "Protocol of the fifth conference," held 06 October 1818, both in ASP, FR, 4:380, 391.

36. Bevans, *Treaties,* 12:58.

37. *Ibid.,* 12:59.

38. Here and below, see: William E. Lass, *Minnesota's Boundary with Canada: Its Evolution since 1783* (St. Paul: Minnesota Historical Society Press,1980), 35-38.

39. John C. Fredriksen, "Porter, Peter Buell," *American National Biography,* vol. 17 (New York: Oxford University Press, 1999), 707-09.

40. Lass, *Minnesota's Boundary with Canada,* 36.

41. Here and below, *Ibid.*

42. Porter to Adams, 12 February 1822, in Letters Received from the U.S. Commissioner, Northern Boundary, Records Relating to International Boundaries, Record Group 76, National Archives and Records Administration, Washington, D.C. Hereafter cited as NB/NARA RG 76; William A. Bird, *The Boundary Line Between the British Provinces and the United States* (Buffalo, N.Y., 1864), 8. Delafield to Porter, 20 April 1822, in Peter B., Porter Papers, roll 7A, frames 0391-0393, originals and microfilm owned by the Buffalo and Erie County Historical Society, Buffalo, New York. On Ferguson, see James Grant Wilson and John Fiske, eds., *Appleton's Cyclopedia of American Biography* (New York: D. Appleton and Co., 1888), 2:433. On Whistler see Harold K. Barrows, "Whistler, George Washington," in *Dictionary of American Biography,* 20:72 (New York: Charles Scribner's Sons, 1936), 20:72. On David Thompson see, "Thompson, David," *Dictionary of Canadian Biography Online* (accessed 10 December 2010).

43. Porter to Adams, 12 February 1822, in Letters Received from the U.S. Commissioner, NB/NARA RG 76; [Joseph Delafield], *The Unfortified Boundary: A Diary of the Survey of the Canadian Boundary Line from St. Regis to the Lake of the Woods . . . ,* ed. Robert McElroy and Thomas Riggs (New York: Privately printed, 1943),63-64.

44. Davidson, *North West Company,* 106.

45. Field maps, 1823, in Thompson Papers; Thompson's report of 20 February 1824, in Boundary Claims, Arguments, and Miscellaneous Documents, 1818-26, NB/NARA RG 76.

46. [Delafield,] *Unfortified Boundary,* , 63.

47. Ferguson to Porter, 02 July 1822, in Porter Papers, 7A, 0439-0443.

48. Porter to Adams, 10 November 1824, in Letters Received from the U.S. Commissioner, and Delafield to Adams, 17 November 1824, in Letters Received from the U.S. Agent, both in NB/NARA RG 76.

49. Here and below, see: Ferguson to Porter, 20 August 1822, in Porter Papers, 7A-0459.

50. [Delafield], *Unfortified Boundary*, 425-429.

51. Here and below, see: Barclay to Canning, 10 March 1824, in FO/5, vol. 187, pp. 229-233; Thompson memorandum, 13 February 1824, Thompson to the board of commissioners, 23 February 1823, both in Boundary Claims, Arguments, and Miscellaneous Documents, NB/NARA RG 76; Thompson's undated report attached to Delafield to Adams, 17 November 1824, in Letters Received from the U. S. Agent, NB/NARA RG 76. Although Thompson's stone monuments have partially collapsed, they are still easily recognizable. (William E. Lass, tour of Lake of the Woods, 19-21 July 2010, organized by David G. Malaher.)

52. Barclay to Canning, 10 March 1824, Planta to His Majesty's Advocate General, 08 December 1824 and Robinson to Canning, 09 December 1824, all in FO/5, 187, pp. 229-233, 328-331.

53. Canning to Barclay, 13 December 1824, in FO/5, Vol. 187, pp. 181-184.

54. Here and below, see: *Ibid.* , and attached memorandum of Tiarks" opinion, FO/5, vol. 187, p, 187.

55. Barclay to Planta, 14, 23 February 1825, in FO/5, vol. 200, pp. 62-65, 68.

56. Barclay to Planta, 16 May 1825, in FO/5,vol.200, p. 76; Barclay to Fraser, 09 April 1825, in Porter Papers, 7A-0523; J[ohann] L. Tiarks, "N.W. Point of the Lake of the Woods," in *American Journal of Science and the Arts (Silliman's Journal}*, 15:43 (1829).

57. Barclay to Canning, 17 February 1826, in FO/5, vol. 215, pp. 127-131; Ferguson to Porter, 30 March 1826, Delafield to Porter, 16 April 1826, both in Porter Papers, 7A-0556, 0561.

58. Here and below, see: Journal of Proceedings for period 16 February 1824–17 October 1826 and for 23 October 1826, attached to Delafield to Clay, 15 November 1826, in Letters Received from the U.S. Agent, NB/NARA RG 76; [Delafield], *Unfortified Boundary*, 67-69; Hale's claim and argument, 05 October 1826, and Delafield's claim and argument, 05 October 1826, in Letters Received from the U.S. Agent, NB/NARA RG 76.

59. Here and below, see: Journal of the New York meeting of the board of commissioners, 04-17 October 1826 and Journal of Proceedings for 17, 23 October 1826, attached to Delafield to Clay, 15 November 1826, in Letters Received from the U. S. Agent. All in NB/NARA RG 76.

60. Journal of Proceedings for 23 October 1826 in Letters Received from the U.S. Agent and Porter to Clay, 02 November 1826, in Letters Received from the U. S. Commissioner, both in NB/NARA RG 76.

61. Here and below, see Journal of Proceedings for 23 October1826, attached to Delafield to Clay, 15 November 1826 and Delafield to Adams, 17 November 1824 , both in Letters Received from the U.S.

Agent, NB/NARA RG 76; John Bassett Moore, *History and Digest of the International Arbitrations to Which the United States Has Been a Party* (Washington: Government Printing Office, 1898), 1:176-188.

62. Here and below, see Porter to Clay, 31 October 1826, in Letters Received from the U.S. Commissioner; David Thompson's sworn affidavit, 03 June 1827, in Report of the British Commissioner on Article 7, 24 December 1827, pp. 4-10. All in NB/NARA RG 76.

63. Here and below, see Lass, *Minnesota's Boundary with Canada*, 54, 60-61.

64. J.R. Baldwin, "The Webster-Ashburton Boundary Settlement," in *Canadian Historical Association Report*, 1938 (Toronto, 1938), 129; Julius W. Pratt, *A History of United States Foreign Policy* (3rd ed., Englewood Cliffs, NJ: Prentice-Hall, 1972), 92.; Howard Jones, *To the Webster-Ashburton Treaty: A Study in Anglo-American Relations, 1783-1843* (Chapel Hill: University of North Carolina Press, 1977), 33-35.

65. Jones, *Webster-Ashburton Treaty*, 15-16; Charles E. Clark, *Maine: A Bicentennial History* (New York: W.W. Norton, 1977), 83.

66. Here and below, see Thomas Le Duc, "The Maine Frontier and the Northeastern Boundary Controversy," in *American Historical Review* 53 (October 1947): 30, 40; Thomas A. Bailey, *A Diplomatic History of the American People* (8th ed., New York: Appleton-Century-Crofts, 1969), 208.

67. Here and below, see Jones, *Webster-Ashburton Treaty*, 90-95; Maurice G. Baxter, "Webster, Daniel," in *American National Biography*, vol. 22 (New York: Oxford University Press, 1999), 865-868.; William Prideaux Courtney, "Baring, Alexander," in *Dictionary of National Biography*, vol. 1 (Reprint ed.; London: Oxford University Press, 1921), 1110-11.

68. Aberdeen to Ashburton, 08 February 1842, in FO/5, vol. 378, pp. 1-4; Wilbur D. Jones, "Lord Ashburton and the Maine Boundary Negotiations," in *Mississippi Valley Historical Review* 40 (December 1953): 479.

69. Jones, *Webster-Ashburton Treaty*, 133.

70. Ashburton to Webster, 16, 29 July 1842, in FO/5, vol. 380, pp. 152, 158-159; Robert Stuart to Webster, 07 July 1842, in *Congressional Globe*, 27 Congress, 3 session, 21; Delafield to Fraser, 20 July 1842, Webster to Ferguson and Ferguson's reply, both dated 25 July 1842—all in *Documents from State Department*, 27 Congress, 3 session, *Senate Documents*, no. 1, pp. 102-106 (serial 413). For the text of the Webster-Ashburton Treaty see Bevans, *Treaties*, 12:82-89.

Robert Lucas. (Courtesy of the State Historical Society of Iowa)

# CHAPTER TWO

## IOWA STATEHOOD AND THE SOUTHERN BOUNDARY

SOON AFTER THE DIPLOMATIC PHASE of Minnesota's northern boundary was ended by the Webster-Ashburton Treaty, Iowa statehood fixed the North Star State's southern boundary. Settlement in eastern Iowa rapidly followed a major land cession by Sauk and Meskwaki (previously called Fox) Indians in 1832. These pioneers were placed in Wisconsin Territory when it was formed by a congressional act of April 20, 1836. Wisconsin Territory was massive. It was bounded on the east by Michigan, on the south by Illinois and Missouri, on the west by the Missouri and White Earth rivers and on the north by the international boundary from present-day northwestern North Dakota to its meeting with the Michigan boundary in Lake Superior. The growth of two population centers divided by the Mississippi River led Congress, in 1838, to divide the territory and in the same act establish Iowa Territory. The new territory encompassed all of the original Wisconsin Territory west of the Mississippi and a line from its source due north to the Canadian boundary.[1]

President Martin Van Buren appointed Robert Lucas of Ohio as the first governor of Iowa Territory. The fifty-seven-year-old Lucas, who was destined to play a prominent role in shaping Iowa, had lengthy political experience. Before being elected Ohio's governor in 1832 and re-elected in 1834, he had served two terms in the state's House of Representatives and seven terms in its Senate. He had a certain national reputation because he had served as the presiding officer of the first Democratic National Convention, held at Baltimore in 1832.[2]

Lucas's ambitious agenda included an attempt to make Iowa a state. He prevailed on the territorial legislature to authorize a public vote, in the election of August 1840, on the question of convening a constitutional convention. He was disappointed when the electorate, fearing statehood would bring increased costs, overwhelmingly rejected the proposition by a vote of 2,907 to 937.[3]

In 1841, President William Henry Harrison, a Whig, replaced Lucas with John Chambers of Kentucky. Chambers, who had served on Harrison's staff during the War of 1812, was an experienced politician with four terms in the Kentucky legislature and three in the United States House of Representatives. Soon after arriving in Iowa, he became a statehood advocate despite the opposition of most of his fellow Whigs. Like Lucas, he persuaded the territorial legislature to authorize a vote on the convening of a constitutional convention. But in the election of August 1842, the majority of the voters in every county rejected the proposal.[4]

However, population growth and an improving economy soon changed public opinion. Following another recommendation by Chambers and legislative authorization, Iowans, in the township elections of April 1844, approved the convening of a constitutional convention by a vote of 6,719 to 3,974.[5]

By the time convention delegates were chosen in the general election of August 1844, a recent census reported the territorial population as 75,150. Nearly all Iowans then lived within sixty miles of the Mississippi River. The vast majority of them supported the Democratic Party, whose convention delegates outnumbered the Whigs fifty-one to twenty-one.[6]

On October 9, the delegates convened in Iowa City, the territorial capital. They organized eleven standing committees, including one on "State Boundaries." Of its nine members, former governor Lucas was the best known. He was a strong advocate of a large-state Iowa. The boundaries finally accepted by the convention are generally remembered in Iowa history as the "Lucas boundaries."[7]

The Boundaries Committee insisted that Iowa should be relatively large and flanked by two great rivers—the Mississippi on the east and the Missouri on the west. Missouri's northern boundary had to be the southern boundary, although there was a dispute between Iowa and Missouri about its exact location. The committee preferred to extend the northern boundary to the present-day Twin Cities. In seeking natural boundaries insofar as possible, the committee recommended that the Missouri be followed upstream from the northwest corner of the State of Missouri to the mouth of the Big Sioux River (the western edge of present-day Sioux City, Iowa). From that point it should proceed up the Big Sioux to:

> the first branch falling into it on the east side, and up that branch to a point where it is intersected by the boundary established in the Treaty of 1830, with the Sac and Foxes, and other Indians, from thence to the St. Peters [sic] river, [Minnesota River] opposite the mouth of the Blue Earth [present-day Mankato, Minnesota], and down the St. Peters to the Mississippi. . . .[8]

The committee's report prompted considerable discussion on the convention floor. There was some sentiment that the northern boundary was too vague and indeed, parts of it were. By the first branch falling into the Big Sioux from the east side, the committee evidently meant the Rock River, which enters the Big Sioux about ten miles north of present-day Hawarden, Iowa. The Indian boundary established by the 1830 treaty referred to an agreement reached at Prairie du Chien, Wisconsin. A reconstruction of a boundary running up the Rock to the treaty boundary in terms of present-day geography would extend through Lyon, Iowa's most northwestern county. A line from the treaty boundary to the mouth of the Blue Earth River would have run northeasterly, in what later became Minnesota, from near Bigelow to Mankato.[9]

In order to make the proposed northern boundary more easily determinable, some delegates moved to amend the committee's proposal. James H. Gower of Cedar County proposed that the forty-fifth parallel be accepted as Iowa's northern limit. Such a line would have given Iowa most of present-day South Dakota east of the Missouri River and all of Minnesota south of the Twin Cities' latitude. Lucas responded that such a demarcation would include "a large range of broken and comparatively valueless country." He also contended that since much of the proposed addition was held by the Sioux Indians "the laws of the State of Iowa could not reach there, and it would become a resort for desperadoes."[10]

Gower's idea that a line of latitude should be the northern boundary appealed to some other delegates. Subsequently, the forty-fourth parallel was suggested, but quickly dismissed. One of the principal arguments against the latitudinal lines was that they would make Iowa a very large, irregularly shaped state, because the Missouri River turned sharply westward near the mouth of the Big Sioux.[11]

A solution proposed by Jonathan C. Hall of Henry County attracted a strong following. He thought the western boundary should leave the Missouri at 42° 30', which would be at or near the Big Sioux. From that point he suggested a line running northeastward to the mouth of the Blue Earth on the St. Peter's River and then down the latter stream to its juncture with the Mississippi. As compared to the boundaries committee's proposal, this demarcation would have resulted in a somewhat smaller state, but would have been more definite.

But several members insisted that Hall was not asking for enough territory on the north. Edward Langworthy, a delegate from the Dubuque area, agreed with Hall about the boundary from the Missouri to the mouth of the Blue Earth, but suggested that from that point it should run northward to the mouth of the "Little Sac" River (i. e. the Watab at present-day Sartell in Stearns County) on the Mississippi. Lucas was even more ambitious. He suggested the line run from the mouth of the Big Sioux to the mouth of the Little Sac. Such a line would have crossed the Minnesota River about forty miles upstream from the Blue Earth's mouth. Proponents of the Little Sac line had their eyes on the Falls of St. Anthony. Ralph P. Lowe of Muscatine County opined that "The Falls of St. Anthony would be a valuable acquisition to the State of Iowa; would add wealth and power. We could not have too much water power." [12]

Most of the support for a Little Sac line came from the northernmost counties. Evidently their delegates saw advantages in giving their locales a more central location in the future state. Conversely, delegates from southern counties did not want to be left on the edge of a very large state. In the spirit of compromise the convention referred the boundaries issue to a select committee, separate from the boundaries committee, representing all twelve electoral districts. The committee's recommendation was accepted by the convention. Its only difference from the boundaries committee proposal was to specify a northern boundary from " 'the mouth of the Sioux or Calumet river; thence in a direct line to the middle of the main channel of the St. Peters River, where the Watonwan river (according to Nicollet's map) enters the same; thence down the middle of the main channel of said river to the middle of the main channel of the Mississippi river. . . . '"[13]

In limiting the state by three navigable rivers, the convention accepted a natural boundaries principle first suggested by Lucas in November 1839.[14]

Obviously the delegates were not familiar with the geography of the St. Peter's River drainage area. In their early deliberations they evidently used a map that correctly showed the northward-flowing Blue Earth as a tributary of the St. Peter's. But when they switched to Joseph N. Nicollet's *Map of the Hydrographical Basin of the Upper Mississippi River*, they misinterpreted the relationships of the Blue Earth, its tributary Watonwan and the St. Peter's. Nicollet placed his label for the "Mankato or Blue Earth R." upstream from the mouth of the Watonwan. Consequently, the delegates assumed the Blue Earth was tributary to the Watonwan and that the mouth of the Watonwan touched the St. Peter's.[15]

Joseph Nicolas Nicollet. (Courtesy of the Minnesota Historical Society)

After the Iowa constitutional convention adjourned on November 1, 1844, the proposed state's constitution was forwarded to Congress with a request that the State of Iowa be created. The boundary stipulations of the constitution were referred to the House Committee on the Territories, chaired by Aaron V. Brown of Tennessee. On February 10, 1845, Brown reported that the committee agreed with Iowa's territorial delegate Augustus Caesar Dodge that

Augustus Caesar Dodge. (Courtesy of the State Historical Society of Iowa)

Iowa's preferred boundaries should be accepted. The committee, he explained, decided "to adhere to the boundary asked for by the people of Iowa, who were there, who had settled the country, and whose voice should be listened to in the matter."[16]

But Alexander Duncan of Ohio challenged the committee's recommendation. He thought Congress, rather than state residents, should determine boundaries. While holding a copy of Nicollet's map in his hand he moved that Iowa's boundaries begin "in the middle of the St. Peter's River at the juncture of the Watonwan River. Then due east to the middle of the Mississippi, south to the northeast corner of Missouri, then west along Missouri's northern boundary to a point due south of the beginning point. Then due north to the point of beginning." In terms of present-day sites, such boundaries would have placed Iowa's northern boundary from Mankato to near Winona on the Mississippi. Iowa's western boundary would have run about five miles east of Fort Dodge and ten miles west of Des Moines.

Duncan's amendment was inspired by Nicollet's recently published *Report Intended to Illustrate a Map of the Hydrographical Basin of the Upper Mississippi River.* Rather than confine himself to topographical observations, Nicollet made some geopolitical recommendations. With respect to Iowa Territory, he observed that its:

> limits are surely very extensive, but as the question of proper limits of this prospective State, destined soon to take its place in the Union, is important to the relations to other States yet to rise, and there being but few persons acquainted with the interior of the broad region embraced by the map, it may not be inappropriate to suggest . . . some views as to the most eligible limits to be given to these several States.[17]

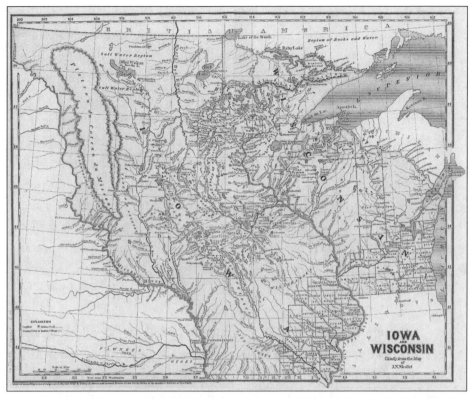

Map of Iowa and Wisconsin drawn chiefly from the J.N. Nicollet map. (Courtesy of the Minnesota Historical Society)

Specifically, Nicollet thought five states should be created immediately west of the existing Mississippi Valley states. The first would be formed west of Arkansas and the second west of Missouri. The third state could be created by "taking about equal portions from each side of the Missouri River, embracing the mouth of the Platte. . . ." Iowa, the fourth state, should be bounded by the Mississippi River on the east, a parallel of latitude passing through the Mankato or Blue Earth River on the north, a meridian line running between the seventeenth and eighteenth degrees of longitude west of Washington, D.C., on the west and Missouri's northern boundary on the south. Nicollet's fifth state, which would be north of both Iowa and the third state, would embrace the area drained by the tributaries that entered the Mississippi from the west as well as the drainage area of the Red River of the North and its tributaries to the international boundary.

Iowa, the only one of the proposed states Nicollet identified by a proper name, was also the only one for which he proposed specific boundaries. Nicollet estimated that his Iowa would have an area of forty to forty-two thousand square miles. Such a relatively small state, he thought, would have a number of advantages. It would provide access to the Mississippi and three of its significant tributaries—the Iowa, Des Moines and St. Peter's rivers. Its compactness would preclude estrangement of "one portion of the people from the other." Thus, they would enjoy a harmonious society. Philosophizing, Nicollet thought his suggested boundaries would not only assure Iowans similar climate, soil, resources and commercial routes, but would also give them "a homogeneity of character and interest highly conducive to their well-being both morally and politically."[18]

Although Duncan and his supporters seized on Nicollet's report as their rationale for reducing Iowa's size, they were too practically minded to believe a smaller Iowa would enhance its citizens' moral well-being. Instead, they were primarily concerned with maintaining a balance between free and slave states. Since Iowa's statehood bid coincided with a Florida statehood attempt, congressmen naturally thought of pairing the two and continuing their tradition of denying both the North and South a decisive advantage in the Senate. Those who wanted to reduce Iowa's size thought there was a possibility Florida would be divided into two states.

Duncan's most vocal supporter was fellow Ohioan Samuel F. Vinton. On February 14, 1845, Vinton addressed the House for an hour. Instead of dealing with the representation of free and slave states, Vinton championed western regionalism. He contended that the congressional tendency to make Mississippi Valley states large deprived that region of Senate representation. Therefore, he thought Iowa should be divided into two states. He believed that the large state favored by Iowans would destine it to "have three or four times as much population as Florida." He insisted that empowering the West would enhance

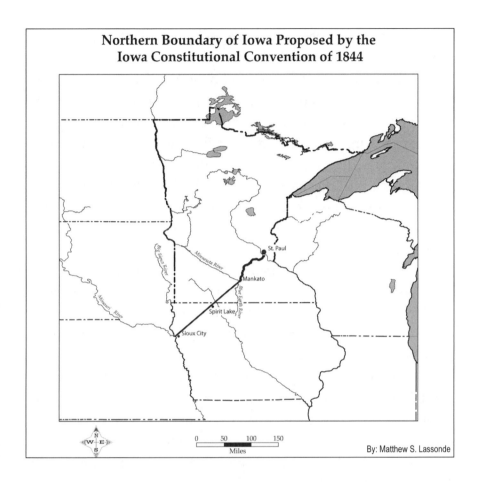

national unity, because unlike the North and South, it was immune to the "spirit of disunion." Consequently, the West "being inseparably connected with both, [because of steamboat commerce on the Mississippi and Ohio] . . . would always hold them together."[19]

Although the representatives refrained from speaking directly about free and slave states, regional contention was obvious. Northerners preferred a small Iowa and Southerners a large one. The strongest opposition to Duncan's amendment was by Brown of Tennessee and James E. Belser of Alabama. Brown stated that Iowa's requested boundaries would not make it too large, because it would be "smaller than Missouri or Virginia, and about the same size as Michigan. . . ." Belser argued that the boundaries proposed by the Committee on the Territories should be accepted, because its area of "some 65,500" square miles would make it slightly smaller than neighboring Missouri.

While not disputing Brown's and Belser's area estimates, Duncan countered that the boundaries proposed by the Committee on the Territories would give Iowa "double or treble the valuable land" of either Missouri or Virginia. "In point of fertility," he insisted, Iowa would have more area "than any two States in the United States."

Duncan's amendment was approved by a decisive House vote of ninety-one to forty on February 14, 1845. The vote was roughly proportional to the size of the slave and free state representation. At that time there were nine slave states that later joined the Confederate States of America. Their combined House membership was seventy-three. The other seventeen states had a total of 164 representatives.[20]

After Duncan had achieved his small state Iowa, Dodge pointed out to the House that Iowa's size was smaller than that recommended by Nicollet. He argued that the House should shift the western boundary from 17° to 17° 30' degrees west of Washington. The change would not only make the House bill consistent with Nicollet's plan, he contended, but would add some 5,000 square miles to Iowa. Duncan, who conceded that the House's intent was to use the Nicollet boundaries, made a friendly amendment to shift its western boundary to 17° 30'. This proposal provoked a long discussion by Brown, Vinton and Dodge, among others. It was then adopted "by general consent." [21]

The "Nicollet boundaries," as they came to be called, provoked no reaction in the Senate. But Congress continued to link Florida and Iowa statehood. On March 3, 1845, "An Act for the admission of the States of Iowa and Florida into the Union" was signed by President John Tyler. The law made an important distinction between the two. Florida was admitted immediately, but the revised Iowa constitution had to be approved by voters in the township elections scheduled for April 7, 1845.[22]

Anticipating an April vote on the constitution, Iowans had debated about the document since the adjournment of the convention. Because the constitution was produced by a convention controlled by Democrats, their party endorsed it. They reasoned that immediate statehood would not only increase Iowa's national stature, but would enable them to solidify their power as well. Conversely, the Whigs generally opposed the constitution, because they believed deferred statehood would enable them to improve their political standing. However, the differences between the Democrats and Whigs did not extend to boundaries. Both parties wanted a large Iowa as a matter of local pride and because access to navigable rivers was commercially important. Consequently, the pro and anti-constitution elements debated mainly about such issues as the division of power among the three branches of government, elected judges and the bill of rights.[23]

But the congressional boundary change became the most emotional issue in the last few weeks before the election. Dodge realized

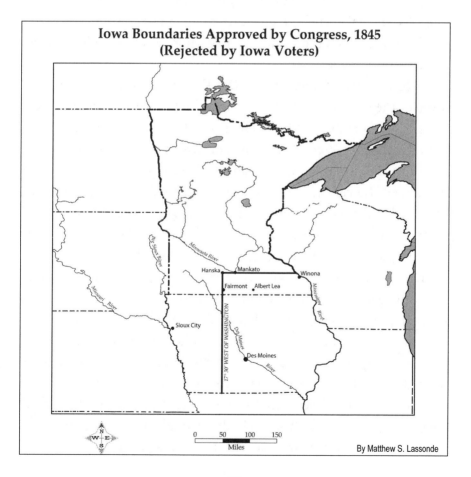

**Iowa Boundaries Approved by Congress, 1845**
**(Rejected by Iowa Voters)**

By Matthew S. Lassonde

the altered boundaries would anger many Iowans, so the day after President Tyler signed the Iowa-Florida Act, he sent a letter about them to his constituents. In attempting to placate Iowans he pointed out that the area encompassed by the new boundaries was 44,300 square miles, which would make their state "larger than the States of New Hampshire, Vermont, Massachusetts, R.[hode] Island, Connecticut, New Jersey, and Delaware combined; larger than the great States of Pennsylvania, Tennessee, Kentucky, North Carolina, Indiana, or Ohio; and nearly as large as the Empire State of New York." Iowa's waterways, he claimed, provided "facilities for navigation and manufactures unequalled by the rivers of any State in the Union."[24]

Quoting directly from Nicollet's report, Dodge explained that Congress instituted Nicollet's recommended boundaries for Iowa, because the lawmakers believed the cartographer had "accurately and scientifically examined the whole country lying between the Mississippi and Missouri rivers."

If Iowans were inclined to reject the congressional changes, he warned, they should realize that the reduction "was effected by the votes of the members of both Houses of Congress, from the North, from the East, *and from the West,* irrespective of party divisions." As evidence of the prevailing bipartisanship in Congress, he stressed that Alexander Duncan was a Democrat but Samuel F. Vinton, whom he described as the most forceful supporter of Duncan's amendment, was a Whig. The "irresistible force" of Vinton's remarks, he wrote, "was admitted by all, except the delegation from the South."

Dodge reported that his effort to retain Iowa's preferred boundaries was futile because the Iowa statehood question had become linked to the proposal to annex the Republic of Texas. The Texas annexation resolution approved on March 1, 1845, worked to Iowa's disadvantage because it stipulated that as many as four additional states could be formed out of Texas. Although the voters of these possible states were to decide whether slavery would be permitted or banned, the general congressional assumption was that they would all become slave states. Fear of additional slave states in the Texas area persuaded many con-

gressmen that a smaller Iowa would enable them to create more coun-
terbalancing Northern states.[25]

In part because of the Texas issue, Dodge was pessimistic about
Iowa's prospects. He concluded that the political opposition to its large
state boundaries was so powerful that regardless of the election results
"we will not be able hereafter under any circumstances, to obtain *one
square mile more*" than contained within the congressional boundaries.[26]

Initially, most Iowa Democrats seemed to agree with Dodge that
attaining statehood was more important than engaging in a boundary
battle with Congress. But dissidents led by five young politicians broke
with their party. All lawyers, the men—Enoch W. Eastman, Shepherd
Leffler, Frederick D. Mills, Theodore S. Parvin and James W. Woods—
vigorously urged rejection of the con-
gressional boundaries in stump speeches
throughout Iowa's election districts.[27]

The thirty-four-year-old Eastman of
Burlington, had arrived in Iowa from his
native New Hampshire less than a year
before the election. Although he was
elected lieutenant-governor (as a Republican) in 1863, he is mainly remembered
for opposing the Nicollet boundaries.[28]

Leffler, a native of Washington
County, Pennsylvania, moved to the Flint
Hills area near Burlington three years before the territory was formed. In 1839,
when he was only twenty-five years old,

Enoch Worthen Eastman. (Courtesy
of the State Historical Society of
Iowa)

he was elected to the first territorial House of Representatives. Subsequently, he served two more terms in the House and four in the Council.
In 1844, he was elected as one of Des Moines County's (the Burlington
area) delegates to the first constitutional convention. His political stature
was greatly enhanced when he was elected president of the convention.
In 1846, when Iowa achieved statehood, he was elected to the national
House of Representatives, where he served three consecutive terms.[29]

Mills moved to Burlington in 1841, the year after he graduated from Yale College in New Haven, Connecticut. His campaign against the congressional boundaries was his only foray into politics. Described as a "brilliant public speaker," he helped sway public opinion. He received a commission as a major in the United States army at the beginning of the Mexican-American War. On August 20, 1846, he was killed in action while leading an assault on Mexico City. Later the Iowa legislature named a county in the southwestern part of the state in his honor.[30]

Parvin, who graduated from the Cincinnati Law School in 1837, at the age of twenty, moved to Iowa the next year as the private secretary of Governor Robert Lucas. He was instrumental in founding the territorial library before being named a federal district attorney in 1839. During his subsequent long career he served variously as a probate judge, United States district court clerk and register of the State Land Office. Deeply interested in education and culture, he promoted the creation of the University of Iowa and the Iowa Historical Society.[31]

Woods moved to Burlington about the time Iowa Territory was created. During the next two decades he earned a reputation as one of Iowa's most famous lawyers and served as clerk of the state Supreme Court. Much of his persuasiveness was attributed to his congenial personality.[32]

In urging rejection of the Nicollet boundaries, Eastman, Leffler, Mills, Parvin and Woods stressed that they would deprive Iowa of "large and valuable" tracts of land adjoining the Missouri and St. Peter's rivers. This would leave the state with "mere imaginary lines, existing only on the face of the map, instead of the great land-marks [sic] traced by the finger of nature." Bordering the Missouri was especially important because commerce from the western portion of the proposed small state "would go to the Missouri and thus make us tributary to the power and influence of a foreign state."[33]

Furthermore, by acquiescing with the "narrow strait-laced limits offered by Congress, we would be reduced at once and forever, to the condition of a fifteenth rate State, shorn of all our glories . . ." But attainment of Iowa's preferred boundaries would eventually make it "one of the largest and most powerful States of the confederacy. . . ."

These large state advocates admonished Iowans to remember that they had nothing to lose by rejecting the congressional boundaries. Defeating the revised constitution would force the issue to be reconsidered by Congress. They reasoned that Congress would always at least offer the Nicollet boundaries but that if Iowans resisted firmly, they would be able to enlarge their state.

Leffler suggested that it might be possible to compromise with Congress by giving up some of the northwest, which he regarded as the least desirable part of the state. Specifically, he recommended conceding an estimated seven or eight thousand square miles. This would be accomplished by shifting the Big Sioux mouth-Blue Earth mouth line eastward to a straight line from the Blue Earth's mouth southwestward to the northwest point of Lake Boyer (present-day Lake View, Iowa) and then following the Boyer River to the Missouri, near present-day Missouri Valley. But Leffler was clear: such a line would be preferable to the Nicollet boundaries but Iowa should settle for it only if there was absolutely no chance in achieving the Lucas boundaries.[34]

In their boundary protest, Iowans never got involved in such national considerations as the balance of free and slave states or the desire to make the West more powerful by creating more states in the Mississippi River valley. Motivated by state pride and the desire for access to the Missouri River, they concentrated on the local issues of greatest concern to them.[35]

Iowa historians have concluded that the boundary question was the decisive issue in the April election. Primarily because of strong opposition to the congressional boundaries, the constitution was rejected by a margin of 996 votes. Eastman, Leffler, Mills, Parvin and Woods came to be remembered as Iowa patriots who saved the state from an interfering Congress. For example, Benjamin F. Gue pronounced their anti-congressional boundaries campaign as "one of the most important public services ever rendered the State."[36]

Dodge, among others, interpreted the election results as a rejection of the congressional boundaries. Desirous of being re-elected to a fourth term as territorial delegate, he adroitly converted to the large state cause. In his "Address to the People of Iowa," written at Burlington on June 23, 1845, Dodge reviewed the history of the congressional change in Iowa's boundaries. "In every stage of the proceeding," he wrote, he "had maintained and defended the boundaries" sought by Iowa. His only regret was "that my efforts were not more successful." Somewhat apologetically, in attempting to explain his circular letter recommendation that Iowans accept the congressional boundaries, Dodge insisted he had been merely reporting the political reality in Congress, rather than personally endorsing reduced boundaries. As for the future, he pledged that "if again sent to Washington as your Delegate, I will go there to carry out your views, opinions, and wishes" on the boundary and other subjects. He assured Iowans he would "devote all my time, talents and energies, towards carrying into effect the voice of those for whom I acted."[37]

While Dodge was campaigning, the territorial legislature authorized another vote on the constitution. In the election of August 4, 1845, Iowans re-elected Dodge but reaffirmed their April vote by again rejecting the constitution.[38]

Dodge returned to Congress determined to fight for a large Iowa with the 1844 constitution boundaries. On December 19, 1845, he introduced a House bill calling for the Lucas boundaries to replace the Nicollet boundaries. In keeping with procedure, the bill was referred to the House Committee on the Territories. Two weeks later, as a demonstration of Iowa's determination, he presented the House with the instructions he had received from the territorial Legislative Assembly to insist Congress accede to Iowa's preferred boundaries unconditionally.[39]

Although Dodge pleaded his case before the Committee on the Territories "a number of times," he could not convince its members to approve the Lucas boundaries. The committee, chaired by Stephen A. Douglas of Illinois, also rejected the 1845 congressional boundaries.[40]

On March 27, 1846, Douglas reported to the House that his committee recommended the Missouri and Big Sioux rivers as Iowa's western boundary and the latitude of 43° 30' from the Mississippi to the Big Sioux as its northern boundary. The proposal was an artful compromise of the

Lucas and Nicollet boundaries. The area of the contemplated state was about midway between the large state favored by Iowans and the small state legislated by the previous Congress. Its compact rectangular shape assured Iowans access to the Missouri River in exchange for relinquishing land north of the latitudinal line.

The selection of the Missouri-Big Sioux line not only provided Iowa with a natural western boundary, but certainly was chosen, in part, to answer Iowa's desire for a western commercial outlet. The reasons for choosing 43° 30' on the north were not as apparent, but the committee seems to have been influenced by developments in Iowa.

Stephen A. Douglas. (Courtesy of the Minnesota Historical Society)

The idea of a northern latitudinal boundary had not only been discussed in Iowa's constitutional convention but had been renewed after Iowans rejected the congressional boundary proposal. In late summer and fall, 1845, there was a movement in the city and county of Dubuque to make the forty-second parallel from the Mississippi River to the Missouri River Iowa's northern boundary. The idea appalled most Iowans because such a line would have fallen about thirty miles south of the Dubuque and created a long, narrow state only about half the size of that authorized by Congress. Supporters of the line apparently wanted to create a situation where Dubuque would be the principal city in a new territory extending north to the international boundary. They were determined enough to circulate a petition and submit it to Congress.[41]

Naturally, those living in the central and southern parts of settled Iowa resisted the northern separatist movement. But some critics saw merit in a northern latitudinal boundary. The *Iowa Capital Reporter* (Iowa City) opined that if Iowans would unite and ask for the forty-third parallel as their northern boundary, "little doubt can exist but such a change can be effected at the next session of Congress." The editor pointed out that such a line would give Iowa access to the Missouri and increase its size by about a third more than that sought by the Dubuque area petitioners. Congress would accept it, the editor reasoned, because it would make Iowa about the same size as the one with the Nicollet boundaries. Congress, after all, was primarily concerned with the size of Iowa, not its shape.[42]

Douglas, well aware of the Iowa suggestions for a latitudinal line, chose to shift it northward to 43° 30', contending that this location was an approximation of the natural divide between the watersheds of the southward-flowing Des Moines and Iowa rivers and the northward-flowing St. Peter's. The actual divide, of course, was a wavy line. Both the headwaters of the Des Moines and Iowa started north of 43° 30' and the Blue Earth, a major tributary of the St. Peter's, rose south of that latitude.[43]

The Douglas bill was not considered by the House until June 8, 1846. In the meantime, its contents became known in Iowa before the second constitutional convention was convened in Iowa City on May 4. Because the first constitution had been twice rejected by the voters, the Legislative Assembly authorized the writing of a new document.[44]

Delegates to the 1846 constitutional convention, which adjourned on May 19, considered only two western and northern boundary scenarios—the Lucas boundaries or the boundaries moved by Douglas. At one point the delegates supported the Lucas boundaries by a vote of twenty-two to eight. But advocates of discretion convinced a majority that attaining statehood was more important than challenging Congress. By a vote of eighteen to thirteen, the convention agreed on a description of Iowa's boundaries that included the Missouri-Big Sioux line on the west and 43° 30' on the north.

This action enabled Douglas to argue during House debates that Congress should endorse the will of the people of Iowa. The strongest opposition to the Douglas boundaries came from Julius Rockwell of Massachusetts, George Rathbun of New York, and Samuel F. Vinton of Ohio.

Rockwell's first preference was for the Nicollet boundaries. But rather than return to that position, he proposed the forty-second parallel as the northern boundary. He was influenced by both the Dubuque petition and the desire to make Iowa smaller. Douglas countered that Rockwell's suggested boundaries would make Iowa some 15,000 square miles smaller than Iowa's original preference. As for the Dubuque petition, Douglas insisted that its signers were nothing more than a discontented minority. Iowans overwhelmingly supported the new compromise boundaries, he noted, and congressional acceptance would enable Iowa to "at once come in as a State of the Union." Rejection would require another convention and constitution "and thus the existing disputes which have been happily terminated would be reviewed and perpetuated...."[45]

In speaking against the bill, Rathbun reiterated most of the contentions advanced in 1845. He argued the proposed Iowa was too large, its valuable land meant it could sustain a large population in much less area than New York, much of which "was broken and utterly worthless," Congress should strive for a balance of free and slave states, and Texas might become five slave states. Furthermore, he claimed Iowans had not rejected the 1844 congressional boundaries *per se*, but had only voted against the constitution that contained them. He believed that "had the question of boundary been separated from the question of constitution, the boundary would have been assented to."

Responding to Rathbun, Dodge insisted Iowans had been "very reasonable" in their boundary demands, which they assumed would be accepted by Congress if they were kept smaller than Missouri. He emphasized that Iowans had always wanted Mississippi and Missouri river lines, but when "they found that Congress had given them, instead of these, mere arbitrary and artificial lines, they rose up as one man, and by an overwhelming vote, rejected the Constitution." He assured the House that if his constituents had been able to vote separately on the constitution and the congressional boundaries, the boundaries "would not have received five hundred votes—nay, I doubt whether one hundred in the whole Territory."

Vinton sarcastically ridiculed the idea of making Iowa larger than the Nicollet boundaries. He knew it was "very natural for the people of the Territory to desire to have a great State; and, if Congress was willing to let the people of Iowa cut and carve for themselves, he did not doubt that they would have their State extend to the mouth of the Columbia." Contending that an Iowa comparable to New York or Pennsylvania was large enough, he made an amendment to make the forty-third parallel its northern boundary. Philosophically, he reiterated his main 1844 contention. A small Iowa was necessary in order to create more western states, which would benefit the nation.[46]

Both Douglas and Dodge spoke against the Vinton amendment. Douglas argued that changing the boundary would require Iowa to hold another constitutional convention, which would delay statehood. Dodge, described as "speaking under obvious excitement," portrayed Vinton as a villain intent on denying Iowa its rightful natural boundaries. He warned that the "people of Iowa would never acquiesce" to boundaries that either cut them off from the Missouri on the west or 43° 30' on the north.

Douglas and Dodge were persuasive. The House defeated Vinton's amendment by a vote of fifty-four "ayes" and sixty-eight "nays." Then the House passed an amendment made by James B. Bowlin of Missouri to describe Iowa's boundaries exactly as they were stated in its constitution.

The House decision sealed the fate of Iowa's boundaries. The Senate accepted the House bill and on August 4, 1846, President James K. Polk signed "An Act to define the Boundaries of Iowa, and to repeal so much of the Act of the third of March, one thousand eight hundred and forty-five as relates to the Boundaries of Iowa." The day before Iowa's voters had approved the 1846 constitution by a vote of 9,492 to 9,036. On December 28, 1846, Polk signed the act admitting Iowa as the twenty-ninth state.[47]

By the time Iowa's northern boundary was surveyed and marked in 1852, the political make-up of the upper Mississippi region had undergone significant changes. Wisconsin was admitted as the thirtieth state on May 29, 1848, and on March 3, 1849, President Polk signed the act that created Minnesota Territory.[48]

The new Minnesota territory encompassed all of the former Iowa Territory left outside the new state as well as that part of the former Wisconsin Territory between the Mississippi and St. Croix rivers. Minnesota's prospects for a burgeoning agricultural economy were boosted by two major treaties between the federal government and the Dakota Indians. By the treaties of Traverse des Sioux and Mendota of July and August, 1851, the four Dakota bands ceded all of their land claims in Minnesota Territory and northern Iowa. Senate approval of the treaties was prolonged and contentious. Consequently, President Millard Fillmore did not proclaim them to be in effect until February 24, 1853. Before year's end most of the Dakota had been moved to two long, narrow reservations straddling the upper Minnesota River.[49]

Because of the slow treaty approval process approximately three-fourths of the Iowa-Minnesota border area was still legally Dakota Indian country when the 1852 boundary survey was conducted. In northeasternmost Iowa, east of the Dakota cessions, Euro-American settlers occupied the area for about thirty miles west of the Mississippi. George B. Sargent of Dubuque, the surveyor general for Iowa and Wisconsin, thought the surveyors might have some difficulty with roving Dakotas. Nonetheless, he did not request an army escort but did provide the surveying party with an interpreter.[50]

Congress saw no urgency in authorizing surveying of Iowa's northern boundary as long as the area north of the state was unorganized territory. But the formation of Minnesota Territory increased the likelihood of conflicting land claims between Iowans and Minnesotans. Consequently, on the same day he signed the Minnesota territorial act, Polk approved "An Act to cause the Northern Boundary of the State of Iowa to be run and marked." The brief measure specified that the boundary determination would be arranged by the "Surveyor-General of Wisconsin and Iowa, under the direction of the Commissioner of the General Land Office."[51]

Although the congressional intent was clear, the General Land Office commissioner could not authorize a complete survey because the act did not include funding. However, in late 1849, while awaiting the next congressional appropriations act, the General Land Office arranged with the army's Corps of Topographical Engineers to have 43° 30' determined and monumented on the west side of the Mississippi. This work was done by Captain Thomas Jefferson Lee. An 1830 graduate of the United States Military Academy, Lee was promoted to captain in the Corps of Topographical Engineers in 1847.[52]

At the north end of Main Street in present-day New Albin, Iowa, Lee determined the latitudinal line astronomically. He marked the point with a 600-pound iron obelisk that stands three feet, eleven inches tall from its base to the top of its pyramidal cap. Each side at the base is ten and a half inches wide, which tapers to seven inches at the lower end of the pyramidal cap. Lee had it inscribed with "Iowa" on its south side, "Minnesota" on its north face, "1849" on its east and "Lat. 43° 30'" on its west. The General Land Office later reimbursed the Corps of Topographical Engineers $1,657.69 for Lee's work, out of the congressional appropriations for measuring and marking the boundary.[53]

In its appropriations act of September 30, 1850, Congress allocated $15,000 for measuring and marking Iowa's northern boundary. But when he was organizing the survey, Sargent requested an additional $15,000. Justin Butterfield, general land office commissioner, endorsed Sargent's plea because most of the boundary area lacked timber for fuel and making monuments and some of it passed through marshes. These features threatened to slow the survey and increase the costs of labor and wagon transportation. On July 21, 1852, when the survey was nearly completed, Congress authorized the requested sum in the Deficiencies Appropriation Act for Year Ending June 30, 1852.[54]

Butterfield outlined the survey's methodology in his letter of February 2, 1852, to Sargent. He emphasized that the boundary had to be determined carefully by celestial observations, because its placement was crucial to the veracity of the rectangular land survey system. He wanted a measurement that was so accurate it would preclude any Iowa-Minnesota land disputes. Butterfield noted that several ranges in eastern Iowa had been surveyed to a line about five miles south of 43° 30'. Therefore, Iowa's northernmost tier of townships would include only thirty sections, which would be numbered seven through thirty-six. According to legend, the subsequent absence of sections one through six just south of the Iowa-Minnesota boundary enabled swindlers to sell them sight unseen to some Indiana and Ohio buyers, who did not realize they had been duped until they arrived to occupy the land. The latitudinal boundary would be designated a correction line, so the Minnesota townships flanking it would be the regular size of thirty-six square miles each. To be certain the land survey was properly connected with the latitudinal line, Butterfield mandated that the Iowa-Minnesota boundary be monumented at all section and half-section points.[55]

As the surveyor-general of Wisconsin and Iowa, Sargent made survey arrangements from his Dubuque office. Andrew Talcott was employed to lead the forty-man party and to serve as its astronomer and chief surveyor. Isaac W. Smith, the "first assistant deputy surveyor," was engaged as the second in command. He directed the survey until Talcott joined the party at Station Washington, forty-nine miles west of Lee's monument.[56]

A Connecticut native, the fifty-five-year-old Talcott had a long experience in the army's Corps of Topographical Engineers and as a civil engineer. After graduating from the United States Military Academy in 1818, he served on the frontier and participated in the construction of various military posts in the East. After resigning his captain's commission in 1836, he worked as a civil engineer. The United States General Land Office employed him as the astronomer for the Michigan-Ohio boundary resurvey of 1837. During the next fifteen years he worked principally as an engineer and construction supervisor for various railroads. His previous experience in the Iowa country may have been a factor in his selection to supervise the boundary survey. In July 1820, he served as the engineer for a small army expedition that reconnoitered an overland route from Cantonment Missouri (later Fort Atkinson), on the right bank of the Missouri River about fifteen miles upstream from present-day Omaha, Nebraska, to Fort St. Anthony, (the predecessor of Fort Snelling). At that time the army wanted to connect its frontier posts by overland trails as well as river routes.[57]

Although Talcott had been out of the army for sixteen years, he was deferentially identified as "Captain Talcott." Evidently he acted more like a military commander than a civilian. One survey veteran recalled that "the organization was conducted along lines of very strict and almost military discipline." Every man had to sign a contract in which he agreed to obey all orders and to refrain from possessing, transporting or drinking any intoxicating liquor.[58]

In late May 1852, after he had joined the survey at Station Washington, Talcott organized four units. He led the headquarters group of ten to twelve men that included a secretary, doctor, interpreter and the commissary and quartermaster services, which David B. Sears supervised. James M. Marsh, Harry Taylor and John S. Sheller led the three surveying parties.[59]

During the nearly three months of fieldwork, Marsh led the advance party. Assisted by eleven men including a topographer, chainmen, flagmen and laborers, he determined a preliminary boundary with a solar compass. The solar compass, patented by William Austin Burt of Mt. Vernon, Michigan, in 1836, was a relatively new instrument. By determining positions from the sun it was much more accurate than the traditional magnetic compass, which was detrimentally affected by local mineral deposits. At the time the boundary survey was being conducted, the General Land Office wanted to compare the results of calculations made by a solar compass operator to those of an astronomer. Since Talcott knew in advance the solar compass measurements would be very near the actual latitude, he also had Marsh reconnoiter the boundary area's natural features. This information enabled him to plan for such things as gathering fuel, caching supplies, crossing streams and establishing astronomical stations.[60]

Talcott established six astronomical stations west of Lee's monument. Spaced at intervals varying from thirty-seven to fifty-one miles, they were named from east to west after presidents of the United States—Washington, Adams, Jefferson, Madison, Monroe and Jackson. Station Jackson was located on the left bank of the Big Sioux River. With the inclusion of Lee's monument, the latitude 43° 30' was precisely determined at seven points.[61]

Theoretically, a line of latitude (or a parallel to the equator) had to curve slightly to the south. But when such a line was connected with a land survey system that used square sections, straight courses had to be calculated between astronomical stations. The most accurate way of doing this was to survey a series of short lines rather than projecting a single straight line from one astronomical station to another.

Surveying the short line courses, which Talcott called the guide line, was assigned to Harry Taylor, whose crew was the same size and composition as Marsh's. In establishing the guide line, Taylor's men had to calculate offsets from the true latitude of 43° 30'. In some instances the variance was as short as a link (7.92 inches, or one one-hundredth of the sixty-six-foot surveyor's chain). Taylor's crew subsequently placed temporary markers at all section and half-section corners. The mile monuments indicated the number of the sections on the Minnesota side that would be platted later during rectangular land surveys.[62]

In Taylor's wake, Sheller and his six-man crew rechecked all distances and marked the boundary. They placed an identifying monument at every section and half-section corner, except when those points fell in lakes or streams. Following Butterfield's instructions, which were relayed to them by Sargent and Talcott, they used wooden posts wherever suitable hardwood was available. The posts at the section and half-section corners had to be four inches square and four and a half feet long, with only two feet above ground level. The posts placed at township corners were the same length, but had to be six inches square.[63]

Generally, in the open country west of Station Washington they monumented the boundary with mounds of earth or rocks covered with soil. The specified height of the conical mounds at township corners was three feet. At all other corners the mounds were to have a height of two and a half feet. Talcott, who stressed the importance of constructing enduring monuments, ordered that whenever possible the mounds were to be made of rocks covered with earth. Each mound was to have a center wooden post inscribed with its sectional location.

Several types of rocks were found over the course of surveying the boundary. In the area east of the Red Cedar River, which was approximately one-third of the boundary distance, limestone, a soft sedimentary rock, was dominant. West of the river, both sandstone and granite were oftentimes found on the surface. Granite, much harder than the other two, was more suitable for mound construction. David B. Sears, whose father supervised the commissary and quartermaster services, wrote that sometimes they had to travel a day or more to obtain granite boulders that weighed as much as a ton. These were moved by "special vehicles" pulled by oxen. In all likelihood they were similar to the rock sleds used by prairie farmers. Sears also noted that a glass bottle containing the survey calculations for that spot was buried under each mound.[64]

All wooden posts, including those in mounds erected at township corners, had distinctive markings. Those at every fourth corner were "deeply cut or branded" with "IOWA" on the south side and "MINNESOTA" on the north. Below each word appeared "43° 30' NORTH." All other township posts were inscribed below the sectional and township identification with "I.B." on the south and "M.B." on the north. Talcott had a special marker erected at the western end of the boundary on the left bank of the Big Sioux River. It was a stone monument made with Sioux quartzite, whose formation underlays much of southwestern Minnesota. The rock was extremely hard, but the monument, has disappeared.[65]

Talcott's surveyors determined that the Iowa-Minnesota boundary from the center of the Mississippi to the center of the Big Sioux was 268 miles, ninety-eight chains and twenty-three links long. Despite some supply and Indian problems they completed their work with dispatch. After entering unsettled country about thirty miles west of the Mississippi, they had to move without benefit of any of the advantages of an established society such as locally available foodstuffs, roads and bridges. After leaving the hilly area on the boundary's easternmost portion they moved through somewhat undulating or flat plains. The flooded West Fork of the Des Moines River was their main barrier, but they safely ferried it.[66]

Equipped with wagons each drawn by three yokes of oxen, a spring wagon and saddle horses, the expedition had to move quantities of rations, equipage and instruments. At Station Washington, Talcott ordered Sears to forward 2400 daily rations (calculated at forty men for sixty days), with half of them being sent and cached at the first crossing of the Des Moines River. Sears was also instructed to transport fifty pounds of personal baggage for each man, 1,000 pounds of instruments and books, grain for the horses, extra harnesses and tools. In addition to traversing the boundary line area on the out and return trips, Sears's men had to make a number of side trips. The two longest were to Lansing, Iowa, on the Mississippi to forward instruments that had been delivered by steamboat, and to Fort Dodge, about seventy miles south of the boundary, to procure additional rations.

Sargent and Talcott planned to supplement the rations with fresh beef. But because of an ample supply of wild animals, the surveyors did not have to slaughter any of the cattle they brought along. A short distance west of the Mississippi they killed their first elk and were able to shoot their first buffalo near the Blue Earth River, about thirty miles west of the expedition's mid-point.[67]

The Dakotas encountered by surveying parties were never openly hostile but, in the words of David Sears, were "unfriendly and suspicious, and often questioned our interpreter as to the purpose of the organization, and the object of running the line." Some of the Dakotas harassed the expedition by stealing cached supplies and destroying fodder. Forewarned about likely thievery, the elder Sears attempted to disguise his caches by building campfires over them, but the Indians were alert to this ruse and found the cached goods by probing with muzzle ramrods. However, Sears discovered a successful technique when he buried supplies under the trail near creek banks, covered the spots with brush and drove wagons across them. This worked because brush matting was often used to firm up the trail in marshy areas. En route to the Big Sioux, Sears had prairie grass cut and stacked for forage on the return trip. To safeguard the stacks from prairie fires, he had fireguards plowed around them. On the return trip he found that Dakotas had burned most of them to the ground.

The cost of surveying and marking the Iowa-Minnesota boundary exceeded the $30,000 appropriated by Congress by $5,347.38. To balance the books the General Land Office raised $3,069.65 by selling survey property and transferred $2,277.73 from its general surveying fund. The survey's three largest expenditures were $18,612.11 for all employees except Talcott, $9,627.28 for provisions, animals, equipment and transportation and $5,000 for Talcott's reimbursement and the cost of astronomical instruments.[68]

With the exception of Lee's iron monument, none of the Iowa-Minnesota boundary markers placed by surveyors in 1849 and 1852 remain. It is likely that some of the wooden posts were destroyed by Dakotas soon after the surveyors withdrew. Natural phenomena such as decay and wind erosion would have obliterated some of them. Additionally, as the country was settled with landholders who claimed specific legal tracts in either Iowa or Minnesota, the markers would no longer serve any purpose and would have been removed for such purposes as road construction and cultivation of the land. However, it is likely some of the markers were still in place when land surveyors worked their way through the Iowa-Minnesota border country in the 1850s.

## NOTES:

1. Wisconsin Territory Act and Iowa Territory Act, *U.S. Statutes at Large*, 5: 10-11, 235.
2. Leigh Ann Randak, "Lucas, Robert," in *The Biographical Dictionary of Iowa*, edited by David Hudson, Marvin Bergman, and Loren Horton (Iowa City: University of Iowa Press, 2008), 325-326; Malcolm J. Rohrbough, "Lucas, Robert," in *American National Biography* (New York: Oxford University Press, 1999), 14: 86.
3. Benj.[amin] F. Shambaugh, *The Constitutions of Iowa* (Iowa City: State Historical Society of Iowa, 1934), 103-104.
4. David A. Walker, "Chambers, John," *Biographical Dictionary of Iowa*, 81-82; Shambaugh, *Constitutions*, 114.
5. Shambaugh, *Constitutions*, 114-116; Benjamin F. Gue, *History of Iowa: From the Earliest Times to the Beginning of the Twentieth Century*, 4 vols. (New York: The Century History Co., 1903) 1:212.
6. Shambaugh, *Constitutions*, 118, 123; Gue, *History of Iowa*, 1: 211.
7. Benjamin F. Shambaugh, comp. and ed., *Fragments of the Debates of the Iowa Constitutional Conventions of 1844 and 1846 along with Press Comments and Other Materials on the Constitutions of 1844 and 1846* (Iowa

City: State Historical Society of Iowa, 1900), 9; Leland L. Sage, *A History of Iowa* (Ames: Iowa State University Press, 1974), 85.

8. Shambaugh, *Fragments of Debates*, 22.

9. For a map showing the boundaries of the 1830 Prairie du Chien Treaty cessions, see Charles C. Royce, *Indian Land Cessions in the United States* (Reprint ed., New York: Arno Press and the New York Times, 1971), Plate CXXXI.

10. Shambaugh, *Fragments of Debates*, 22-23.

11. Here and below, *Ibid.*, 23-24.

12. Shambaugh, *Fragments*, 24.

13. Shambaugh, *Constitutions*, 157.

14. *Ibid.*,

15. Nicollet's map printed from an original copy (St. Paul: Minnesota Historical Society, 1976).

16. Here and below, *Congressional Globe*, 10 February 1845, 14:269.

17. Here and below, 28 Cong., 2 sess., House doc. 52, p. 73 (Serial 464).

18. *Ibid.*, 74.

19. Here and below, *Congressional Globe*, 14 February 1845, 14: 269, 273, 279.

20. *Ibid.*, 14:273, *Biographical Directory of the United States Congress 1774-2005* (Washington: Government Printing Office, 2005), 127-29.

21. Dodge, "Address to the People of Iowa," 23 June 1845, in *Fragments*, 257; *Congressional Globe*, 14 February 1845, 14: 273. The Washington meridian, which was then used by American cartographers, passed through the center of the White House. It was 77° 02' 12.48" west of the Greenwich prime meridian. The Greenwich meridian was made the international standard for determining time by International Meridian Conference held in Washington, D.C. in 1884. (Joseph Hyde Pratt, "American Prime Meridians," *Geographical Review* 32 (April 1942): 234-35.)

22. Act to Admit the States of Iowa and Florida, *U. S. Statutes at Large*, 5:742.

23. Shambaugh, *Constitutions*, 170-72; Gue, *History of Iowa*, 1:217.

24. Here and below, "Letter of Augustus C. Dodge to His Constituents, *Iowa Capital Reporter* (Iowa City), 29 March 1845, reprinted in Shambaugh, *Fragments*, 232-34.

25. *Ibid.*, 235; "Joint Resolution for Annexing Texas to the United States," 01 March 1845, *U.S. Statutes at Large*, 5: 797-98.

26. Shambaugh, *Fragments*, 235.

27. Gue, *History of Iowa*, 4:84; Sage, *History of Iowa*, 88.

28. Gue, *History of Iowa*, 4: 84.

29. *Ibid*, 4: 167: *Biographical Directory United States Congress*, 1436.

30. Gue, *History of Iowa*, 4: 194.

31. *Ibid.*, 4: 210; William R. Krueger, "Parvin, Theodore Sutton," in *Biographical Dictionary of Iowa*, 398-400.

32. *Report of the First Annual Meeting of the Iowa State Bar Association, Held at Des Moines, Iowa, June 27 and 28, 1895* (Davenport, IA: Egbert, Fidlar, & Chambers, 1895), 45-46.

33. Here and below, Shambaugh, *Fragments,* 252.

34. *Ibid.*

35. Shambaugh, *Constitutions,* 182.

36. *Ibid.* , 177; Gue, *History of Iowa,* 4: 84.

37. Shambaugh, *Fragments,* 256-57, 259.

38. Louis Pelzer, *Augustus Caesar Dodge* (Iowa City: State Historical Society of Iowa, 1908), 121.

39. *Congressional Globe,* 19 December 1845, 15:86; Pelzer, *Dodge,* 122.

40. Here and below, *Congressional Globe,* 27 March, 8 June 1846,15: 86, 939.

41. Shambaugh, *Fragments,* 261-64.

42. *Iowa Capital Reporter,* 22 October 1845, reprinted in Shambaugh, *Fragments,* 264.

43. *Congressional Globe,* 8 June 1846, 15: 938.

44. Here and below, Shambaugh, *Constitutions,* 185-88, 204-05.

45. *Congressional Globe,* 8 June1846, 15:938-39.

46. Here and below, *Ibid.,* 940; "The Boundaries of Iowa. Remarks by Mr. A.C. Dodge, June 8, 1846," Appendix to the Congressional Globe, for the First Session, Twenty-Ninth Congress: Containing Speeches and Important State Papers," p. 668.

47. *U.S. Statutes at Large,* 9:52; Shambaugh, *Constitutions,* 210.

48. *U.S. Statutes at Large,* 9: 233, 403.

49. Charles J. Kappler, *Indian Affairs: Laws and Treaties* (Washington: Government Printing Office, 1904), 2: 588-93; Roy W. Meyer, *History of the Santee Sioux: United States Indian Policy on Trial* (Lincoln: University of Nebraska Press, 1967), 89; William E. Lass, *The History of Traverse des Sioux* (St. Peter, MN: Nicollet County Historical Society Press, 2011).

50. "Survey of the Iowa-Minnesota Boundary Line," *Annals of Iowa* 16 (January 1929): 502.

51. *U.S. Statutes at Large,* 9:410.

52. "Survey of the Iowa-Minnesota Boundary Line," 488; Francis B. Heitman, *Historical Register and Dictionary of the United States Army,* 2 vols. (Washington: Government Printing Office, 1903), 1: 625.

53. J.S. Dodds (ed.) *et al., Original Instructions Governing the Public Land Surveys of Iowa: A Guide to Their Use in Resurveys of Public Lands* (Ames: Iowa Engineering Society, 1943), 524; Author's inspection of Lee monument, 03 November 2009; *Report of the Secretary of the Interior Relative to Iowa's Northern Boundary Survey,* December 27, 1853, 33 Cong., 1 sess., Senate Ex. Doc.10, serial 694;

54. *U.S. Statutes at Large,* 9:535, 10:22; *Iowa's Northern Boundary,* 32 Cong., 1 sess., House Ex. Doc. 66, serial 641.

55. "Survey of the Iowa-Minnesota Boundary Line," 483-87; Hildegard Binder Johnson, *Order Upon the Land: The U.S. Rectangular Land Survey and the Upper Mississippi Country* (New York: Oxford University Press, 1976), 124; Otto Knauth, "Reporter Tells Story of Iowa-

Minnesota Boundary Survey," *Dis-Closures* (Fall 1989). 17. (*Dis-Closures* was published by the Minnesota Society of Professional Surveyors. Knauth's article was reprinted from the *Des Moines Sunday Register*, 12 July 1970. During the rectangular land survey of Iowa's northernmost townships, they proved to have a north-south distance of about 4.75 miles. Therefore, all of the sections (seven through twelve) abutting the Iowa-Minnesota boundary have about 490 acres as compared to 640 for full sections. (Trevor Wolf, Winnebago County, Iowa, assistant engineer, letter to William E. Lass, 29 December 2010.)

56. Dodds, *Original Instructions*, 528.

57. Albert Watkins, "Three Military Heroes of Nebraska," *Nebraska History and Record of Pioneer Days* 2 (October-December 1919): 5; Heitman, *Historical Register,* 1: 943; James Grant Wilson and John Fiske, eds., *Appleton's Cyclopaedia of American Biography* (New York: D. Appleton and Co.,1889) , 6:24.

58. "Survey of the Iowa-Minnesota Boundary Line," 502.

59. Dodds, *Original Instructions* ,536.

60. *Ibid.* , 531-32; Terry S. Reynolds and Barry C. James, "Burt, William Austin," in *American National Biography*, 4: 60-62.

61. Dodds, *Original Instructions*, 537.

62. "Survey of the Iowa-Minnesota Boundary Line," 493.

63. Here and below, *Ibid.* , 485-87.

64. *Ibid.* , 500,503.

65. *Ibid.* , 487; Johnson, *Order Upon the Land,* 124.

66. Here and below, Dodds, *Original Instructions,* 537; "Survey of the Iowa-Minnesota Boundary Line," 490, 502.

67. Here and below, "Survey of the Iowa-Minnesota Boundary Line," 502.

68. *Report of the Secretary of the Interior Relative to Iowa's Northern Boundary Survey.* In terms of 2012 dollars, the 1852 dollars shown in the text would each be worth an estimated $27.50. ("Consumer Price Index (Estimate) 1800-," Accessed 30 January 2013.

## Minnesota-Wisconsin Boundary Possibilities

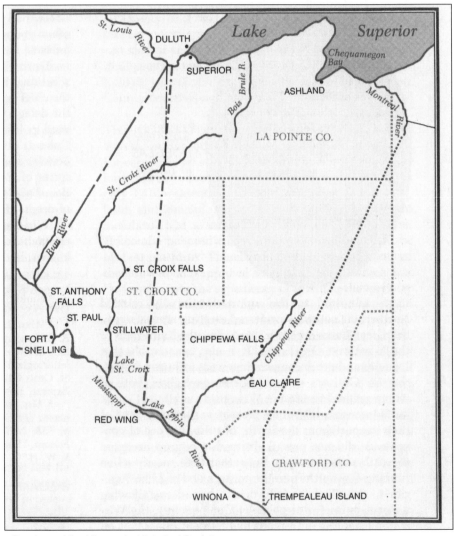

Courtesy of the Minnesota Historical Society

# CHAPTER THREE

## FORMING THE EASTERN BOUNDARY WITH WISCONSIN

N O ONE LIVING WITHIN THE BOUNDS of Minnesota had a hand in shaping its northern and southern boundaries. But by the time the Minnesota-Wisconsin boundary was determined, with the advent of Wisconsin's statehood process, some pioneers in the Stillwater-St. Paul area tried to influence the shaping of both Wisconsin and Minnesota.

By 1838, when Wisconsin Territory's western boundary was fixed at the Mississippi River and a due north line from its source to the international boundary, forces that would soon cause dramatic changes in the Upper Mississippi region were at work. Shortly after Wisconsin Territory was established in 1836, its political leaders began scheming for statehood. Men such as Henry Dodge, the first territorial governor, were very familiar with the statehood process in the Northwest Territory. Ohio, Indiana, Illinois and Michigan, the states already created out of the territory, had all moved relatively rapidly from territorial to statehood status because of population booms preceded by Indian land cessions.

The groundwork for cessions in the Upper Mississippi area was laid by the 1825 Treaty of Prairie du Chien. Among other things, it established a boundary between Dakota and Ojibwe lands. From a point near what would become Osceola, Wisconsin, on the lower Chippewa River, the dividing line extended northwestward across the St. Croix and Mississippi to the mouth of the Buffalo River, a tributary of the Red River. Ostensibly, the federal government intended the boundary to be a deterrent to intertribal warfare. Although it never served that purpose, it facilitated later cessions by legally identifying respective tribal claims.[1]

When Dodge was named governor, Wisconsin's economy was based on agriculture and lead mining it its southern counties. Both farmers and miners wanted to be able to obtain lumber from the vast pineries on Indian land to their north. Thus, Indian land cessions would not only open a lumbermen's frontier, but would benefit all Wisconsinites. In 1837, pinelands were ceded by treaties with the Ho-Chunk (i.e. Winnebago), Ojibwe and Dakota. Only the Ojibwe and Dakota treaties applied to lands in the future Minnesota.[2]

Dodge, acting in his capacity as territorial *ex-officio* superintendent of Indian Affairs, negotiated with Ojibwe chiefs and warriors at Fort Snelling. On July 29, the Ojibwe leaders agreed to cede a vast tract of land. It encompassed about one-third of the later state of Wisconsin and that part of Minnesota between the St. Croix and Mississippi rivers north of the 1825 boundary line and south of a line drawn eastward from the mouth of the Crow Wing River to the north end of Lake St. Croix[3]

After the Ojibwe treaty, Lawrence Taliaferro, head of the St. Peter's Agency, led a delegation of Mdewakanton Dakota chiefs and headmen to Washington, D.C. Taliaferro wanted the Dakota to cede their lands east of the Mississippi, which he insisted they were no longer using, so part of the government's reimbursement could be used to promote their transition to a farming society. But his superior, Dodge, was primarily interested in a Dakota cession to open more forest lands. On September 29, 1837, the Mdewakanton leaders signed a treaty negotiated by Secretary of War Joel R. Poinsett. They agreed to sell all their lands east of the Mississippi and south of the 1825 boundary.[4]

Senate approval of the Ojibwe and Dakota treaties was customarily slow. They were finally proclaimed to be in effect by President Martin Van Buren on June 15, 1838.[5]

Combined, the two treaties added some five thousand square miles of land between the St. Croix and Mississippi to the public domain. The "Delta Area," as it was sometimes called because of its shape, was a magnet for New England lumbermen, land speculators and independent Indian traders. Newcomers joined with the established American Fur Company's traders and some settlers expelled from the Fort Snelling reservation to establish new communities in the southernmost part of the Delta Area.

The genesis of St. Paul was the tiny outpost of Pig's Eye, located about four miles down the Mississippi from Fort Snelling. While anticipating approval of the Dakota and Ojibwe treaties, fort commander Major Joseph Plympton began planning to evict civilian squatters from the military reserve. A survey conducted in October 1837, showed that 157 civilians who had no role in the fort's official activities were living on the reserve. Some of them were French-Canadians who drifted west with the ever-shifting frontier, and others were exiles from Lord Selkirk's Red River Colony. Plympton complained that they and their animals were a threat to the reservation's timber and pasturage resources.[6]

Soon after he received news of the Dakota treaty's approval, Plympton evicted the civilians from reservation grounds. Their cluster of shelters near Pierre Parrant's grog shop was named Pig's Eye in 1839, after Parrant's nickname. Two years later, the French-born Roman Catholic priest Lucian Galtier built St. Paul's chapel there. Since the place was the Mississippi's practical head of navigation, its name evolved over the course of a few years to St. Paul's Landing and then St. Paul.

Joseph R. Brown. (Courtesy of the Minnesota Historical Society)

Meanwhile, lumbermen and other promoters moved into the St. Croix valley. Franklin Steele, a storekeeper at Fort Snelling, built a sawmill at the falls of the St. Croix River. Downstream from the falls, agents for a lumbering company located a sawmill site at Marine on St. Croix. Near the head of Lake St. Croix, Joseph R. Brown, who had lived in the area for two decades as a drummer boy, dragoon, and fur trader, platted the townsite of Dacotah.[7]

The assemblage of squatters, fur traders, speculators, and lumberjacks in the Lake St. Croix-St. Paul area had little, if any, feeling for

Wisconsin. They had nothing in common with the farmers and lead miners of the southern counties. Even those who came from the East had not necessarily passed through the settled portions of the territory. It is understandable that they felt alienated from Wisconsin, with its political center at distant Madison.

The straggling outposts on the upper Mississippi gained a certain sense of unity and identity from the formation of St. Croix County in January 1840. In keeping with the tradition of creating extraordinarily large counties on the edge of the frontier, St. Croix County was massive. It encompassed all of Wisconsin Territory west of a north-south line about forty miles east of the lower St. Croix River and running from Lake Superior to the Chippewa River. The 1840 federal census reported the new county had 809 non-Indian residents, with 351 of them located between the St. Croix and Mississippi.[8]

Brown led the way in giving St. Croixians more control over their own affairs. While trading and farming on Gray Cloud Island in the Mississippi below St. Paul, he was named a justice of the peace for Crawford County in the fall of 1839. Through this position, Brown gained status and became acquainted with political leaders in Prairie du Chien, the county seat. When he lobbied the territorial legislature for the creation of St. Croix County out of the northern portions of Crawford County, the political powers in Prairie du Chien supported him. He correctly reasoned that county structure would not only provide political opportunities for himself and others, but would also give the area a certain degree of independence in local matters.[9]

The leading Jacksonian in a predominantly Democratic area, Brown was the first representative of St. Croix County. As a member of the territorial House of Representatives in Madison, he learned much about the workings of frontier politics and cultivated the friendships of men who might help him in promoting the upper Mississippi area.

From the beginning, Brown and other St. Croixians probably wanted their area excluded from the future state of Wisconsin. They knew that a state could have only one capital, one penitentiary, and one major university, and Madison had those secured. Inclusion within

Wisconsin thus offered no opportunities for important public institutions on the upper Mississippi. Lingering separatist yearnings of St. Croixians were stimulated in 1846, after Congress approved the Wisconsin Enabling Act, the first step in the statehood process.

Wisconsin's statehood bid was prompted by a booming population of 155,000, more than triple what it had been only four years earlier. This growth assured favorable congressional action for Wisconsin.[10]

There was some difficulty, however, over the enabling act's boundary provisions. Morgan L. Martin, Wisconsin's territorial delegate to Congress, adhering to the strongly expressed desires of the Wisconsin legislature, proposed that the state include all that remained of the old Northwest Territory. But the House Committee on the Territories, chaired by Stephen A. Douglas of Illinois, preferred a much smaller state. On May 11, 1846, Douglas reported to the House that the committee recommended that Wisconsin's western boundary be the Mississippi River and a north-south line between it and the western end of Lake Superior. Such a boundary, Douglas noted, "would leave as much of the northwest territory out of the State of Wisconsin as in it, so as to form a new State equal to it in size." Obviously the committee was influenced by the same beliefs that caused Congress to restrict Iowa's size.[11]

The committee's proposal caused a sharp clash over a Northwest Ordinance provision on the House floor between Douglas and George G. Dromgoole of Virginia. The Northwest Ordinance of July 13, 1787, specified that "not less than three nor more than five states" were to be formed out of the Northwest Territory. Douglas insisted that the stipulation was not binding on Congress, because it had been "superseded and virtually annulled" by a constitutional clause that authorized Congress "to admit new States into the Union, without restriction as to number or size." Dromgoole, however, held that the restriction was inviolable. Thus, the State of Wisconsin had to include all of the remaining Northwest Territory. Supporting Dromgoole, Martin argued that the Northwest Ordinance provision was "irrepealable" by Congress. Only the people of Wisconsin, he held, had the power to alter it. Dromgoole, Martin and others who claimed the ordinance could not be changed by Congress came to be known as the "Fifth State" advocates.[12]

Martin's contention that the people of Wisconsin should be the final authority on boundary matters somehow appealed to the representatives. The House approved of his proviso to the Wisconsin bill authorizing the Wisconsin constitutional convention to adopt such boundaries as it deemed expedient. But proponents of a small state Wisconsin led by John A. Rockwell of Connecticut, Allen G. Thurman and Samuel F. Vinton of Ohio, and Paul Dillingham Jr. of Vermont mounted a counterattack. They charged that the House had unwittingly authorized Wisconsin to extend its western boundary even beyond the limits of the Northwest Territory. They feared such a state would be too large and irregularly shaped, with a long, uninhabited, and potentially vulnerable western frontier. Once alerted to the implications of Martin's proviso, the representatives did an abrupt about-face. Acting on Rockwell's motion, they rejected Martin's proviso.[13]

As in the case of Iowa, congressional bickering between the fifth-state and sixth-state sponsors reflected the broader sectional antagonism between the North and South. As a matter of course, Southerners wanted relatively few large Northern states admitted to the union. Northerners naturally preferred creating more states in the Great Lakes region by exceeding the limitations of the Northwest Ordinance.

Wisconsin's fifth-state promoters garnered most of their support from the South, but this alliance of convenience did not prevail. Instead, Congress accepted the sixth-state principle, but rather than specify a line running due south from the western end of Lake Superior to the Mississippi, favored a boundary following waterways insofar as possible. Consequently, the Wisconsin Enabling Act, signed by President James K. Polk on August 6, 1846, provided that the northwestern boundary from the point where it entered Lake Superior at the mouth of the Montreal River would run

> to the middle of Lake Superior; thence through the centre of Lake Superior to the mouth of the St. Louis River; thence up the main channel of said river to the first rapids in the same, above the Indian

village, according to Nicollet's map; thence due south to the main branch of the River St. Croix; thence down the main channel of said river to the Mississippi.[14]

Congressmen left no record of the precise reasons for this boundary. But Joseph N. Nicollet's "Hydrographical Basin of the Upper Mississippi" map, which was their geographic authority, portrayed the possibility of shaping northwestern Wisconsin primarily by natural boundaries. Once they accepted the Mississippi and St. Croix on the west and Lake Superior and its main source—the St. Louis River—on the north, they had only to close the boundary gap. Nicollet's map showed the shortest way of connecting the St. Croix demarcation with the St Louis River would be a north-south line from near the Indian village on the right bank of the St. Louis. Above the village Nicollet showed "Falls and Rapids." So by designating the first one, Congress presumably used a natural starting point for determining the short overland boundary to the St. Croix.[15]

The northwestern boundary seemed reasonable to Congress, but it offended both fifth-state believers and St. Croixians, who wanted a boundary well east and south of the St. Croix River. In Stillwater, the hotbed of St. Croix separatism, the boundary became the main issue in the election of a delegate to the Wisconsin constitutional convention.

Although Brown laid the foundation for St. Croix politics, he was not a factor in this controversy. When his grandiose plans for Dacotah failed, Brown left the St. Croix Valley in 1842 to trade with Dakota Indians in the Lake Traverse-Coteau des Prairies region. By the time he returned to the valley four years later, Stillwater, the principal settlement on the St. Croix, had replaced Dacotah as the county seat, and other young men were eagerly promoting their own political ambitions.[16]

During the campaign to elect delegates to the constitutional convention, William Holcombe emerged as the chief proponent of separatism. As a candidate for the delegacy from St. Croix County, Holcombe had a good political base. After moving to Stillwater from Galena, Illinois, in 1839, he became involved in lumbering, steamboating, and land investment. By the spring of 1846, when he was serving

William Holcombe. (Courtesy of the Minnesota Historical Society)

as both clerk of the board of county commissioners and as county register of deeds, Holcombe plunged into local politics.[17]

Whether or not Holcombe proposed a specific western boundary for Wisconsin during the campaign is not known, but his general views on the subject were clear. He wanted a sixth state to be formed out of the Old Northwest but he wanted it to be much larger than the one envisioned by some members of Congress. Wisconsin should be small enough, he believed, that another state of roughly equal size could be created between it and the Mississippi River. Stillwater would be the probable capital of such a state.

Not unexpectedly, Holcombe's greatest support came from Stillwater and nearby Lake and Marine precincts on the west bank of the St. Croix. In the election of September 7, 1846, Holcombe easily defeated his opponent, Joseph Bowron, by a vote of one-hundred-fourteen to seventy-seven. Bowron, a resident of St. Croix Falls on the east side of the river, supported the enabling act boundary. Bowron easily won his home precinct and swamped Holcombe by a twenty-three to three vote in St. Paul. The vast majority of St. Paul voters evidently preferred being left not too far out of Wisconsin to being left well out and losing a future state capital to Stillwater.[18]

At least in his public utterances, Holcombe saw the election returns as a sweeping mandate for his boundary views. While in Madison, he spoke of the people of his county as if they were or one mind and never expressed any misgivings about his lack of support on the east side of the St. Croix and in St. Paul. Holcombe's local prestige was boosted yet more when, on September 7, 1846, he was re-elected as both clerk of the St. Croix County board of commissioners and register of deeds.[19]

The constitutional convention was convened on October 5. Once seated in Madison, Holcombe schemed to advance his chief interest. As the lone delegate from an isolated frontier county with only 1,419 residents, Holcombe had to be enterprising, bold, and forceful. Although the large convention (124 members) had a standing committee on boundaries, Holcombe believed that a select committee would be his best platform. Therefore, he proposed and received the convention's approval to establish one, which was "to inquire into the expediency of dividing the territory of Wisconsin, and locating such line of division as shall equitably divide the same into two states."[20]

The convention took this action for various reasons. Some members approved of Holcombe's idea, others believed he should not be rejected summarily, and some perhaps saw the proposal as a way of opening other boundary questions and ultimately adding northern Illinois to Wisconsin. In December 1838, Governor Henry Dodge of Wisconsin Territory, endorsing a petition by the territorial legislature, claimed that the northern boundary of Illinois, which had been admitted to statehood twenty years earlier, was slightly more than sixty-one miles too far north. According to the Northwest Ordinance, asserted the petitioners, Wisconsin's rightful southern boundary should be drawn due west from the southern end of Lake Michigan. Congress failed to act on Wisconsin's complaint but the southern boundary issue subsequently aroused considerable political fervor in Wisconsin, which carried into the constitutional convention.[21]

That attainment would have probably caused them to accept a more restrictive northwestern boundary. Then too, in the early stages of the convention there was a natural tendency for the predominantly Democratic group to be gracious to a fellow Democrat.

Since Holcombe had a special interest in the question of equitably dividing the territory, it seemed only proper that he chair the select committee. Interestingly, the committee endorsed Holcombe's initial proposal even though it later appeared to be too rash for the convention.

Holcombe wanted a northwestern boundary for Wisconsin that would run from the center of the Mississippi River channel just south of Trempeleau Island (about eleven miles downstream from present-day Winona), due north for half a degree (about thirty-four and a half miles). From that point it was to follow a direct line northeasterly to the headwaters of the Montreal River, then down that stream to Lake Superior.[22]

Such a boundary would have reduced Wisconsin by over one-sixth of the area delineated in its enabling act, cut if off entirely from Lake Superior, and left outside of the state areas where such key cities such as Chippewa Falls, Eau Claire, and Superior later developed.

Since Holcombe's immediate concern was limiting Wisconsin, he never had to describe the shape of the state that he hoped to see created to its northwest. If this sixth state's eastern boundary proved to be the Trempeleau Island-Montreal River line, then the Mississippi River would be a probable western boundary. Such a state would have provided maximum access to Lake Superior and the Mississippi and would also have been appealing to lumbermen and merchants in an age dominated by water transportation. The nucleus of such a state would have been the St. Croix Valley, with Stillwater or some place nearby as its capital. Some people thought Holcombe had yet grander schemes to include land west of the Mississippi and even Upper Michigan in Wisconsin's "sister state," which would be named Superior.[23] In his formal remarks to the convention, Holcombe never used any name for the area to be created to Wisconsin's northwest. However, there was a certain tradition that Superior was the name preferred by St. Croix separatists before and during the first constitutional convention.

Holcombe supported his proposal with reasoning that must have appeared logical to his supporters. Wisconsin was too large, he claimed, and was out of proportion to other states whose small size assured their region heavy representation in the Senate. He cautioned that Wisconsin should think of the advantages of a sister state to the northwest when its sectional needs were considered in Congress. Effective government, he asserted, should be close to the people. A "remote location" over 300 miles to Madison, Wisconsin's capital, he warned, will continue to be as it has been a source of vexation and to a great degree destructive of the very end which a good government has it view. It would seem, therefore, to be unreasonable to include the Lake Superior country, simply to gratify a feeling of state pride, at the expense of the perpetual disadvantages and vexations that would unavoidably grow out of it.

He strongly implied that not only would the people of the north be better off without Wisconsin, but Wisconsin would be better off without them. His one premise that proved to be convincing was that the proposed congressional line along the St. Croix was unacceptable because a divided valley tended to "alienate the interests of society, perplex the trade and business of the river, and retard the growth of the settlement."[24]

Holcombe insinuated that the people he represented had been maltreated. "If these things are to remain so," he debated, "what use is it to declare in our bill of rights that all government proceeds from the people? Has this proceeded from the people? No, Mr. Chairman. They of St. Croix never knew anything about it; there were no consultations with them." The obvious redress, according to Holcombe, was to adjust the boundary to the preference of that distant minority, but the convention decided otherwise.

After persuading the select committee, Holcombe attempted to convince the convention to accept his boundary as an amendment to the one in the enabling act. But when he submitted the committee's recommendation on November 12, vigorous opposition dismayed him. Several speakers thought the Trempeleau Island-Montreal River line might endanger the statehood bill in Congress, and others thought Wisconsin would simply lose too much land and too much of the Mississippi River. Only Moses M. Strong of Mineral Point spoke for Holcombe, because he thought the proposed line was "better" than the enabling act provision. Sensing a need to marshal further support, Holcombe withdrew his motion.[25]

When Holcombe tried again on November 27, his motion was defeated by a vote of fifty-one to twenty-nine. Strong, however, moved that the Holcombe boundary be submitted to Congress as the "preference of the state of Wisconsin." This tactic of accepting the enabling act boundary to avoid a clash with Congress but offering another option as a "preference" confused and temporarily disarmed Holcombe's opponents. Consequently, Strong's motion passed by a forty-nine to thirty-eight vote. The victory was short-lived, because the convention reversed itself after the question was reconsidered.

During the reconsideration it was evident that some delegates wholeheartedly accepted Holcombe's arguments. John H. Tweedy of Milwaukee, for example, argued that not only was the land coveted by Holcombe of no agricultural or mineral value to Wisconsin, but he also asked: "What . . . is the object of government? To cover territory, or to protect men?" Tweedy believed that Wisconsin would be tyrannical if it spurned the expressed will of the people of the St. Croix.[26]

Even though he had some support, Holcombe must have been concerned about the general tenor of the boundary debates. An element in the convention, including former territorial governor James D. Doty, clamored for Wisconsin's rights to all that remained of the old Northwest Territory—rights they insisted were "fixed and established" by the Northwest Ordinance. These claimants of an utmost Wisconsin also concerned the dominant moderates, who found the enabling act boundary acceptable. While the latter thought the expansionists were unreasonable, they apparently saw Holcombe as too extreme in the other direction. Inclined to regard the enabling act line as a compromise, they consistently rejected both Holcombe and the fifth-state group.[27]

Whatever plans Holcombe had were dashed by the reconsideration of Strong's motion. Any future state northwest of Wisconsin would have to include land west of the Mississippi. But Holcombe persisted in his beliefs that the St. Croix Valley should not be divided by a state boundary following the river and that St. Croixians should be left out of Wisconsin. Therefore, only four days after his Trempeleau Island-Montreal River line was lost, he proposed as "the preference of the state of Wisconsin" a line from the international boundary in the middle of Lake Superior opposite the mouth of the "Burnt Wood" [Bois Brule] River to the river's mouth and then on a direct course to the head of Lake Pepin in the Mississippi. Such a line, he pleaded, would not affect much territory, but would leave his constituents unified. Despite the seeming reasonableness of his proposal, the convention rejected it by a greater margin than it had the previous one. On the same day the convention also denied another fifth-state effort to claim all of the remaining Old Northwest for Wisconsin.

Holcombe evidently lobbied hard to convince delegates to leave at least the immediate St. Croix Valley outside of Wisconsin. On December 9, again relying on the "preference of Wisconsin" ploy, he moved for the approval of a line southwardly from the first rapids above the mouth of the St. Louis River to a point an unspecified number of miles east of the most easterly point of Lake St. Croix, and from that spot to the head of Lake Pepin. Although the number of miles was actually left blank, the motion was approved by a forty to thirty-eight vote. Holcombe certainly had reached an understanding with delegates that his expectation would be modest, because the constitution as finally accepted designated the point as fifteen miles east of the most easterly point of Lake St. Croix.[28]

Most of the delegates who supported Holcombe sincerely wanted Congress to approve the boundary change. Not content with just including the alteration in the constitution, thirty-three of them signed a petition requesting Congress to approve the change. Their justification included the familiar Holcombe contentions that the St. Croix area was isolated "from the more civilized part of the world" and that its citizenry should be unified. They informed Congress that since four-fifths of St. Croixians lived west of the St. Croix River it would benefit the entire valley if the remaining one-fifth was also left outside of Wisconsin and be included in a new territory.

Although the proposed alteration in Wisconsin's northwestern boundary fell far short of Holcombe's original aspirations, he nonetheless salvaged a unified St. Croix Valley. The boundary change, however, had to be accepted by Congress, and Wisconsin's voters would have to approve the constitution before the decision was final. Wisconsin's request provoked little congressional discussion; Congress was willing

to accommodate Wisconsin, since it was uncharacteristically requesting a reduction. On March 3, 1847, "An Act for the Admission of the
State of Wisconsin," approving the boundary change and specifying
that Wisconsin would be admitted to the union as soon as its voters
approved the constitution, became law.[29]

In the meantime, Morgan L. Martin on December 23, 1846, had
proposed the organization of Minnesota Territory. Sympathetic to fur
traders, he apparently thought the organization of a new territory on
Wisconsin's western flank would hasten Dakota Indian land cessions,
which in turn would enable the natives to pay off their debts to the
traders.[30]

Martin's bill was well-received in the House of Representatives.
No one even bothered to inquire about the population of the presumed
territory. Oddly, the members were primarily concerning about the territory's name. The Committee on the Territories, chaired by Stephen
A. Douglas, favored the name "Itasca." After Martin, on the House
floor, moved to restore the name Minnesota, which he rendered "Minesota," various representatives suggested "Chippewa," "Jackson" (for
Andrew Jackson) and "Washington" (in honor of George Washington).
Martin prevailed. On February 17, 1847, the House approved the creation of "Minesota Territory." The territory's boundaries were detailed
in the House bill. On the east it was bounded by Michigan in Lake
Superior and Wisconsin's western boundary as defined in the subsequent congressional act of March 3, 1847. Iowa's northern boundary
as far west as 95° 30" (about fifteen miles southeast of present-day
Worthington, Minnesota) was its southern boundary. Its western
boundary ran in a direct line running northwest from 95° 30" on the
Iowa boundary to the point where the 100th longitude intersected the
international boundary, and its northern boundary followed the
Canada-United States boundary eastward and southeastward to
Michigan's northwestern corner in Lake Superior.[31]

In sharp contrast to the representatives, senators were very critical
of the Minnesota bill. Chester Ashley of Arkansas, chairman of the
Judiciary Committee, to which the bill was referred, merely moved to

consider rather than approve it. In response to questions from George Evans of Maine and Jabez W. Huntington of Connecticut, Ashley responded that the territory had an estimated population of 6,000, but also revealed that no census had been taken and that the territorial inhabitants themselves had not initiated the bill. After William Woodbridge of Michigan opined that the territory did not even have 600 residents, the Senate on March 3, 1847, tabled the bill.[32]

If Wisconsin voters had accepted the constitution as submitted to them in the April 6, 1847, election, the St. Croix Valley would have become part of the newly suggested Minnesota Territory. But the document was rejected by a vote of 20,231 to 14,116 following a long, emotional campaign. Newspapers stimulated interest by ardently attacking or defending certain provisions, and former delegates to the constitutional convention exacerbated differences in vitriolic public debates. The storm over the constitution was caused, in particular, by two provisions: one would have granted property rights to women, and the other would have forbidden the chartering of banks. Although the furor over these stipulations is difficult to understand today, it was in keeping with the times. Women's rights was a relatively new concept which sharply divided reformists and conservatives, and anti-bank sentiment was strong in frontier areas still smarting from ruinous speculation mania.[33]

Although the northwestern boundary provision did not provoke statewide debate, it was an issue in certain areas. Principal opposition came from Crawford County. Rather than sympathizing with the separatist aims of the St. Croix people, important leaders at Prairie du Chien were distressed at the prospect of being left near the northwestern edge of Wisconsin, since the eastern and western sections were characterized by different political philosophies. The eastern part, dominated by New Englanders, was more receptive to change, while the western area still reflected the Southern conservative outlook of the old lead mining frontier. Thus, westerners saw any attempt to limit them geographically and, ultimately, demographically as a step toward inevitable eastern dominance. This reasoning caused men such as Hercules L. Dousman, the famous Prairie du Chien fur trader, to champion

Wisconsin expansion. He later wrote that "the People in this part of the Country voted against the *old* Constitution, mostly on account of the Northern boundary."[34]

St. Croix County voters narrowly approved the constitution sixty-five to sixty-one, a turnout considerably smaller that that of the Holcombe-Bowron election.[35]

St. Croix County voters did not regard the election as solely a referendum on the boundary provision. They were also concerned about the other controversial provisions that caused the rejection of the document. There is also the possibility that some voted against the constitution with the hope of winning an even larger share of Wisconsin in a subsequent constitutional convention. Actually, any acceptance margin was a significant accomplishment in a statewide perspective: St. Croix County was only one of five counties out of a total of twenty-five whose voters favored the constitution. In all likelihood the voters of St. Croix County would have rejected the constitution if it had not contained a somewhat favorable boundary provision.[36]

After the election setback, advocates of statehood took several months to reassess their position and win new converts. Not until October did a special session of the territorial legislature authorize a new election of delegates to a second constitutional convention. Striving to make the second convention more efficient than the first, legislators reduced the number of delegates to only sixty-nine, with St. Croix and neighboring La Pointe County named as a single district with one seat.[37]

Holcombe may have wanted to serve again but his political fortunes declined during 1847. By the time the first convention adjourned on December 16, 1846, Holcombe was one of the best-known men in the St. Croix Valley. During the campaign for constitutional approval he was considered a possible rival of Henry H. Sibley, the area's leading fur trader, for the delegacy of the future Minnesota Territory. But St. Croix County voters decisively rejected Holcombe on September 6, 1847, when he stood for re-election as clerk of the county commissioners and register of deeds. William E. Watson won both positions by votes of ninety-two to sixty-six and ninety-three to sixty-three, respectively. On the same ballot Holcombe was barely elected one of Stillwater's justices of peace.[38]

Most St. Croixians accepted Holcombe's boundary views but they no longer thought he was the man to represent them, so they turned to George W. Brownell, who also stood for St. Croix separatism. Opposing Brownell was Holcombe's old foe Joseph Bowron. Brownell, who in 1846 had moved to the St. Croix Valley from Galena, where he had edited a newspaper and discovered some lead deposits, was a native of Florida, Montgomery County, New York. He was a wagonmaker in Syracuse

George W. Brownell. (Courtesy of the Minnesota Historical Society)

before moving to Missouri in about 1834, where he worked as a lead miner, geologist, and mineralogist. His achievements as a geologist brought him to the attention of some prominent Bostonians, including Caleb Cushing, Rufus Choate, and Robert Rantoul, Jr. Cushing, who was best known for negotiating the first commercial treaty between the United States and China in 1842, and his associates had organized the St. Croix and Lake Superior Mining Company in 1845. Their grand scheme included opening copper mines on the upper St. Croix and developing water power and timber resources at both St. Croix Falls and the Falls of St. Anthony. When Brownell arrived in the St. Croix Valley he was already associated with these Eastern capitalists. As company geologist, Brownell prospected for copper on the upper tributaries of the St. Croix River and headed the firm's mining and land departments.[39]

For reasons of their own, the Bostonians promoted St. Croix separatism. Like many residents of the St. Croix Valley, they did not share professions or outlooks with the people of southern Wisconsin. Thus, they naturally feared political domination by farmers, merchants, and lead miners. Eastern capitalists were hardly popular in a region so critical of the moneyed element, whose constitutional convention delegates agreed to prohibit bank chartering. As developers, Cushing and his associates wanted a state government that would facilitate their claiming of copper, timber and water power sites. Then, too, there was the vital matter of state taxation. A government in Madison controlled by probable opponents would not be nearly as likely to grant tax concessions as one located in the St. Croix Valley. To what degree the Bostonians hoped to dominate a new St. Croix Valley-centered state is not clear, but there was a persistent belief in the valley that Cushing himself wanted to become governor of such a state. Since a new state held the promise of major financial gains, the Bostonians easily accepted the valley rhetoric about people controlling their own destiny. Such talk suggested the very essence of American democracy and disguised less lofty motives.

Until Brownell's election the aims of Cushing and his associates were not well-known. There was no significant distrust of the Bostonians during the first constitutional convention, despite the possibility that Cushing and his partners had influenced the sixth-state movement in Congress during Wisconsin's Enabling Act. Cushing had toured the Lake Superior-St. Croix Valley region in 1846 to assess company progress and prospects. He returned home by way of Madison, which he visited when the first constitutional convention was in session. It is quite likely that the purpose of his visit was to meet with Holcombe and lobby for St. Croix separatism.[40]

Brownell defeated Bowron in the election of November 19, 1847, more decisively than had Holcombe. But, despite his victory of 137 to ninety, Brownell, like Holcombe before him, was rejected by the majority of St. Paulites, who did not want a capital in the St. Croix Valley. Brownell's greatest margins were in the Stillwater area, but Bowron narrowly won St. Paul and the two precincts on the east side of the St. Croix River.[41]

Hoping to accomplish more than Holcombe, Brownell prepared to argue his case. His dramatic gesture of walking to Madison on snowshoes to emphasize the remoteness of the St. Croix Valley brought him some attention, but little else. When the convention opened on December 15, Brownell, probably at his own request, was named to the fifteen-member committee on general provisions, which included boundary matters.[42]

But the nature of the northwestern boundary became an issue before the committee could act. On December 21, Daniel G. Felton, a Prairie du Chien lawyer and court clerk representing Crawford and Chippewa counties, proposed the expansion of Wisconsin to the west of the enabling act boundary. Felton resolved that Wisconsin would accept the enabling act line, but preferred one running from the foot of the St. Louis River rapids directly southwest to the mouth of the Rum River on the Mississippi (about twenty miles upstream from St. Paul) and then down the main channel to the Illinois state line.[43]

Brownell never recovered from Fenton's bold initiative. When the general provisions committee endorsed the Rum River line only two days after it had been first suggested, Brownell's only recourse was to file a minority report. In the report, which he read on December 27, he reiterated all of Holcombe's familiar arguments about St. Croix isolation, the rights of the people to govern themselves, and the advantages to Wisconsin of a sister state. He graciously acknowledged his predecessor by referring to his premises as the Holcombe Amendment.

Brownell was given another opportunity to defend his views when he offered the Trempealeau Island-Montreal River line as an amendment to the Rum River line. His assertion that the voters of St. Croix County favored the Trempealeau Island line was vigorously challenged. Fenton pointed out that the first constitution, which he insisted was a referendum on the boundary, was only narrowly accepted in St. Croix County.[44]

Sensing the expansionist mood of the delegates, Fenton extolled the advantages of the Rum River line. It would, he contended, gain for Wisconsin an immense pine forest, which he pronounced to be "the best probably in the world." Wisconsin would also secure one side of the "splendid water power" at the Falls of St. Anthony as well as control of the ground, through which a railroad connecting the heads of navigation of the Mississippi and the Great Lakes would be built.

Fenton's public utterances were attuned to the "best interests of Wisconsin" theme but he also had an ulterior motive. As an ally of the powerful Hercules Dousman, Fenton wanted to force the cession of Dakota lands west of the Mississippi. As Fenton and Dousman reasoned, a Wisconsin boundary on the Rum River would create agitation for a new territory west of that line, which, in turn, would cause the negotiation of a major Dakota Indian cession. Such a treaty would benefit Dousman, a creditor of the Dakota, because the Indians would have money after selling their lands.[45]

The Brownell-Fenton debate on January 7, 1848, unleashed a wave of expansionist sentiment. Many speakers agreed with Fenton that Wisconsin should include the promising timber and presumed copper ore lands and the abundant water power of the upper country. As a group they were obviously more aware of the potential worth of the St. Croix Valley than the delegates to the first convention had been, and they were more inclined to be acquisitive. Probably because of the activities of Cushing's company and the direct link between Cushing and Brownell, the delegates had no patience with the latter's claim that the St. Croix Valley was "worthless" to Wisconsin.[46]

During the polemics the Rum River line advocates came to look like moderates. The vocal fifth-state faction attempted to revive Wisconsin's "ancient rights" to all that remained of the Northwest Territory. In response, Rum River supporters argued that there was a hazard in asking for too much, because such a course of action would cause Congress to approve the enabling act boundary and nothing else.

After listening to the delegates Brownell certainly realized his amendment would fail. Nonetheless, he moved its acceptance on January 10. As soon as it was rejected by a fifty-two to five vote, Brownell proposed the Bois Brule River-Lake Pepin line as an amendment. Only Brownell and one other delegate voted for it; fifty-three opposed it. Later in the day, Brownell voted against the Fenton resolution, but it was included in the constitution by an overwhelming margin of fifty-three to three.

The expansionists must have prided themselves on their masterful ploy. Not only would the Rum River line gain Wisconsin valuable resources, but it would, ironically, fulfill the St. Croix contention that the valley should not be divided. Wisconsin would have all of it and more. The delegates realized Congress would determine the final boundary, so when the constitution and accompanying documents were sent to Washington it was clearly stated that Wisconsin accepted the boundaries described in the Enabling Act of 1846, but was proposing the Rum River line as the "preference of the State of Wisconsin"[47]

After St. Croixians were spurned in Madison, they appealed to Congress. Brownell and Holcombe both wrote to John Tweedy, who had succeeded Martin as Wisconsin's territorial delegate, urging him to support their cause. As they well knew, Tweedy, as delegate to the first constitutional convention, had been sympathetic to Holcombe's pleas. Brownell insisted that "the interests of the people of the St. Croix should be regarded as well as a mere feeling of pride of territory on the part of the new state," and he warned Tweedy: "You will doubtless receive a petition from out people setting forth their remonstrance" to the boundary proposal. Holcombe believed that Tweedy should make a full explanation to Congress "as an act of Justice to this county."[48]

Even as Brownell and Holcombe wrote, the promised petition, which had been drafted by William R. Marshall and made public at a meeting held in St. Paul on January 24, 1848, was being circulated. Henry H. Sibley, a likely candidate for the delegacy of the new territory to be formed northwest of Wisconsin, actively solicited signatures despite efforts by Dousman and Fenton to persuade him that the Rum River line would benefit all traders, including himself.[49]

The petition was signed by about 350 men, described as residents within the limits of "Minnisota" Territory, who objected to the Rum River line and offered a substitute, running from Chequamegon Bay on Lake Superior due south to the Chippewa River and then down it to the Mississippi River. The "Chippewa River boundary," as it came to be called, would have run from present-day Ashland to just east of Chippewa Falls. They pointed out the geographic and economic identity of the upper Mississippi, St. Croix and Chippewa River areas, and argued that the proposed Rum River line would make Minnesota's outlook "forlorn indeed." Appealing to the sympathies of Congress, the petitioners stated they had "full confidence that your honorable bodies will consult the wishes of those who are most interested in a solution of this question, and will not do so much violence to the feelings of the people of this region as to leave them within the limits of Wisconsin, in utter disregard of their prayers and remonstrances."[50]

The extent of Tweedy's assistance was to present the Minnesota petition to the House of Representatives. Despite his earlier support for St. Croix separatism, Tweedy was squarely caught between the proponents and critics of the Rum River line. Dousman assured Tweedy that the "only objection to this boundary, comes from the Speculators & office seekers on the immediate bank of Mississippi River above the mouth of the St. Croix;—they want & expect the seat of Government of the contemplated new Territory to go there, & almost every other man has a Town plat laid out & ready prepared for the Capitol." He also noted that many of the petitioners were "Half Breeds & Canadians," and stressed the importance of St. Anthony Falls to Wisconsin, the acquisition of which would curtail the plans of the Boston company which was said to "have laid out a large City," intended to be the capital of the Northwest.[51]

The circulation of the Minnesota petition created some excitement in the St. Croix country before the March 13, 1848, vote on the second Wisconsin constitution. In Wisconsin as a whole, the document was not nearly as controversial as the first one had been. It did not include any reference to married women's property rights and remanded the matter of chartering banks to a special election. Wisconsinites approved the constitution by the overwhelming margin of 16,759 to 6,384. The estrangement and bitterness in St. Croix County was shown by its vote, 259 to seventeen, against acceptance.[52]

The St. Croix County vote reflected none of the ambivalence of the first constitutional election. It was clearly a mandate on the boundary question and was the largest vote recorded in the county to that time. The unprecedented returns were caused by the agitation of the petitioners and the creation of new precincts at Snake River and Rice River to augment the earlier ones of Stillwater, St. Croix Falls, Marine Mills, St. Paul, Lake St. Croix, and Willow River. While the vote was not factored in the outcome, it did bolster St. Croix unity and the determination of its leaders to fight for their cause in Washington.

Brownell and ostensibly Cushing tried a direct appeal to Congress. Brownell evidently went to the nation's capital, where he prepared an elaboration of Minnesota's boundary grievance. The seven-page document, which was printed at the office of the *Congressional Globe*, included the verbatim text of Brownell's and Holcombe's minority reports to the Wisconsin constitutional conventions, in addition to a preface by Brownell. Its title, "Boundaries of Wisconsin," belied its contents, which were in keeping with the subtitle, "Reasons Why the Boundaries of Wisconsin, as Reported by the Committee for the Admission of that Territory into the Union as a State, Should Not Be Adopted."[53]

The Minnesota protest sparked a long, sometimes acerbic debate in the House over Wisconsin's northwestern boundary. Minnesota's chief spokesman was Representative Robert Smith of Alton, Illinois. On May 9, 1848, he proposed to amend the boundary recommended by the House Committee on the Territories. Caleb B. Smith (Indiana), chairman of the committee, had moved to create the State of Wisconsin with its Enabling Act boundaries. But Robert Smith argued that Wisconsin should be curtailed on the northwest. He wanted a boundary very close to Holcombe's original motion. He proposed that the demarcation start at Lac Vieux Desert on the Upper Michigan-Wisconsin boundary. From there it was to run about fifteen miles southwest to Trout Lake. From the lake the boundary would be drawn southwest on the direct line to Trempeleau Island's highest point. Smith argued for minority rights and local self-determination. He knew some of the men of the St. Croix area and found them to be energetic, intelligent, and resourceful, he reported, and a desirable nucleus for a new state. Smith's concern for frontier democracy was no doubt inspired by some of his relatives who were living in the St. Croix valley.[54]

Rather than reject the constitution because of the boundary question and again refer the matter to Wisconsin, representatives were swayed by the reasoning of Caleb B. Smith and Tweedy that a compact had been concluded between Congress and the state of Wisconsin, because Congress had made a specific boundary offer in the enabling act and Wisconsin had accepted it. On May 11, the House, by a vote of forty-six "yeas" and ninety-four "nays," rejected Robert Smith's amendment. Evidently, the Enabling Act boundaries, which they approved later in the day, seemed to be a reasonable compromise between Smith's preference and the Rum River line. The Senate accepted the House bill with no changes in the boundary provisions and on May 29, 1848, President James K. Polk signed the act admitting Wisconsin as the thirtieth state. Thus, in less than two years the question of Wisconsin's northwestern boundary had come full circle.

Although St. Croixians of the Holcombe-Brownell persuasion seethed about the "injustice" done to them with a St. Croix boundary, they recognized that they had to be primarily concerned with organizing Minnesota. This was accomplished quickly. On March 3, 1849, President Polk signed the act that created Minnesota Territory. Its boundaries were specified as:

> Beginning in the Mississippi River, at the point where the line of forty-three degrees and thirty minutes of north latitude crosses the same, thence running due west on said line, which is the northern boundary of the State of Iowa, to the north-west corner of the said State of Iowa, thence southerly along the western boundary of said State to the point where said boundary strikes the Missouri River, thence up the middle of the main channel of the Missouri River to the mouth of the White-earth River, thence up the middle of the main channel of the White-earth river to the boundary line between the possessions of the United States and Great Britain; thence east and south along the boundary line between the possessions of the United States and Great Britain to Lake Superior; thence in a straight line to the northernmost point of the State of Wisconsin in Lake Superior; thence along the western boundary line of said State of Wisconsin to the Mississippi River; thence down the main channel of said river to the place of beginning. . . ."[55]

Although Michigan was not mentioned in this act, it bordered the new territory in Lake Superior from the point where the international boundary as drawn from the west reached the lake, to Wisconsin's northernmost point.[56]

Congress provided for the surveying and marking of the Minnesota-Wisconsin meridian boundary by a $600 appropriation in its Appropriations Act for Year Ending June 30, 1851. George B. Sargent, surveyor general for Iowa and Wisconsin, decided to have the work done at the same time the Iowa-Minnesota boundary was being surveyed. In late May 1852, he ordered deputy surveyor George R. Stuntz to leave the Iowa-Minnesota boundary survey and proceed to northwestern Wisconsin to perform rectangular land surveys and determine the meridian boundary.[57]

George Stuntz.(Courtesy of the University of Minnesota Duluth Library Archives)

The thirty-one-year-old Stuntz, later best remembered as one of Duluth's founders, was a native of Erie County, Pennsylvania. After a farm boyhood he studied mathematics, engineering and surveying at Grand River Institute in Ohio. From there he moved to Wisconsin to work as a land surveyor. While thus engaged, he became acquainted with Sargent.[58]

When Stuntz arrived at the head of Lake Superior in July 1852, the area was still part of the fur trading frontier. The old American Fur Company, which was then controlled by Pierre Chouteau, Jr., and Company of St. Louis, Missouri, had its main Lake Superior base at La Pointe on the west side of Madeline Island. At Fond du Lac, the traders' traditional name for the locale where the St. Louis River flowed into Lake Superior, the company had a trading post and warehouse. Stuntz arranged to use this facility as his surveying headquarters.

During his survey of the Minnesota-Wisconsin meridian boundary, Stuntz was assisted by eight men. They were A.C. Stuntz, the assistant deputy surveyor, two chainmen and five axemen-laborers.[59]

As Stuntz's party started moving up the St. Louis River in mid-October, he worried about locating the beginning of the meridian boundary because of the imprecise specifications in Wisconsin's Statehood Act. He thought the congressional wording about the start of the meridian line was "vague and indefinite." First he had to locate an Indian village and then the first rapids above it. Fortunately, nineteen miles above the river's mouth he found "the Indian village of Fon Du Lac [sic] on the North side of the River; containing 50 or 60 cabins and lodges and 3 or 4 good houses, 2 trading houses and a mission building." He also reported "that on the Wisconsin side opposite this Village several families of French and Indians live in a half civilized manner. Hunting and fishing being their only occupation."[60]

About a mile above the village he reached the foot of the lowermost rapids, where he had to interpret the congressional intent of "at the first rapids." Did this mean the foot, head or midpoint? He decided that Congress had intended to fix the northern end of the meridian line at the lower end of the rapids. He determined that the rapids, which were approximately 660 feet long, ran almost due north-south along the western side of a loop. However, the exact foot lay a few yards around the northern end of the loop. If he had started the meridian line precisely at the foot he would have created a situation that left an extremely narrow strip between the meridian line and the loop. Opting to follow a natural boundary insofar as possible, he ran the northern end of the meridian line through the western side of the loop. Rather than systematically explain this decision, Stuntz tersely observed that he had located the north end of the meridian line "near the foot of the rapids." The effect of Stuntz's decision was to give Wisconsin a slight strip of land along the course of the meridian boundary. His certainly did not take this action to benefit Wisconsin. Rather, he made a commonsensical decision based on a local geographic feature.

Stuntz's survey determined that the meridian line from the center of the St. Louis River to the center of the St. Croix River was forty miles, seventy-five chains and eighty-four links long. For the first sixteen miles it ran through generally level forestland of red clay with white pine, white cedar, birch and spruce as the most common trees. At that point it crossed the divide separating the St. Louis and St. Croix watersheds. South of the divide the sandy soil had "a succession of swamps many of which are filled with rich deposits of peat." Stuntz found the timber in that portion was "small and not valuable for lumbering except in the vicinity of the St. Croix River where a few valuable groves of White Pine are found."

Stuntz marked the boundary by cutting a trace through the forest. His crew erected wooden posts at the half-mile and mile intervals unless those sites were in water. Additionally, nearby trees were marked with "M.B." or "W.B." with the blazes facing the boundary. Stuntz placed his southernmost monument on the right bank (north side) of the St. Croix about four miles below the mouth of the Namekagon River.

On December 15, 1852, Stuntz filed his sworn report with Sargent in Dubuque. Sargent and the United States surveyor general were obviously satisfied that Stuntz had fixed the meridian line efficiently and correctly. Either official had the discretion to order a resurvey if they decided there were errors in procedure or conclusions in the original survey.

― · ― · ― · ― · ― · ― · ― · ― · ― · ― · ― · ― · ―

## NOTES:

1. Kappler, *Indian Affairs,* 2: 250-55.
2. Alice E. Smith, *The History of Wisconsin, vol. I: From Exploration to Statehood* (Madison: State Historical Society of Wisconsin, 1973), 132, 147. 499-500.
3. *Ibid.,* 491-93; Royce, *Indian Land Cessions,* plate 64.
4. Kappler, *Indian Affairs,* 2: 493-94; Meyer, *History of the Santee Sioux,* 58.
5. Kappler, *Indian Affairs,* 2: 491, 493.
6. Here and below, J. Fletcher Williams, *A History of the City of Saint Paul, and of the County of Ramsey, Minnesota,* vol. iv of *Collections of the Minnesota Historical Society* (St. Paul, 1876), 80, 85, 111.

7. James Taylor Dunn, *Marine on St. Croix: From Lumber Village to Summer Haven 1838-1968* (Marine on St. Croix: Marine Historical Society, 1968), 1; Nancy and Robert Goodman, *Joseph R. Brown Adventurer on the Minnesota Frontier 1820-1849* (Rochester, MN: Lone Oak Press, 1996), 185.

8. Here and below, Goodman and Goodman, *Brown*, 160,174-77,186; Smith, *History of Wisconsin*, 1: 470.

9. W.H.C. Folsom, *Fifty Years in the Northwest* ([St. Paul]: Pioneer Press Co., 1888), 34; Justice of the Peace Docket, Crawford County, of Joseph R. Brown, Oct. 31, 1839-Oct. 5, 1841, Joseph R. Brown and Samuel J. Brown Papers, MHS.

10. Smith, *History of Wisconsin*, 1: 466.

11. William Francis Raney, *Wisconsin: A Story of Progress* (New York: Prentice-Hall, 1940), 92; *Congressional Globe.*,14 January, 11 May, 10 June 1846, 15: 196, 789, 953; Moses M. Strong, *History of the Territory of Wisconsin from 1836 to 1848* (Madison: Democrat Printing Co., 1885), 484.

12. *Congressional Globe*, 8, 10 June 1846, 15: 941, 953.) "The Northwest Ordinance," in Henry Steele Commager, ed., *Documents of American History, vol. I: To 1898* (7th ed.; New York: Appleton-Century-Crofts, 1963), 131.

13. *Congressional Globe*, 10 June 1846, 15: 952-53.

14. *U.S. Statutes at Large*, 9:56.

15. Nicollet's map.

16. Goodman and Goodman, *Brown*, 217, 229.

17. Mrs. Andrew E. Kilpatrick, "William Holcombe," *Collections of the Minnesota Historical Society*, , vol.10, pt. 2 (St. Paul, 1905), 858; MHS Scrapbook, 1: 36; Folsom, *Fifty Years*, 103; Folsom, "Early Elections and Other Historical Sketches," vol. 5, W. H. C. Folsom and Family Papers, 1836-1944, MHS.

18. Nancy Goodman, ed., *Minnesota Beginnings: Records of St. Croix County, Wisconsin Territory 1840-1849* (Stillwater, MN: Washington County Historical Society, 1999), 35-36,297; Folsom, "Early Elections," 5:66, Folsom Papers.

19. Goodman, *Minnesota Beginnings*, 35-36.

20. Folsom, *Fifty Years*, 104. Of the 1,419 inhabitants of St. Croix County on the census date of June 1, 1846, there were 914 white males, 496 white females, seven black males, and two black females. *Madison Express*, August 11, 1846; Milo M. Quaife, ed., *The Convention of 1846*, vol. 27 of *Collections of the State Historical Society of Wisconsin* (Madison, 1919), 320.

21. Reuben G. Thwaites, "The Boundaries of Wisconsin," *Collections of the State Historical Society of Wisconsin*, vol. 11 (Madison, 1888), 496-501.

22. Quaife, *Convention of 1846*, 560.

23. Thwaites, "Boundaries of Wisconsin," 489; William H. C. Folsom, "History of Lumbering in the St. Croix Valley, with Biographic

Sketches," *Collections of the Minnesota Historical Society,* vol. 9 (St. Paul, 1901), 295.

24. Here and two paragraphs below, Quaife, *Convention of 1846,* 565-566.

25. *Ibid.,* 444, 560, 581-582.

26. *Ibid.,* 582-583.

27. Here and below, *Ibid.*, 605-608.

28. Here and below, *Ibid.*, 685, 732; John Porter Bloom (comp. and ed.), *The Territorial Papers of the United States,* vol. 28: *The Territory of Wisconsin 1839-1848* (Washington: National Archives and Records Service, 1975), 1024-1025.

29. *U.S. Statutes at Large,* 9:178.

30. *Congressional Globe,* 23 December 1846, 16: 71.

31. *Ibid.,* 20 January, 17 February 1847, 16: 218, 441, 444-45; "An Act Establishing the territorial government of Minasota [sic]," 18 February 1847, in "Territorial Papers of the United States Senate,1789-1873." Microfilm roll 14 (NARS): Minnesota, February 18, 1847-June 16, 1860. New Mexico, December 14, 1840-August 21, 1854. In the House and Senate records Minnesota was variously spelled Minesota (the commonest version), Minnesota and Minasota.

32. *Congressional Globe,* 03 March 1847, 16: 572; Handwritten note at end of "Minasota" Territory bill in "Territorial Papers of Senate."

33. Smith, *History of Wisconsin,* 664. For detailed particulars, see Milo M. Quaife, ed., *The Struggle Over Ratification 1846-1847,* vol. 28 of *Collections of the State Historical Society of Wisconsin* (Madison, 1920).

34. William R. Marshall, "Reminiscences of Wisconsin—1842 to 1848," *Magazine of Western History* 7 (January, 1888), 249. Hercules Dousman to Henry Hastings Sibley, 28 January 1848; Henry Hastings Sibley Papers, 1815-1891, MHS, microfilm copy in Memorial Library, Minnesota State University, Mankato; Dousman to John H. Tweedy, 15 February 1848, John Hubbard Tweedy Papers, State Historical Society of Wisconsin.

35. Goodman, ed., *Minnesota Beginnings,* 45.

36. Quaife, *Struggle over Ratification,* 698; Milo M. Quaife, ed., *The Attainment of Statehood,* vol. 29 of *Collections of the State Historical Society of Wisconsin* (Madison, 1928), 191.

37. Quaife, *Attainment of Statehood,* 1-5.

38. D[aniel] G. Fenton to Sibley, 17 March 1847, Sibley Papers; Goodman, ed., *Minnesota Beginnings,* 49; Marshall, "Reminiscences of Wisconsin," 248; Quaife, *Attainment of Statehood,* 923; H[orace] A. Tenney and David Atwood, *Memorial Record of the Fathers of Wisconsin* (Madison: D. Atwood, 1880), 188.

39. Alice E. Smith, "Caleb Cushing's Investments in the St. Croix Valley," *Wisconsin Magazine of History* 28 (September, 1944): 7-10; Alice Elizabeth Smith, *James Duane Doty: Frontier Promoter* (Madison: State Historical Society of Wisconsin, 1954), 308; Marshall, "Reminiscences," 248;

Folsom, *Fifty Years,* 104. On Cushing's interest in St. Anthony Falls, see Lucile M. Kane, *The Waterfall That Built a City: The Falls of St. Anthony in Minneapolis* (St. Paul: Minnesota Historical Society, 1966), 16.

40. Smith, "Caleb Cushing's Investments," 10.

41. Goodman, ed., *Minnesota Beginnings,* 54.

42. Smith, *History of Wisconsin,* 673; Quaife, *Attainment of Statehood,* 206.

43. Here and below, Quaife, *Attainment of Statehood,* 225,242, 261, 902.

44. Here and below, *Ibid.,* 455, 458.

45. Fenton to Sibley, 24 December 1847, 14 February 1848, and Dousman to Sibley, 28 January 1848, Sibley Papers.

46. Here and two paragraphs below Quaife, *Attainment of Statehood,* 455-468, 475.

47. Quaife, *Attainment of Statehood,* 475, 888

48. Here and below, Brownell to Tweedy, 31 January 1848, and Holcombe to Tweedy, 10 February 1848, Tweedy Papers.

49. *Wisconsin Herald* (Lancaster), 26 February 1848; Dousman to Sibley, 28 January 1848, John McKusick to Sibley, 02 February1848, Fenton to Sibley, 14 February 1848, Sibley Papers; Return I. Holcombe, *Early History—Minnesota as a Territory,* 347, vol. 2 of Lucius F. Hubbard et al., *Minnesota in Three Centuries 1655-1908* (New York: Publishing Society of Minnesota, 1908).

50. *Memorial of Citizens of the United States Residing within the Limits of the Territory of Minnisota* [sic] . . . , 30 Cong., 1 sess. Senate Miscellaneous Document 98, p. 1-2 (serial 511).

51. Dousman to Tweedy, 15 February 1848, Tweedy Papers.

52. Smith, *History of Wisconsin,* 669, 676; Goodman, ed., *Minnesota Beginnings,* 59.

53. A copy of the pamphlet, printed 20 April 1848, is in the MHS library.

54. Here and below, *Congressional Globe,* 09, 11 May 1848, 17: 743, 754-55, 772, 785; *U. S. Statutes at Large,* 9: 233; B[enjamin] H. Cheever to John H. Tweedy, February 2, 1848, in Bloom, *Territory of Wisconsin,* 1153.

55. *U.S. Statutes at Large,* 9:403.

56. For detailed coverage of the formation of Minnesota Territory, see: William E. Lass, "The Birth of Minnesota," *Minnesota History* 55 (Summer 1997): 267-79.

57. *U.S. Statutes at Large,* 9:535; "Survey of the Iowa-Minnesota Boundary Line," 494; Burleigh Keith Rapp, "The Life of George R. Stuntz," typewritten manuscript in Minnesota Historical Society, St. Paul, p. 10.

58. Here and the paragraph below, Dwight E. Woodbridge and John S. Pardee, eds., *History of Duluth and St. Louis County,* 2 vols. (Chicago: C. F. Cooper & Co., 1910),229, 393-394.

59. "Catlin Butler & Lyons, Superior, Wisconsin, October 1852. A Part of the Survey of State Line Between Wisconsin State & Minnesota Territory by George R. Stuntz," typewritten copy in Stuntz, George

Papers, Northeast Minnesota Historical Center, University of Minnesota, Duluth, folder 2, p. 1.

60. Here to the end of the chapter, *Ibid.*, p. 7-10.

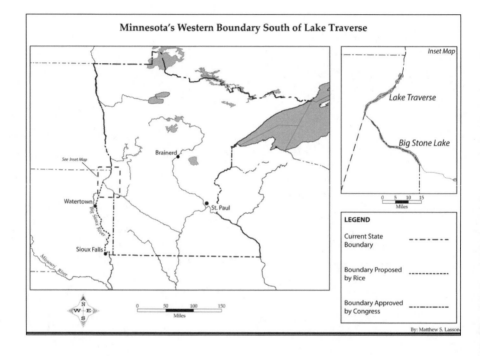

Minnesota's Western Boundary South of Lake Traverse

Inset Map

Lake Traverse

Big Stone Lake

See Inset Map

Brainerd

Watertown

St. Paul

Big Sioux River

Sioux Falls

Missouri River

0   5   10   15
Miles

LEGEND

Current State
Boundary

Boundary Proposed
by Rice

Boundary Approved
by Congress

N
W   E
S

0      50     100     150
Miles

By: Matthew S. Lasson

# CHAPTER FOUR

## DETERMINING THE WESTERN BOUNDARY

B Y THE TIME MINNESOTA TERRITORY WAS created in 1849, the northern, southern and eastern boundaries of the future state had been established. The fixing of the western boundary occurred when Minnesota was admitted to the union as the thirty-second state on May 11, 1858. During its late territorial phase, a time of spectacular growth, the final shape of the state was debated between advocates of a north-south state and an east-west state.

When Alexander Ramsey, a former Pennsylvania congressman, assumed his duties as Minnesota Territory's first governor, statehood appeared to be very remote. On September 4, 1849, in his inaugural message to the legislature, Ramsey reviewed the territory's status and prospects. The vast realm, extending from the Mississippi and St. Croix rivers westward to the Missouri and White Earth rivers, encompassed an estimated 166,000 square miles. The white and mixed-blood population, as reported in a census taken during the summer of 1849, was a meager 4,535. Most of these people lived between the St. Croix and Mississippi in the Stillwater-St. Paul-St. Anthony area. Other than this concentration, the only assemblage of note was in the Red River valley at Pembina near the international boundary. Lumbering and fur trading were the main economic activities.[1]

Ramsey and other promoters recognized that agriculture was the key to Minnesota's future growth and prosperity. But the best farming area was the Dakota Indian lands west of the Mississippi. Acquiring it was Minnesota Territory's highest priority. James Madison Goodhue, the territory's first newspaper editor, aroused public calls to force the Dakotas from their homeland, which he publicized as the "Suland." Ramsey hoped Dakota cession treaties could be negotiated during the territory's first year. However, the fur traders who were both the creditors and advisers of the natives managed to delay negotiations until they were in a position to recoup their trading losses.[2]

After these frustrating delays, the federal government was ready to negotiate with the four Dakota bands during the summer of 1851. In July, Luke Lea, federal commissioner of Indian affairs, and Ramsey, the territorial *ex-officio* superintendent of Indian affairs, working as co-commissioners, coerced Sisseton and Wahpeton chiefs and headmen into signing the Treaty of Traverse des Sioux. The following month they concluded the Treaty of Mendota with the Mdewakanton and Wahpekute. Under the two treaties the United States acquired all of Minnesota Territory south of the 1825 boundary line, west of the Mississippi and east of a line formed by the Red, Bois des Sioux and Big Sioux rivers, and a straight course from Lake Traverse to the point where the Big Sioux entered Lake Kampeska (the western edge of present-day Watertown, South Dakota).[3]

The greatly anticipated opening of the ceded lands was delayed by a Senate investigation into fraud charges brought against Ramsey. As a result, presidential proclamation of the treaties did not occur until February 24, 1853. But after this legal opening the reluctant Dakotas had to be persuaded to vacate the land. By the end of 1853, most of them had moved to upper Minnesota River reservations.

In the meantime, opportunistic townsite promoters and other trespassers were not deterred by legal niceties. In 1852, some Sooners started the communities of Red Wing and Winona in the Mississippi River Valley and Henderson, Mankato and Traverse des Sioux in the Minnesota River valley. Reportedly, about 5,000 whites took up claims in the Minnesota Triangle—the land south of St. Paul between the Mississippi and Minnesota rivers.[4]

Despite the lure of rich farmland, Minnesota Territory's growth was initially deterred by its remoteness from the eastern United States and its reputation for harsh winters. But reaching Minnesota became much easier after the completion of the Chicago and Rock Island Railroad to Rock Island, Illinois, on February 22, 1854. Wishing to celebrate their feat of linking Atlantic coast cities with the Mississippi by rail and to promote the Upper Mississippi region, the line's proprietors arranged the Rock Island Railroad Excursion of 1854. In June, about a thousand guests, including such dignitaries as ex-president Millard Fillmore, several state governors and some prominent journalists and authors traveled from Rock Island to St. Paul in five crowded steamboats. During their whirlwind round trip, which took only five and a half days, they were greeted and entertained by Governor Willis A. Gorman and shown area sights, including the scenic Falls of St. Anthony, Hiawatha Falls, Fort Snelling and Lake Calhoun. The resultant newspaper and magazine publicity, which generally lauded Minnesota's prospects, helped attract thousands of settlers.[5]

In 1855 and 1856, Minnesota Territory's population boomed. On January 9, 1856, in his annual message, Governor Gorman informed the legislature that on the basis of an 1855 census and "from statistics gathered from other reliable sources," Minnesota contained "fully seventy-five thousand souls," which was more than double the 35,000 he had mentioned in his 1855 message. On January 14, 1857, Gorman happily reported that the gains of 1856, which brought the population to "about 180,000 souls," far surpassed that of the previous year.[6]

Gorman attributed Minnesota's gains to its rich soil, unsurpassed water power, extensive pineries, the commerce of the Mississippi, Minnesota and St. Croix rivers and "the inexhaustible copper mines of Lake Superior." He could just as well have added that Minnesota was benefitting from improved transportation, national prosperity and a wave of speculative mania that inflated territorial property values.

The population surge coincided with national events that greatly affected Minnesota's political character. The uneasy calm in the lingering sectional slavery controversy effected by the Compromise of 1850 was shattered by the Kansas-Nebraska Act. Approved by a Democratic Congress in the spring of 1854, the measure was inspired by the desire to open new territory to facilitate the construction of a transcontinental railroad to California. It provided for the establishment of Kansas and Nebraska territories, with the fate of slavery in each to be decided by the voters. Significantly, it expressly repealed the Missouri Compromise of

1820, under which slavery was banned in Louisiana Territory north of 36° 30", with the exception of Missouri. This provision, which created an opportunity for the expansion of slavery, provoked an angry reaction against both the act and its chief sponsor—Stephen A. Douglas, one of the nation's most prominent Democrats.[7]

Reaction to the act created great political turmoil throughout the North and West. In most states anti-act groups allied with such minority parties as the Know-Nothings and Prohibitionists to present Fusionist tickets in the state elections of 1854. But in Michigan and Wisconsin, the act's main critics—antislavery Democrats and Free Soilers, who insisted slavery in Kansas would deny land to small farmers, united to organize the Republican Party during the summer. [8]

The aims of the new party were clear—the Kansas-Nebraska Act should be repealed, Congress should forbid slavery in all territories, the Fugitive Slave Law should be repealed and slavery should be abolished in the District of Columbia. These desires proved to be appealing in the general elections. Republicans won Michigan and Wisconsin. Elsewhere, they had to share gains with Fusionist tickets. However, the election, a major setback for Democrats, made Republicanism much more appealing. Following the election the party attracted many more supporters, including most Whigs.

As the Kansas-Nebraska issue became regular fare for Minnesota's newspapers, some slavery opponents, who styled themselves as the "friends of freedom," met in St. Anthony on July 4, 1854. They appointed a committee to arrange a meeting of those opposed to the extension of slavery. Subsequently, the committee arranged for a statewide Republican assembly held on March 29-30, 1855.[9]

The meeting, attended by some 200 participants, affirmed the national Republican Party's demand for banning slavery in all territories. They called themselves Republicans but refrained from organizing a state party. Showing an eagerness to engage in Minnesota politics, the conclave agreed to hold a July convention to select a candidate for territorial delegate.

On July 25, ninety-four Republican delegates met in St. Paul. At this convention they completed the organization of the Minnesota

Republican Party and nominated William R. Marshall to challenge the Democratic incumbent, Henry M. Rice, for the territorial delegacy. In the October 9 general election Rice was re-elected by a plurality. Marshall finished a respectable second by outpolling David Olmsted, the candidate of an anti-Rice Democratic faction.

The election results clearly showed that for the first time in its brief history, Minnesota had two major political parties. During their early rivalry Minnesota's transition to statehood was the paramount issue.

Statehood happened much faster than Minnesota's political leaders envisioned. Despite the ongoing population surge, Governor Gorman, in his 1856 message, recommended "the propriety and public policy of our remaining a Territory for a few more years, without manifesting too much eagerness to assume the mantle of State Sovereignty."[10]

Henry M. Rice. (Courtesy of the Minnesota Historical Society)

Gorman apparently thought the statehood process would be started when he asked the legislature to authorize a constitutional convention. This method, used by Iowa, conceivably would have made him as important in shaping Minnesota as Robert Lucas had been in Iowa.

But before year's end, Gorman was undercut by public opinion and his rival Henry M. Rice. In his letter of January 29, 1856, John Esaias Warren, who had served as the territorial district attorney for a time in 1854-1855, challenged Gorman's stance. Warren insisted Minnesota had been a territory "long enough." He believed statehood would cause a great population increase, which, in turn, would stimulate the economy. Furthermore, Minnesota would be enabled to make its own laws and would have stronger representation in Washington. Statehood would also facilitate the construction of railroads.[11]

Warren's opinion was especially significant because of his relationship with Rice. The historians of Minnesota's constitution observed that "Warren appears to have been close to Rice both in political and railroad matters, and it is not impossible that the latter spoke through Warren in the matter of statehood." Not coincidentally, Warren's comments were published in the St. Paul *Pioneer and Democrat*, the territory's principal Rice organ.[12]

Warren did not suggest the shape of Minnesota when he recommended statehood. But several weeks earlier he had written to the *Pioneer and Democrat* about the importance of railroads, and in particular, one linking St. Paul with the head of Lake Superior. Warren thought the future city that would inevitably arise at the southwestern end of Lake Superior would benefit St. Paul, which would then have a vital rail/lake connection with the East. Warren's support for a St. Paul-Lake Superior railroad presaged his later advocacy of a state that would extend from Iowa to the international boundary.[13]

Joseph Rolette. (Courtesy of the Minnesota Historical Society)

By the time Warren urged statehood, some other Minnesotans had contemplated the shape of their future state. The *Shakopee Independent* on December 1, 1855, in calling for the State of "Dacotah" to be organized to Minnesota's west, concluded that the Big Sioux and Red rivers should be the Minnesota-Dacotah boundary. Opposition to this aim of a north-south state first came from the Red River valley. On February 15, 1856, veteran Indian trader Joseph Rolette, a councilor from the Pembina district, proposed an east-west division. He wanted the territorial legislature to request Congress for a division of Minnesota into two territories by a boundary following 45°10" from the St. Croix to the Missouri. Such a demarcation would have run only about sixteen miles north of downtown St. Paul.[14]

The Council was unimpressed. Its only response to Rolette's bill was to read it and order it to be printed.

Rolette obviously hoped that his action would lead to the creation of the State of Minnesota south of his proposed line and another state to its north. Presumably, he thought a northern territory separate from Minnesota would benefit his area. The new territory would bring increased federal aid, make government more accessible to its people and solve the problem of trying to unite the seemingly disparate economic interests of the agricultural southern half and the lumbering-fur trading northern half.

Throughout the subsequent contention over Minnesota's boundaries, there was some northern support for an east-west state. However, the best-organized and most vocal demands for such a state came from the southern communities of St. Peter and Winona.

Many St. Peterites and Winonans thought an east-west state would improve their chances of getting a federal land grant for a railroad linking their communities. In the spring of 1856, both towns intensified their efforts to promote the recently chartered Transit Railroad.[15]

The proposed line would not only connect their towns but be linked with Chicago on the east and extended westward to the Missouri River. The Transit Railroad had the potential for transforming southern Minnesota. It would make Winona and St. Peter important depots and would modernize transportation for a wide belt through Minnesota's prime agricultural area. As Minnesota's first railroad, it would also conceivably shift economic and potentially political power away from St. Paul, the territory's largest city.[16]

The promotion of the Transit Railroad transcended Democratic-Republican rivalry. In St. Peter, an "immense number of the citizens of St. Peter, Traverse des Sioux and surrounding country" attended a pro-railroad rally on March 28. They passed a series of resolutions calling for the speedy construction of the Transit Railroad from Winona to St. Peter. About the same time, both Winona newspapers—the Democratic *Winona Argus* and the *Winona Republican*—endorsed the idea of sending a delegate to Washington to lobby Congress for a Transit Railroad land grant.

As the population continued to surge in 1856, calls for statehood by territorial newspapers became more frequent. But as Earle S. Goodrich, editor of the *Pioneer and Democrat*, reported, there was much difference of opinion among Minnesotans about both when Minnesota should become a state and what its boundaries should be. Goodrich observed that "while many favor an eastern and western division of the territory, the sentiments, we think, of a majority of the people, is decidedly averse to a division of this character." The favorite plan, he noted, was for a north-south state with its western boundary "running up the valley of the Red River to its source, and thence south to the Iowa line."[17]

Goodrich explained the advantages of the north-south state. It "would give us a State great not only in territorial extent, but in all the elements of wealth and prosperity. We would have a lake coast of over one hundred miles in extent, and the Mississippi, Minnesota, and St. Croix rivers would furnish facilities for intercommunication such as few States can boast." Furthermore, such a state would embrace "agricultural, mineral, and lumbering resources of inexhaustible extent."

However, Daniel Sinclair the editor of the *Winona Republican*, denounced the idea of a north-south state. He claimed that its proponents, who were mainly concerned with keeping St. Paul as the capital, ignored the value of southern Minnesota and the drawbacks of the north. Protesting that a north-south state would block Minnesota from the agricultural lands west of the Big Sioux, they observed that:

> every person who knows anything about the character of these two regions [North and South], knows that Southern Minnesota is one of the very finest agricultural regions in the West, while that of the north is almost worthless for agriculture or anything else. The northern region is filled with a succession of swamps, lakes and barren ridges.

He dismissed a Lake Superior port as insignificant compared to a Chicago railroad connection. Furthermore, he insisted that the claims of northern Minnesota's mineral wealth were false, because copper mining existed only in nearby areas outside of Minnesota. He conceded that the northern pineries were valuable but felt Minnesota would benefit from them even if they were in another state.[18]

Although he endorsed an east-west state, Sinclair did not suggest its northern boundary. But he did insist that an east-west state would require a capital other than St. Paul. He assumed the statehood process would be initiated by the territorial legislature, which would provide for an election of delegates to a constitutional convention.

The *St. Peter Courier,* a Democratic paper owned by the St. Peter Company, also supported an east-west state. Like Sinclair, its editor thought such a long, narrow state was more achievable if Minnesotans took the initiative in applying for statehood. The *Courier* warned that Minnesotans should not let Congress propose state boundaries. Suggesting a timetable, the editor believed the territorial legislature, which would be convened in January 1857, should authorize an April census, a July constitutional convention, an October ratification vote by the people and the submission of the constitution to Congress in the winter of 1857-1858.[19]

The Winona and St. Peter scheme for a Minnesota legislative statehood initiative was undercut by Henry M. Rice, Minnesota's territorial delegate. Rice preferred to follow the statehood method used by Wisconsin by which Congress legislated state boundaries. Fortunately for the north-south state advocates, Rice acted before the territorial legislature convened. On December 24, 1856, he introduced the Minnesota enabling bill in the House of Representatives.[20]

In starting the enabling process, Rice displayed his characteristic shrewdness. He not only moved before the territorial legislature convened but was able to link the state authorization bill and a drive for major congressional railroad land grants to a north-south shaped Minnesota. Furthermore, he was assured of congressional support. Several months prior to the bill's introduction, Lewis D. Campbell, chairman of the House Ways and Means Committee, told Rice it was time for Minnesota to apply for statehood so it could pay its own expenses. As Campbell and Rice well knew, there was a congressional element that would support statehood for no other reason than saving the federal government the expense of administering the territory.[21]

The western boundary proposed by Rice followed natural boundaries insofar as possible. From the international boundary it was to run up the Red and Bois des Sioux rivers to Lake Traverse, their southernmost source. From the head of Lake Traverse (its southern end) a direct overland line was to be drawn to the point where the Big Sioux River entered Lake Kampeska. From that point the boundary would run down the Big Sioux to the Iowa boundary. Other than wanting natural boundaries, Rice was apparently motivated to extend Minnesota to the western edge of the land ceded by the Sisseton and Wahpeton Dakota by the Treaty of Traverse des Sioux.[22]

Following its customary practice, the House referred the Minnesota bill to its Committee on Territories. On January 31, 1857, committee chairman Galusha A. Grow of Pennsylvania reported a substitute bill to the House. The committee had changed the boundary south of the Lake Traverse head. From that point it was to run on a direct line across the continental divide to the head of Big Stone Lake. Then the demarcation would be through the center of Big Stone Lake to its southern outlet. From that spot the boundary would be overland due south to Iowa. Under questioning from Muscoe R.H. Garnett of Virginia, Grow responded that the difference between the original bill and the substitute "can be but a few hundred square miles at most."[23]

Grow never explained why his committee adjusted Minnesota's western boundary. Significantly, he reported to the House that Minnesota Territory west of the proposed state boundary be organized as "Dacotah " Territory. Rice did not oppose the alteration and in all likelihood probably endorsed it heartily. Both Grow and Rice were evidently influenced by lobbyists who aspired to create townsites and control the territorial government in the area left out of Minnesota.

In 1856-1857, at least a dozen Minnesotans were in Washington lobbying Congress for various causes. Some went there to assist Rice, others went to seek an east-west state, many of them worked to get a congressional railroad land grant and one of them, William H. Nobles, sought funds for a federal military road connecting Fort Ridgely on the upper Minnesota River with South Pass on the crest of the Rocky Mountains in present-day southwestern Wyoming. This road was intended to be the first stage of a northern overland route to California, which would add to the importance of St. Paul as an outfitting point.[24]

Nobles and his backers wanted much more than just a wagon road. The road would facilitate a new mail route to California and would enhance the development of settlement west of Minnesota. Nobles and some other prominent Minnesotans, including Joseph R. Brown, one of Minnesota's most influential Democratic politicians, regarded the Falls of the Big Sioux River (present-day Sioux Falls, South Dakota), as the most promising townsite. In Rice's original proposal, the falls would have been divided by Minnesota's western boundary. But under the change by the House Committee on Territories the entire falls, which were hailed for their water power potential, would be placed entirely within the proposed Dacotah Territory. Brown spent most of the winter in Washington lobbying for various things, including his own appointment as the Dakota Indian agent. Considering his reputation as a conniving deal maker and his interest in the area west of Minnesota, he is the most likely initiator of the boundary change.[25]

The scheming to develop the area west of Minnesota became very clear soon after Congress approved the western boundary recommended by Grow. On March 6, 1857, the Minnesota territorial legislature incorporated the Minnesota, Nebraska and Pacific Mail Transportation Company, which was empowered to convey "United States Mail, passengers, or other matters, between the eastern boundary of the Territory of Minnesota and the Pacific." Its incorporators included Brown, Nobles, and Edmund Rice, brother of the territorial delegate. Two and a half months later the legislature incorporated the Dakota Land Company, which was authorized to establish townsites in the southwestern part of the proposed

State of Minnesota and the Big Sioux valley. Brown and Nobles were the most famous of its nine incorporators.[26]

Rice's bill brought the debate over Minnesota's shape into sharper focus. North-south state proponents immediately recognized that they had gained a tactical advantage, because Rice had proposed a specific western boundary. Furthermore, they knew Rice was very influential. His fellow congressmen tended to regard him as Minnesota's official spokesman because he was the elected delegate. Aside from his official position, Rice's supporters believed he would use his considerable wealth (an estimated $250,000 in 1857) to host social affairs at his Washington home, which was reported to be "one of the finest dwellings in the city." While Rice refrained from giving public orations, he was widely acknowledged to be a persuasive deal maker.[27]

When news that the enabling bill had been referred to the House Committee on Territories reached Minnesota, Earle S. Goodrich, editor of the St. Paul *Pioneer and Democrat,* believed Rice would foil "these speculators in town lots" who were "a tremendous lobby influence at Washington, exerting its strength in favor of an east and west division of the Territory." Goodrich enthused "Ho! Then for the future state of Minnesota, extending from the British line on the North, to the Iowa line on the South, and having within its borders a greater extent of valuable land and a greater amount of navigable water, than any other state in the Union."[28]

Once the enabling act boundaries were proposed, east-west state advocates became more strident in their denunciation of the allegedly worthless North that they insisted would be a drag on the agricultural South. But they also took out their wrath on Rice, whom they portrayed as part of the St. Paul cabal, which scorned public opinion. Daniel Sinclair, of the *Winona Republican*, claimed that two-thirds of Minnesotans favored an east-west division near the forty-fifth parallel. He thought the interests of the south and the north, which,

> is nothing more than a succession of pine barrens, swamps, and
> marshes . . . can never be made to harmonize. But in the face of
> such facts as these, we find a set of men from St. Paul and vicinity,

among whom is the *St. Paul and Bayfield delegate*, Mr. Rice, using all their influence and energies to secure such a division of our Territory as must ever prove a source of trouble to its inhabitants. We trust the eyes of Congress will be opened to the magnitude of this nefarious scheme, before it is placed beyond a practical remedy. In so doing they may blast Mr. Rice's prospects of the Senatorship from the new state, but they will confer an unspeakable favor upon the masses of Minnesota.[29]

Venting frustration over Rice's initiative, the *St. Peter Courier* contended that an east-west state was vital to St. Peter's future. Such a state would facilitate the construction of the Transit Railroad and lead to the removal of the capital from St. Paul.[30]

The linkage of an east-west state, a land grant for the Transit Railroad and relocating the capital to St. Peter was advanced as the core philosophy of an informal alliance of Gorman Democrats and Republicans in the territorial legislature.

The legislature strongly objected to the western boundary provision in the enabling bill by memorializing Congress. On January 21, 1857, the House by a vote of twenty-five to ten approved the memorial introduced by Eli B. Barrows of Pleasant Grove, in Olmsted County. By an eleven to four vote, the Council followed suit the next day. The memorial contended that a north-south state would produce "political conflicts and rivalries" because the northern and southern sections have "no community of interests." Seeking justice "for and on behalf of the people of the Territory," the memorial stated that the imposition of Rice's proposed boundary "would be a violation of their sovereign rights as a people, and tyrannical in the extreme." Therefore, the memorialists asked Congress to authorize the people of Minnesota to determine its boundaries.[31]

The memorial was a rather extraordinary document. By asserting that the people had sovereign rights in boundary matters, it challenged the very idea that Congress had the power to determine state limits. The memorial was a watershed event in the contention over shaping Minnesota. After it, the east-west advocates consistently claimed that the ultimate authority in the United States was "squatter sovereignty."

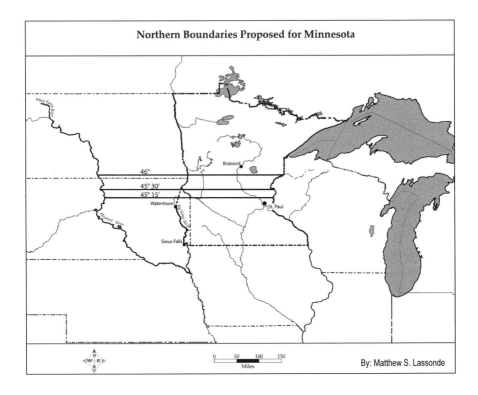

Northern Boundaries Proposed for Minnesota

By: Matthew S. Lassonde

The memorial served to energize opposition to the enabling act boundaries, but had little impact in Congress. It was received too late to even be considered by the House of Representatives, which approved the enabling bill with the western boundary alteration on January 31. When the Senate considered the House bill only Senator George W. Jones, an Iowa Democrat, spoke for the memorialists. Jones was apparently influenced by his nephew William Ashley Jones, the editor of the *Winona Argus.*[32]

The younger Jones, through his Democratic newspaper, represented the prevailing Winona-area sentiment by routinely advocating an east-west state and lambasting Rice and St. Paul. Among other things, he insisted that the only plausible reason for a north-south state was "that it would tend to retain the seat of government at St. Paul and the control of the State, in the hands of a few political jugglers thereabouts, nineteen twentieths [sic] of whom expect to be Senators, Congressmen, Governors, Judges, etc."[33]

On February 21, after Stephen A. Douglas asked the Senate to consider the bill authorizing Minnesota to proceed with the statehood process, Jones objected to the boundary provision. He proposed to amend it with: "Provided, that the convention to form the constitution for said State shall submit to the people whether the foregoing boundaries shall be adopted, or whether the state shall embrace all that portion of the present Territory which lies south of the forty-sixth degree of north latitude." Jones explained that he had voted for the bill in the Senate Committee on Territories, but was offering the amendment "at the instance of some ten or twelve citizens of Minnesota, who have spent a portion of the winter at Washington city." He added that he had also been informed that the Minnesota legislature had petitioned Congress not to adopt a north and south boundary. Jones thought his amendment "would accommodate the great mass of the people," because a division at forty-six degrees latitude would divide the territory into "about equally" two parts. Apparently there had been some informal discussion about the matter, because Senator John B. Thompson of Kentucky observed that the "part thus cut off is to constitute the suggested future State of Superior."[34]

The Senate overwhelmingly rejected the Jones amendment. Most senators were apparently influenced by Douglas, the chairman of the Committee on Territories, and Andrew P. Butler of South Carolina, who objected to Congress relinquishing its power to establish state boundaries.

Although never mentioned in its deliberations, the Senate had another major reason for routinely approving of the Minnesota enabling bill on February 25. By the time it received the bill from the House, the Senate was deeply involving in considering a large railroad land grant to Minnesota predicated on the north-south shape.

The appeal of railroads was not lost on Rice and other promoters, who believed St. Paul and nearby communities would be Minnesota's economic hub. They recognized the dire consequences that a single railroad such as the Transit Railroad across southern Minnesota would have on the St. Paul-St. Anthony-Minneapolis district. Their solution was to ask Congress for a magnanimous land grant that would subsidize a statewide system of railroads, including one along the proposed Transit

Railroad route. Such a grant would not only benefit a future north-south state but would also undermine those who thought an east-west state was necessary to lead to the construction of the Transit Railroad.

On February 7, 1857, Senator Robert A. Toombs of Georgia reported that he had received a petition from "James Shields and other citizens of Minnesota" requesting railroad grant lands. The petititioners stated that Minnesota had been denied grants even though adjoining states had received them. Toombs, who enthusiastically supported the request, claimed Minnesota had a large population of 180,000 to 200,000.[35]

Shields, the only Minnesotan specifically mentioned by Toombs, proved to be an important lobbyist for the railroad land grant bill. Very prominent in the Minnesota Democratic Party, Shields was already well-known when he moved from Illinois to Minnesota Territory in 1855. He had been a major general during the Mexican-American War and later (1849-1855) represented Illinois in the United States Senate. He entered Minnesota as the leader of a colony of Irish immigrants which established the community of Shieldsville in Rice County.[36]

The Minnesota railroad land grant request was easily approved by Congress. Its backers compromised any potential Southern opposition by including land grants for Alabama railroads. The act of March 3, passed less than a week after the enabling act, gave Minnesota Territory 6,000,000 acres (about eleven percent of the future state's area), which was to be re-granted to railroads. The territory received all odd-numbered sections in a six-mile width on each side of the following routes:[37]

1) "From Stillwater, by way of Saint Paul and Saint Anthony, to a point between the foot of Big Stone Lake and the mouth of Sioux Wood River, with a branch via Saint Cloud and Crow Wing, to the navigable waters of the Red River of the north, at such point as the Legislature of said Territory may determine. . . ."

2) "From Saint Paul and from Saint Anthony, via Minneapolis, to a convenient point of junction west of the Mississippi, to the southern boundary of the Territory in the direction of the mouth of the Big Sioux River, with a branch, via Faribault, to the north line of the State of Iowa. . . ."

3) "From Winona, via Saint Peters [sic], to a point on the Big Sioux River, south of the forty-fifth parallel of north latitude" with a connecting route from La Crescent up the Root River valley to a point near Rochester.

Passage of the land grant act created great excitement in Minnesota. Railroads were universally appealing. Satisfaction with the act not only transcended differences among the Democratic factions but even gave Democrats and Republicans a matter on which they could agree. While realizing the grant would bolster a north-south state, even east-west advocates applauded it. The *Winona Republican* , for example, recognized six men it deemed "the most active and influential in securing the passage of the Land Bill." They were Rice; Shields; William R. Nobles; Henry Titus Welles, a St. Anthony lumbering entrepreneur; Richard Chute, who had a financial interest in developing Falls of St. Anthony water power; and Henry D. Huff, a Winona townsite owner.[38]

Some communities that benefitted particularly from the grant demonstrated their gratitude. At a Stillwater celebration on March 19, James Shields, Robert Toombs and Henry M. Rice, identified as "present delegate and future Senator," were lauded for their roles. In Minneapolis, citizens of both political parties honored Henry Titus Welles at a public dinner. At St. Peter, in response to a call by the *Courier*, "a large and enthusiastic meeting" at the Alma House led to the planning of the "Grand Railroad Celebration and Illumination" to celebrate the grant. Rice, Shields, Toombs and Stephen A. Douglas were the most prominent invited guests.[39]

Public enthusiasm was reflected in the territorial legislature, which eagerly accepted the land grant and designated routes for specified railroads. In May, during their special session, lawmakers made the most of the discretion granted to them by Congress. They designated Breckenridge, the northernmost eligible point, as the western end of the route, which ran from Stillwater to a point between the foot of Big Stone Lake and the mouth of the Sioux Wood (i.e. Bois Brule) River. Furthermore, they extended a branch that was to run to navigable waters of the Red River all the way to St. Vincent, in the northwestern corner of the future state.[40]

While Congress was considering the enabling and railroad grant bills, east-west advocates in the territorial legislature fought back. About a week after a majority of legislators sent their January 1857, memorial to Congress, Republican councilor Clark W. Thompson of Houston County made a bold move to initiate the statehood process in Minnesota. He proposed that the legislature authorize a constitutional convention. His action was supported by a parallel bill in the House of Representatives. As an ardent east-west state champion, Thompson obviously hoped such a convention would agree on an east-west configuration and a resultant boundary showdown with Congress. Editor Earle S. Goodrich of the *Pioneer and Democrat* warned that acceptance of Thompson's idea would assuredly delay statehood. Most legislators, apparently agreeing with this judgment, refused to support Thompson.[41]

East-west legislators also tried another tack—moving the capital from St. Paul to St. Peter. A bill calling for capital removal to land owned by the St. Peter Company was introduced in the House on February 5, 1857. [42]

The capital removal bill provoked a sharp, acrimonious debate. Its critics immediately questioned the authority of the legislature to even consider such a bill. Their position was strengthened by a ruling from Lafayette Emmett, the territorial attorney general. In reviewing pertinent legislation, Emmett ascertained that the territorial organic act specified that the legislature should first meet in St. Paul. The same measure empowered the legislature to designate a temporary capital and determine the method of establishing a permanent capital by a vote of the people. The first legislature had named St. Paul as the temporary capital, but until 1857, had never acted to create a permanent capital.

Despite Emmett's position that a vote of the people was the only authority for capital removal, the St. Peter supporters acted as if the organic act had no meaning. A coalition of pro-removal Gorman Democrats and Republicans narrowly won Council and House approval. The removal sentiment was fueled not only by a desire for an east-west state but by hatred for St. Paul, the territory's largest city and economic center and a Democratic bastion.[43]

Minnesota newspapers, with the exception of those from St. Peter and Winona, lambasted the capital removal attempt as a nefarious scheme by speculators flaunting the public will. It was well-known that Governor Gorman was a major stakeholder in the St. Peter Company. As for legislative support, a common press explanation was that some legislators had been bribed with promises of St. Peter town lots.

The skullduggery charges helped create an "anything goes" political climate in the legislature. Many who wanted St. Paul to remain the capital believed the courts would ultimately block any capital removal effort. But others, including Councilor Joseph Rolette, wanted to prevent the legislature from passing a removal act. As chairman of the Council's Committee on Enrolled Bills, Rolette disappeared with the enrolled capital removal bill. In the meantime, both houses approved a substitute bill but Council President John B. Brisbin of St. Paul refused to sign it because of alleged irregularities. Nonetheless, Gorman approved it.

However, Rolette's antics had cast a shadow over the entire proceeding. St. Paul's supporters proclaimed Rolette to be the capital's savior. But pro-removal forces, who worried about the legality of the legislative action, tried to portray him as the archvillain.

Those who wanted an east-west state and capital removal were frustrated by their inability to influence Congress and by Rolette's stunt. Consequently, their self-appointed spokesman, William C. Dodge, an owner of the *Winona Republican*, appealed for public support. In his deceptively titled pamphlet, *Address of the Majority Members of the Legislature to the People of Minnesota*, Dodge pointed out that a decided bipartisan legislative majority favored an east-west boundary. But since Congress had ignored the boundary memorial, the *Address* was an appeal to the highest possible authority—the people themselves.[44]

Dodge also noted that east-west state advocates had tried to assure equitable representation of all portions of Minnesota in the pending constitutional convention. Specifically, they had proposed a reapportionment bill for election of delegates based on a new census. As they well realized, recent history was on their side. The first apportionment of the territorial legislature set its size at nine councilors and eighteen representatives but an 1855 reapportionment based on a new territorial census increased the Council to fifteen members and the House of Representatives to thirty-nine. Many of these gains were in the area south of St. Paul, where east-west sentiment was the strongest. East-west state advocates believed an 1857 census and apportionment, which would be sharply influenced by the population boom, would give them a clear majority in the constitutional convention. But this aim, although outwardly fair, ran afoul of the Enabling Act, which specified that Minnesota's voters were to choose two constitutional convention delegates for each "representative district" in a June 1 election. Given that pending deadline, those who favored an east-west state simply did not have enough time to gain approval for a new census and subsequent reapportionment.[45]

Recognizing that prevailing in the June 1 election was the last hope for an east-west state, Dodge tried to incite a public reaction to Rolette's prank. Most of his address was a condemnation of Rolette and St. Paul. The *St. Peter Courier* published a verbatim copy of the address and William Ashley Jones of the *Winona Argus* wished it could be placed in the hands of every Minnesotan, because that would prevent the "suicidal" advocacy of a north-south state.[46]

The address helped sharpen the debate between proponents of the north-south and east-west states that had been raging since the details of Rice's enabling bill became public. The campaign to influence the outcome of the June 1 election of delegates featured area rather than party differences, sharply contrasting views of the two possible state configurations, and basic disagreement over the authority to establish state boundaries.

The strongest case for the north-south state emanated from St. Paul and such nearby communities as Minneapolis, Shakopee and Stillwater. Demands for an east-west state came mainly from southern Minnesota, with St. Peter and Winona as the leading centers. The St. Peter and Winona promoters, especially, regarded an east-west state, the building of the Transit Railroad and capital removal as interrelated goals. North-south sentiment was somewhat stronger among Democrats and east-west support more prevalent among Republicans, but this was only because the Democrats dominated the St. Paul vicinity and the Republicans southern Minnesota. St. Paul Republicans led by John P. Owens, editor of the *Daily Minnesotian*, wanted a north-south state, but in St. Peter and Winona, both Democrats and Republicans campaigned for an east-west state.

However, there were notable exceptions to the prevailing sentiment in the St. Paul area and in southern Minnesota. Some Republicans in St. Anthony, led by William W. Wales, a member of the territorial council, and the *St. Anthony Republican* wanted an east-west state. Owens denounced the *Republican* as the organ of the "Gorman Republican clique" and labeled Wales, Governor Gorman and Saint Andre Durand Balcombe, a councilor from Winona, as the leaders of the "Squatter-Sovereign-Gorman clique." Balcombe, Gorman and Wales were generally scorned in St. Paul because they were also the most zealous champions of capital removal.[47]

In the South, St. Peter's support for an east-west state was vigorously opposed in Henderson, only about fifteen miles distant. Opinion in Henderson was greatly influenced by its founder Joseph R. Brown, who also owned the *Henderson Democrat*, the town's only newspaper. Brown, one of Minnesota's leading Democratic politicians, regularly supported St. Paul with regard to the future state's shape and capital removal. In a long letter to the *Henderson Democrat*, Brown first observed that the legislators who voted for capital removal professed to be motivated by the desire to get an east-west state. But he observed, "I cannot see how we can hope to get an east and west line that will give us a State worth living in." He assumed that a state south of 45° 30" could not extend beyond the western boundary specified in the Enabling Act. Thus, Minnesota would be a small state of only 30,000 square miles with agriculture as its only resource. Brown believed the Minnesota River Valley would benefit most from the proposed north-south state, because it would be advantageously situated between the northern pineries and the great prairie to its southwest, which extended into Nebraska and Kansas.[48]

Another major criticism of an east-west state was made by John M. Berry of Faribault, a member of the territorial House of Representatives. In objecting to the claim by the *Faribault Herald's* editor that the majority of Minnesotans favored an east-west state, Berry opined that boundaries should be established "with reference to the greatest good of the whole, for this generation and all generations to come, for our present circumstances, and for every variety of circumstance which time may develop." Berry insisted that many who originally favored an east-west state had been converted to the north-south pattern, because it would provide a compact state which would assure "the greatest State in all the elements of true greatness and universal prosperity. . . ."[49]

Other than the southern counties, east-west state sentiment was the strongest in Minnesota's northernmost settlements. By the time of the state shape dispute, the farming frontier had extended up the Mississippi River valley beyond St. Cloud and Sauk Rapids to Little Falls. Some people in this area felt the same sense of estrangement from St. Paul as many southern Minnesotans did. Although they actually lived in the central part of proposed north-south state, inhabitants of the St. Cloud-Sauk Rapids-Little Falls region saw themselves as northerners. Evidently, they believed an east-west state would not only free them from St. Paul's dominance but would create an opportunity for their community to become the capital or the site of some other significant public institution.

Northern support for an east-west state did not necessarily improve the prospects of achieving it. Although they agreed on the general notion of such a state, east-west proponents differed on specific details. Southern Minnesotans believed they would be more persuasive if they called for a roughly equal division of Minnesota Territory at either 45° 30 or 46°. To the dismay of some northerners, either line would have left them in Minnesota. Consequently, they wanted a more southerly demarcation. The *Northern Herald* of Little Falls proposed 45° 15", but the editor of the Sauk Rapids *Frontiersman* wanted the boundary placed at 45° 20".[50]

In their attempts to rally public support, east-west and north-south advocates exhibited sharp differences. The east-west promoters emphasized agriculture as the key to future growth and prosperity. Further, they insisted an east-west state would best facilitate railroad construction, because the nation's main commercial lines would naturally run east-west. They also stressed the fertility of the land between the Enabling Act's western boundary and the Missouri River. Bordering the Missouri, they insisted, would give Minnesota vital steamboat routes on both its eastern and western sides. As part of glorifying agriculture, the east-west champions disparaged the north, which they portrayed as a barren wilderness unfit for development. [51]

North-south promoters insisted that their proposed square and compact shape was superior to an east-west configuration, which would create an odd southern projection between the Big Sioux and Missouri rivers. Further, they contended that a diverse economy based on the three pillars of agriculture, lumbering and mining would lead to a more prosperous state. They certainly had tangible proof of the value of lumbering, because it had been done for two decades in the St. Croix Valley. But their claim to mining was based only on the assumption that it would also be discovered and developed commercially in the northeastern part of the north-south state, because copper had been found in the Lake Superior regions of Michigan and Wisconsin. A key part of the north-south argument was their insistence that access to Lake Superior and the Red River valley would lead to the construction of railroad links with St. Paul, which, in turn, would cause the development of the regions along their routes.[52]

The aspect of the north-south and east-west controversy that created the greatest fervor was about who had the right to establish state boundaries. Supporters of the north-south state held that Congress had the authority to establish state boundaries. Hence, they supported Rice and the Enabling Act's western boundary provision. Those who wanted an east-west state insisted that a vote of the people should negate a congressional action. They called this acclaimed people's power "squatter sovereignty."

The battle lines between the two sides were clearly drawn when the legislature approved its memorial to Congress. Newspaper editors who wanted a north-south state ridiculed the idea of squatter sovereignty. John

P. Owens of the *Daily Minnesotan* wanted to enlighten "our political friends in the Legislature and elsewhere who are at present disposed to be wildly led in the swamps of political heresy by that new-fangled will-of-the-wisp known as 'Squatter Sovereignty.'" Owens strongly endorsed a letter from a correspondent who likened squatter sovereignty to actions hostile to American democracy, including Shays's Rebellion, the Whiskey Rebellion and the South Carolina nullification ordinance. "Junius," the letter writer, claimed that the territorial legislature showed utter ignorance and disregard for the federal union under which Congress had the legal authority to establish state boundaries.[53]

Earle S. Goodrich of the *Pioneer and Democrat* made a distinction between "Squatter Sovereignty" advanced by "Black Republicans" and "Popular Sovereignty," a Democratic doctrine. He thought squatter sovereignty was like a mob action but popular sovereignty was the right of people to self-government. He believed such a matter of state boundaries in which the federal government had a vital interest was never intended to be part of popular sovereignty. He asserted "the very idea of a boundary implies the existence of two interested parties."[54]

East-west state spokesmen insisted that the people should decide the state's boundaries because Congress, and specifically Rice, had flaunted public opinion. The *St. Peter Courier* and the *Winona Argus*, the leading promoters of an east-west state, consistently claimed that the overwhelming majority of Minnesotans wanted an east-west state. The *St. Peter Courier* published an opinion that two-thirds of all Minnesotans favored an east-west line between forty-five and forty-six degrees latitude and that "Southern Minnesota is almost unanimous" in that regard.[55]

When he became aware of the Enabling Act's western boundary, William Ashley Jones of the *Argus* charged that Rice had sprung a surprise, because the previous boundary opinions had differed only with respect to the placement of the east-west line. He wrote, "we are confident, at least, that not more than one to a thousand of the citizens of Minnesota, ever heard of the proposition of a North and South line seriously proposed." He saw the Rice proposal as "this secretly concocted and treacherous movement, this stealthy, midnight, and assassin-like charge upon an unsuspecting and unguarded constituency." The entire scheme of a north-south state, he alleged, was designed to create a state that would have two sections divided by the Mississippi River. Such a shape would enable Rice of St. Paul to become a United States senator from the east side. He believed the appropriate response to Rice's disdain for public opinion was for the people to assert themselves. In trying to rile public opinion, he commented: "Are you, men of Minnesota, a set of asses of such lamentable ignorance that you cannot say how you would divide the territory, or is it true that our Delegate in making that assumption has outstepped the bounds of his authority."[56]

As east-west promoters realized quite well, once the Enabling Act was passed the only opportunity the people had to change the boundaries was through the pending constitutional convention. The *St. Peter Courier* claimed that if the constitution so authorized, the people had the right to vote on an alternative to the boundaries "which his lordship, Mr. Henry M. Rice would fasten upon us."[57]

Although the shaping of the state was an issue in some districts during the campaign for the election of constitutional convention delegates, it was overshadowed by the Democratic and Republican debate over slavery. The positions each party assumed after the Kansas-Nebraska Act were further inflamed and hardened by the Dred Scott Decision of March 6, 1857. In holding that Congress did not have the power to control the expansion of slavery, the United States Supreme Court's majority ruling struck at the very core of an essential Republican tenet. Consequently, many party members intensified their demands to not only prohibit slavery in the territories but to abolish the institution of slavery. Democrats, accustomed to their majority status in the state and the nation and as defenders of the *status quo*, responded by ridiculing Republicans as "nigger lovers" and "Black Republicans."[58]

The acrimonious debate over slavery created an atmosphere in which members of both parties usually regarded the other side as enemies rather than political rivals. With this background, the elected Democratic and Republican delegates were in no mood to cooperate when they opened the constitutional convention on July 13, 1857, in St. Paul.

With each side determined to dominate the convention, they could not even agree on the opening meeting time and presiding officer. This and the roughly equal size of both party delegations and disputes over election results in some districts caused the Democrats and Republicans to hold separate constitutional conventions. The Democratic and Republican wings chose their own presiding officers. The Democrats selected Henry H. Sibley, a veteran fur trader who had served as Minnesota Territory's first delegate to Congress. The Republicans chose Saint Andre Durand Balcombe, who had represented the Winona district in the 1857 Council.[59]

In both conventions there was some contention over the north-south and east-west state. The overwhelming majority of the Democratic and Republican delegates favored acceptance of the Enabling Act boundaries. However, small but very vocal minorities tried to make a case for an east-west state. Support for an east-west state was somewhat stronger in the Republican convention. Most of its delegates were from the agricultural south, whose citizenry was most supportive of an east-west state.

On the opening day of the Republican convention the delegates, by a vote of forty-one to fifteen, accepted John W. North's motion to form a constitution in accordance with the Enabling Act. In a seeming contradiction, they also approved a motion by David A. Secombe of St. Anthony to create a five-man committee on the name and boundaries of the state. Some delegates questioned the need for such a committee, because acceptance of the Enabling Act, they reasoned, obviously included acceptance of its boundaries. But by consensus, the delegates concluded that the committee could decide if acceptance of the act had resolved the boundary question.[60]

Oscar F. Perkins (Rice County) chaired the committee, which also included Samuel W. Putnam (St. Anthony), Thomas Wilson (Winona), Lucas K. Stannard (Chisago County) and Simeon Harding (Olmsted County). On July 24, Perkins reported that the committee recommended acceptance of the Enabling Act boundaries, with Wilson as the lone dissenter. When the convention began considering the report, Wilson moved for a northern boundary of forty-six degrees latitude from Wisconsin to the Missouri River.[61]

He was strongly supported by Lewis McKune of Waseca County, who thought such an east-west state would "include nearly all the inhabited portion of Minnesota, and nearly all that can ever become populous. By adopting this boundary we not only get rid of large tracts of unfertile lands, but of conflicting interests, which will require distinct and separate legislation." But Wentworth Hayden (Hennepin County) countered that it was important to adhere to the Enabling Act, because failure to accept it could jeopardize statehood prospects. He also contended that lumbering, mining and agriculture would not conflict, but "will necessarily combine us what we desire to be—a prosperous and powerful state."[62]

Determined to prevail, Wilson tried to dominate the floor debate. He insisted that the people, especially those of Winona, Houston and Fillmore counties, favored his east-west line and that St. Paul's political leaders would dominate a north-south state. He orated, "I never wish them to have any control in any State of which I am a citizen. But how can we deprive her [St. Paul] of it, without changing our boundaries." Responding to Wilson, George Watson of Freeborn County said Wilson's comment about the people's preference in Fillmore County was false. Two-thirds of the county's residents, he reported, wanted a north-south line. Stannard also spoke against Wilson's motion. He argued that such an east-west state would disenfranchise some of his constituents. He thought a variety of pursuits "tends to promote happiness" and that Wilson's proposed boundary would exclude "trappers, hunters, and lumbermen," who were Minnesota's only inhabitants when the pineries of the St. Croix were opened in 1838. Watson and Stannard were convincing. The delegates defeated Wilson's proposal by a vote of fifteen "yeas" and thirty-seven "nays." All of Wilson's supporters were from the southernmost two tiers of counties.[63]

After Wilson's setback, one of his allies, Amos Coggswell of Steele County, tried a more radical approach by proposing to change both the northern and western boundaries of the Enabllng Act. He wanted forty-six degrees on the north and ninety-seven degrees on the west. His longitudinal line on the west would have run about twenty miles west of present-day Sioux Falls, South Dakota. Such a state, he reasoned, would be nearly square in shape and about the size of Iowa. It was important to him that Minnesota become an agricultural state, because the "northern region will never be settled up by a permanent home abiding population." The delegates were so unimpressed with Coggswell's proposal that they did not even deign to consider it.[64]

After the rejection of the Wilson and Coggswell proposals the delegates assumed they had settled the boundary question by their approval of North's motion. But on August 10, E. Page Davis of Nicollet County proposed that the boundary proposition of forty-six degrees on the north be submitted to their constituents when they voted on the constitution. Davis did not choose to debate the merits of the east-west and north-south states but said he only wanted the people to be given the opportunity to exercise their "squatter sovereignty" rights. In support of his position he presented a newspaper article, resolutions from a St. Peter meeting and a letter from a constituent. The gist of the article from the *St. Peter Free Press* of July 29, 1857, was that a north-south state would ruin the Republican Party and that the people should have the right to express their choice on the boundary. The resolutions from the mass meeting at St. Peter on August 3, 1857, reiterated the newspaper's position. Davis stated that the constituent letter, which supported the resolutions, was only an example and that he could produce additional letters. Davis insisted that with the acceptance of his proposal, "we can go into Nicollet county [sic], and into Le Sueur county [sic], and obtain nearly every vote in favor of this Constitution, while without it, I assure this Convention that our Constitution will receive but very few votes."[65]

The Davis proposal led to a long and sometimes sharp debate. Davis's most vocal supporters were Coggswell, Balcombe, who identified himself as a consistent supporter of the east-west state, and Wilson, who was still seething about the Enabling Act boundaries. Wilson reported that when he was in Washington during the previous winter, he had lobbied the House Committee on Territories for an east-west northern boundary but that unspecified forces deceitfully convinced the committee that Minnesotans preferred a north-south state. Thomas Foster of Dakota County, a vigorous supporter of the north-south state, scornfully responded that Wilson was misleading about his Washington lobbying. He pointed out that Wilson and other opponents of the Enabling Act boundaries were also in Washington to lobby for a railroad grant. Winona had gotten its share, so Wilson should be satisfied.[66]

Other than Foster, the leading opponents of the Davis proposal were North, W.H.C. Folsom of Chisago County, Perkins, chairman of the Boundaries Committee, and Thomas J. Galbraith of Scott County. Their main contentions were that the convention should not do anything that could delay or abort Minnesota's admission to the union, the convention had already approved the Enabling Act boundaries, there was no evidence of strong voter support for an east-west state, squatter sovereignty was contrary to the Enabling Act, and the railroad grant lands north of forty-six degrees were very important to Minnesota's future.[67]

During the consideration of the Davis proposal, Wilson inferred that Davis might be trying to revive the plan to move the capital to St. Peter. Wilson said he had opposed the capital removal scheme because it was "impolitic and unwise." Davis assured the delegates there was absolutely no linkage between his proposal and any plan to make St. Peter the capital. He stated that since Willis A. Gorman, whom he called "the father" of the capital removal effort had abandoned it, there was no prospect of St. Peter ever becoming the capital.[68]

As Davis and all the other delegates knew, Gorman's change of heart was not the real reason for the capital removal scheme's death knell. The dubiously passed removal bill specified that the capital was to be transferred from St. Paul to St. Peter on May 1, 1857. When the incumbent Democratic administration made no effort to abide by the act, the president of the St. Peter Company filed suit in federal district court. On July 12, Judge Rensselaer R. Nelson ruled that the capital would remain in St. Paul. Nelson determined that the legislature had exceeded its authority in approving the capital removal act and that the act was invalid because of legal irregularities in enacting it.[69]

The delegates were generally satisfied that Davis was not trying to revive capital removal but were greatly concerned that his proposal, if included in the constitution, would cause Congress to reject Minnesota statehood. Under pressure, Davis agreed to change his proposal. His revision stipulated that if the people voted for an east-west state their desire would be submitted to Congress as a memorial separate from the constitution. Congress could then decide if it wanted to revise the constitution by establishing a forty-six degrees latitude northern boundary from Wisconsin to the Missouri River.[70]

Charles E. Flandrau. (Courtesy of the Minnesota Historical Society)

Davis's contention that the people should have a role in determining the boundaries was persuasive. By a vote of thirty to twenty-eight, the convention approved his motion. But after a short delay, the delegates, by a vote of thirty-two to twenty-one, approved a motion by John W. North that the Davis motion be reconsidered. In the reconsideration vote the Davis motion was defeated by a vote of thirty-one to twenty-six. The result demonstrated the decisive north-south schism on the boundary question. The entire fourteen-man Hennepin County delegation voted against the Davis proposal. They were joined by all of the delegates from north of Minneapolis and St. Paul as well as nearly all those in the counties immediately south of those cities. With only two exceptions, all of Davis's support came from the southernmost two tiers of counties.[71]

As the Republicans went through the process of accepting the Enabling Act boundaries, the Democratic convention was rejecting an attempt to form an east-west state. Charles E. Flandrau of Traverse des Sioux, Nicollet County, led the effort to change the Enabling Act boundaries. Apparently, his election from a predominantly Republican district resulted from his willingness to support an east-west state. Several weeks before the June 1 election, the county's Democrats were urged to attend a meeting at Traverse des Sioux to organize support for constitutional convention delegates who would strongly support an east-west state.[72]

Unlike the Republicans, the Democrats felt no urgency in addressing the state boundary question. Their convention was three weeks old before George W. Becker (Ramsey County), chairman of the Boundaries Committee, recommended acceptance of the Enabling Act boundaries.

Flandrau moved to amend Becker's motion by calling for a forty-sixth parallel northern boundary from Wisconsin to the Missouri River. Such a demarcation, he explained, would benefit both the North and South. The people of the northern territory, he stated, "want a condition in which they can arrange their own matters and not be overborne by the more populous South, which has always preponderated in the Territory and has always appropriated all the Federal donations, and all the Federal patronage." The principal advantage to the South, he thought, would be access to Missouri River navigation.[73]

Former Governor Gorman, one of Ramsey County's delegates, responded that the north-south state was vital because of the railroad grant lands. He reported that before the railroad grant act, he had favored an east-west state because the original railroad grant plan was for a line from Winona to the Missouri by way of St. Peter. But after the grant was greatly expanded, he estimated that Minnesota would lose thirty to fifty million dollars as the result of the boundary proposed by Flandrau.[74]

Before the vote on his amendment, Flandrau tried to sway the delegates by reporting on public opinion. He claimed the people of Nicollet County were "almost unanimously " in favor of an east-west line. The argument was unconvincing and his amendment was defeated by a vote of thirty-six to six. His five supporters were all from southern counties.[75]

Sensing that a line somewhat south of forty-six degrees would attract northern support, Flandrau moved to amend Becker's motion by a northern boundary at 45° 30". This prompted Henry C. Waite of St. Cloud to propose a line at 45° 15". Flandrau's new amendment would have placed Minnesota's northern boundary only about four miles south of St. Cloud, but Waite's would have left St. Cloud about twenty miles north of an east-west Minnesota. Because he got the votes of delegates from Benton and Pembina counties, Waite's amendment fared better than either of Flandrau's proposed lines. Even so, it was decisively rejected by a vote of thirty-two to ten. The convention then promptly defeated Flandrau's proposed 45° 30" line by thirty-three to nine. This action cleared the way for the consideration of Becker's main motion to accept the Enabling Act boundaries. It was approved by a margin of nearly four to one.[76]

Acceptance of the Enabling Act boundaries seemingly resolved the question of shaping of the state. But ten days later, Flandrau moved that the boundary of 45° 30" on the north from Wisconsin to the Missouri River be voted on by the people, separate from the constitution, on the same day they voted on the constitution. The idea was very popular in the St. Peter area and Flandrau was no doubt determined to show his constituents that he was putting up a good fight.

In their last stand, Flandrau and his small coterie of supporters again tried to invoke the people's will. Flandrau contended a "very large portion" of the people in the territory favored an east-west line. He reported: "I am told by gentlemen who know that there are whole counties which will poll thousands of votes where this is regarded as the all important question." Waite and James C. Shepley, another Stearns County delegate, also spoke about public desire for an east-west state. Waite stated that "the whole northern portion of the Territory" wanted it and Shepley said his constituency "almost unanimously" favored it.[77]

In response, two Ramsey County delegates, George L. Becker and Lafayette Emmett, said they opposed Flandrau's amendment because the people had expressed their preference in the June 1 election. Becker stated that "a large and overwhelming majority of the members of the Constitutional Convention were sent here because of their known opposition to this measure, and because they had publicly expressed that opposition. . . ." Emmett's judgment was that the east-west boundary proposition was "signally defeated" in the delegate election.[78]

The convention did not even show Flandrau the courtesy of voting on his proposal. After some parliamentary maneuvering led by the clever Joseph R. Brown, the resolution was tabled by consensus. No one tried to bring it off the table before the convention adjourned eight days later.[79]

Even without the tabling maneuver, Flandrau's proposal would have been doomed. By the time he introduced it, the Democrats and Republicans had agreed to name a compromise committee to reconcile their differences and produce a single constitution. Since both convention wings had accepted the Enabling Act boundaries, the committee naturally incorporated them in its document. After the Democrats and Republicans agreed on the constitution there no was no further contention about Minnesota's boundaries.

Why was the north-south state accepted? One reason is because it was a specific proposal initiated by the territorial delegate. Although Congress changed Rice's western boundary slightly, north-south state backers did not object. Throughout the boundary contention they consistently supported the Enabling Act boundaries. The east-west state advocates, on the other hand, never had a common goal. They all wanted an east-west state but could not agree on the exact placement of its northern boundary. The forty-sixth parallel boundary was the most popular proposal. It was supported by the 1857 territorial legislature and was the first line introduced in both the Democratic and Republican constitutional conventions. However, the forty-sixth parallel was unacceptable to those in the area between it and 45° 10", Rolette's suggestion. So east-west proponents in the St. Cloud-Sauk Centre-Little Falls area usually wanted 45° 15 or 45° 20". The notion of using 45° 30" was proposed as a compromise in both constitutional conventions.

East-west state sentiment was at its zenith when the 1857 territorial legislature sent its memorial to Congress, but that swell was undercut by the railroad land grant act. After Minnesota received the massive grant, a clear majority in both parties wanted a north-south state. Given the nature of the grant, Minnesota simply could not afford to create an east-west state.

The failure of the capital removal effort also reduced support for an east-west state. As long as southern Minnesotans were thinking of the Transit Railroad as the only land grant line and St. Peter as the capital, an east-west state was appealing to many.

It is also possible that the tone of the east-west and north-south debate caused some people to become converted to the Enabling Act boundaries. Generally, north-south champions waged a positive campaign with the emphasis on a potentially rich state with a diverse economy built on agriculture, lumbering and mining. But east-west proponents were extremely negative about the north, which they portrayed as a backward land that would never develop a prosperous society.

Lastly, becoming a state was extremely important to Minnesotans. The argument that refusal to accept the Enabling Act boundaries would jeopardize statehood was very persuasive in molding public opinion. Despite their sharp differences on other issues, both political parties were pro-state. Statehood sentiment was certainly reflected by the vote on the constitution in the first general state election, held on October 13, 1857. The canvassed vote was 30,055 in favor of the constitution with only 571 opposed. Anything supported by over ninety-eight percent of the electorate is certainly a sweeping mandate. The election results raise a question about the veracity of the claims that masses of Minnesotans wanted an east-west state. Even if many people changed their minds in the several months before the election, it would seem that if the east-west sentiment was as strong as its backers claimed, there would have been a more substantial protest vote.[80]

Within a year after Minnesota attained statehood, the federal government began the process of surveying and marking its western land boundary. On March 3, 1859, Congress included $5,000 for the survey in its annual appropriations act.[81]

Thomas A. Hendricks, commissioner of the United States General Land Office, decided to personally supervise the survey rather than assign it to Charles L. Emerson, the federal surveyor general of Min-

nesota. On April 30, 1859, five days after advising Emerson of his decision, Hendricks sent survey instructions to Chauncey H. Snow and
Henry Hutton, whom he had engaged to conduct the survey. Several
weeks later, Snow and Hutton were employed by Commissioner of Indian Affairs Albert B. Greenwood to survey the boundaries of the
Dakota Indian reservations in the Upper Minnesota River valley. The
following summer they surveyed the boundaries of the two reservations
before commencing the western boundary determination. They evidently did both the reservation and state boundary surveys as part of
the same expedition from St. Paul. Their determination of the Upper
Sioux reservation boundaries carried them northwestward to the head
of Big Stone Lake, only several miles from the starting point of the
western boundary survey.[82]

Assisted by five chainmen and flagmen, Snow and Hutton worked
on the western boundary survey from July 11 to August 4, 1859. During the first several days they surveyed from their starting point at the
head of Lake Traverse to the foot of Big Stone Lake. Pursuant to their
instructions they erected iron monuments at the heads of Lake Traverse and Big Stone Lake. The approximately four-mile straight-line
course between the two monuments first crossed the continental divide, which separated the Hudson Bay and Gulf of Mexico watersheds.
About a mile from Lake Traverse it also crossed the Little Minnesota
River, which flowed into Big Stone Lake. The continental divide was
not readily discernible. Snow and Hutton found the terrain between
Lake Traverse and Big Stone Lake to be a grassy, "low flat hollow."[83]

Proceeding southeastward along the Dakota side of Big Stone
Lake, Snow and Hutton determined the boundary along the lake's meander line and referenced it with onshore wooden posts. At the point
where the meander line touched the lake's southeast shore, which they
concluded was the lake's foot, they erected another iron monument.

The three iron monuments placed by Snow and Hutton on the
boundary's first section all had the same composition and dimensions.
Made with cast iron shells three-fourths of an inch thick, the hollow
monuments each weighed over 400 pounds and were six feet tall. They

tapered from a twelve-square-inch square base to a seven-square-inch top and were buried three feet deep. Each was uniquely inscribed with one-inch high raised capital letters. The side of the Lake Traverse post facing the lake was marked "Initial Point." Its opposite side, which faced Big Stone Lake, was inscribed "B.S. Lake 1859." The east and west sides, like those of the next two iron monuments, were inscribed respectively as "Minnesota" and "Dakota." The south side of the post at the head of Big Stone Lake was labeled "B.S. Lake" and its opposite side "1859." The monument at the foot of Big Stone Lake was marked "1859" on its north side and "South" on its south face.

Once they erected the monument at the foot of Big Stone Lake, Snow and Hutton embarked on their second phase—determining and marking a due south line from the monument to Iowa's northern boundary. As they were instructed, the due south line prescribed by Congress in Minnesota's Enabling Act, like any other due south line, had to be a meridian line. Thus, they had to determine the longitude at their starting point and reaffirm it at appropriate intervals and the intersection with Iowa's northern boundary.

At the foot of the Big Stone monument, Snow and Hutton determined their meridional location by five series of observations of the eastern elongations of Polaris, the North Star. Seventy-two miles south, when they stopped to cut wooden posts along a portion of Lake Benton about twelve miles east of their station, they verified the meridian by observations on three successive nights. The surveyors made their third and fourth meridian determinations twenty miles south of the station west of Lake Benton and at their intersection with Iowa's northern boundary.[84]

As they moved along the 124-mile course from Big Stone Lake to Iowa, Snow and Hutton's crew set wooden boundary posts in earthen mounds at one-mile intervals. They had been instructed to erect cedar posts, if possible, but if they could not procured, to use some other durable wood. Apparently, the surveyors never found any cedar. The only trees mentioned with any frequency in their field notes were bur oak, cottonwood and elm, which were found only along creeks and large lakes.[85]

The lack of trees along the boundary required Snow and Hutton to haul posts many miles. They cut posts at only two places—"Izuzah" Creek (the present-day Whetstone River), a mile south of Big Stone Lake, and Lake Benton. They never described their wooding operations, but cutting trees and fashioning posts obviously required many toilsome hours in the summer heat.

The pyramidally topped posts were eight feet tall and six inches square. They were dug in three feet below ground level. The first three and a half feet above ground were enclosed in a mound usually made from soil obtained from trenches dug on the east and west sides. The posts all bore carved inscriptions—"MINNESOTA" on the east, "DAKOTA" on the west, "1859" on the south, and on the north face an identifying number showing their distance from the starting point such as "1.M," "24.M" and "115.M."

At their intersection with Iowa's northern boundary, which they determined was precisely 124 miles, one chain and ten links south of their starting point, Snow and Hutton erected an iron monument. In referencing its location relative to the public land survey, they determined Minnesota's southwest corner was five chains, twenty-three and fifty-six one-hundredths links (about 345.5 feet) west of the corner of sections thirty-four and thirty-five, Township 101 North, Range forty-seven West. This iron monument, with the same dimensions as the first three, was inscribed on its north side "W.B. MINN.," "IOWA" on the south, and "43° 30" on the east and west.[86]

In addition to surveying and marking the boundary, the General Land Office required Snow and Hutton to report on the nature of the borderlands area. The office routinely included this stipulation for all boundary and rectangular land surveys in order to assess agricultural prospects.

Snow, Hutton, and their superiors realized that the borderland was hardly *terra incognita*. Two decades prior to their survey, the celebrated explorer and cartographer Joseph N. Nicollet had traveled through parts of southwestern Minnesota. Snow and Hutton were provided with a copy of Nicollet's map, so in advance of their work they were aware of such features as the Coteau des Prairie, Lake Benton and Pipestone Creek.

Furthermore, during the last years of Minnesota Territory, various surveys including those of the Nobles Road, the Transit Railroad and the public land survey provided information about Minnesota's southwestern prairie lands. Nonetheless, Snow and Hutton were the first to reconnoiter a meridian line course from Big Stone Lake to Iowa.[87]

In their cryptic field notes, Snow and Hutton made some observations about natural features, soil types, manmade trails and boundaries. The Coteau des Prairies and Lake Hendricks were the most prominent natural features they encountered. They began ascending the coteau, the long ridge separating the watersheds of the Minnesota and Missouri rivers, twenty-seven miles from Big Stone Lake. Until they started descending from it thirty-eight miles farther south, they passed through land they variously described as "high rugged country" and "high rolling prairie." They did not mention the coteau's numerous ponds and rocks but did evaluate most of its soil as "2nd rate." Generally, they found the soil both north and south of the coteau to be "1st rate." About two-thirds of their way across the coteau, they reached the north shore of a mile-wide lake, which they named Lake Hendricks in honor of the General Land Office commissioner. This was their most important discovery. The large lake, about six miles long east-west, was not shown on Nicollet's map. Snow and Hutton skirted Lake Hendricks but referenced the boundary line across it by wading in from the north shore and setting a post in a mound. Near the lake's southern shore they referenced the boundary by marking a blaze on a lone tree.[88]

With respect to manmade features, Snow and Hutton noted the Upper Sioux reservation's southern boundary, the Nobles Road and the Transit Railroad route. They crossed the reservation boundary nearly nine miles south of Big Stone Lake. About eight miles southwest of Lake Benton they reached the "Ft. Ridgely and South Pass Wagon Road." This federally funded road was surveyed in 1857, under the superintendency of William H. Nobles. Its name belied its extent. The Nobles Road was surveyed only as far as Fort Lookout (near present-day Chamberlain, South Dakota) on the Missouri River. Twenty-seven miles south of the Nobles Road, the surveyors crossed the Transit

Railroad route. Evidently, this route was surveyed in 1858 as a step in the company's plan to construct a line from Winona to the Big Sioux River via St. Peter and New Ulm.[89]

In their field notes Snow and Hutton did not describe their trip from Minnesota's southwestern corner to St. Paul. Assuming average rates of wagon travel, they must have arrived in the capital by about August 17. But they and their assistants delayed filing sworn statements that they had performed the survey in accordance with their instructions and contract until October 29, 1859.[90]

Meanwhile, Joseph S. Wilson, acting commissioner of the General Land Office, had been advised by an unspecified party that Snow and Hutton had completed the boundary survey. For some reason, Wilson suspected that they had not performed in accordance with their instructions. Therefore, on October 15, before he received Snow and Hutton's official report, he ordered Emerson "to cause a thorough and scientific examination of this survey to be made at once, by a competent and faithful Deputy [sic], who is in no way interested in the result, further than a just determination as to whether the work has been thoroughly and properly done." The cost of this work was to be covered by the $800 balance of the $5,000 boundary survey appropriation.[91]

Wilson and Emerson obviously knew that winter could arrive early on the northern plains, but the commissioner wanted the resurvey completed before passing final judgment on Snow and Hutton's work. Emerson negotiated a contract with Ehud N. Darling, an experienced public lands surveyor. On November 8, 1859, Darling and his two assistants, outfitted with two mule-drawn wagons, left St. Paul for Big Stone Lake. Traveling via Henderson, Fort Ridgely and the first crossing of the Minnesota River seventeen miles above the fort, Darling took twelve days to reach the foot of Big Stone Lake. About sixty miles above the Minnesota River crossing, the party got caught in snowstorm that left six to eight inches on the ground.[92]

Darling and his assistants worked six days making the round trip from the foot of Big Stone Lake to the head of Lake Traverse. Proceeding up the east side of Big Stone Lake, they reached "Big Stone

Lake City" after sixteen miles. Despite its pretentious name, the "city" was apparently nothing more than the residence of P.J. McClelan. Darling stored most of his equipment and supplies with McClelan while he went on to Lake Traverse. At the Lake Traverse head, Darling found that the Indians had tried to pull up the iron monument. He also found that the snow was three feet deep and that he could not locate the Lake Traverse meander post or any posts in mounds on the line between Lake Traverse and the head of Big Stone Lake. At the head of Big Stone Lake he located the iron monument, but could not find any meander post. He surmised that the meander post "has probably been thrown away by the Indians as there was a good many about the lake."

During the night of November 27, only hours after his return to the foot of Big Stone Lake, Darling began the meridian line phase of his work. From the monument he made two observations on Polaris and the next day made "a number of observations on the sun." Once he was satisfied that the iron monument was correctly located at the foot of Big Stone Lake, he started moving south along the meridian line.[93]

Averaging nearly fifteen miles a day, Darling's small party reached Iowa's northern boundary on December 6. Its movement was more of a trip along the boundary than a resurvey. Darling's brief field notes mentioned only the miles traveled each day and the numbers of the boundary markers they encountered. At Iowa's boundary, Darling tarried long enough to make two observations of the meridian and determine the iron post's location relative to the public land survey.

Darling and his men reached St. Paul on December 17, after an eleven-day trip from Minnesota's southwest corner. They first traveled eastward to Jackson on the Des Moines River by way of Spirit Lake. From Jackson they moved northeastward via Lake Crystal, Mankato, the Big Woods and Shakopee.

When he sent Darling's field notes to Samuel A. Smith, the new commissioner of the General Land Office, Emerson observed that he had "confidence in the general correctness thereof and that his examination has been faithfully and carefully made." Emerson particularly lauded Darling for his resurvey of the direct line between the iron monuments at the heads of Lake Traverse and Big Stone Lake. He pointed out that Darling had discovered that Snow and Hutton had not run a straight line course between the two points as specified in their instructions. Darling determined the distance was 348 chains, fifty links, whereas Snow and Hutton had measured it as only 294 chains, sixty links. A difference of over five-eighths of a mile was a considerable error. Furthermore, Darling found that Snow and Hutton had not marked the line despite their instructions to erect wooden posts in mounds as one-mile intervals. Because of Darling's findings, Emerson recommended that the Lake Traverse-Big Stone line be re-checked and monumented by one of his public land surveyors. Emerson noted that the Snow and Hutton had correctly placed the four iron monuments and that Darling had also concluded the meridian line from the foot of Big Stone Lake to Iowa had been "well run and established." But in another criticism of Snow and Hutton he reported that they had not dug quadrangular trenches around the mounds as instructed, but had only excavated on the east and west sides.[94]

Wilson had a mixed reaction to Darling's report. He accepted Darling's conclusion that the survey by Snow and Hutton on the Lake Traverse to Big Stone Lake line was inadequate. Hence, he ruled that Snow and Hutton would have to resurvey and monument that line at their own expense. But Wilson was bothered by Darling's hasty trip along the meridian line. Consequently, he ordered Emerson to have Darling submit a supplemental report containing a more detailed explanation about his work on that section.[95]

In his brief supplemental report, Darling conceded he had not systematically resurveyed the meridian line. He wrote that he tested only about a third of the line by solar compass, but did not do any chaining. Most of his work consisted of checking on the boundary posts. He inspected all of them except numbers fifty-six, one-hundred-nineteen and one-hundred-twenty and determined that the post and mound of number two had been destroyed. Evidently he was not even following the boundary line at the sites of the three markers he did not inspect.[96]

Darling blamed his failure to conduct a rigorous resurvey on limited appropriations and bitterly cold conditions. He explained that he simply did not have enough funding for the time required for chaining the entire line. He also had to hurry, he claimed, because of his concern for his men's safety. The temperatures at times reached thirty degrees below Fahrenheit and one assistant suffered from frosted fingers and nose and the other had his nose and ears frosted.

Darling's supplemental report satisfied Smith that the meridian line survey by Snow and Hutton was acceptable. On February 4, 1860, he authorized the payment of Darling's account.[97]

On July 23, 1860, Hutton resurveyed and monumented the boundary between Lake Traverse and Big Stone Lake. He determined that the line, which crossed the Little Minnesota River twice, was 349 chains and forty-three links long (4.397 miles). At exactly the one-, two- and three-mile points from the Lake Traverse iron monument Hutton erected earthen mounds with wooden posts in their centers three and a half feet high. He did not monument the four-mile point because it was located in a "floating marsh" within sight of the iron monument at the head of Big Stone Lake. The sides of the posts facing Lake Traverse were marked respectively "1M," "2M," and "3M." The northeast and southwest sides of the posts were inscribed, respectively, with "MINN." and "DAKOTA." Hutton dug pits, two and a half feet deep, at right angles to the boundary eight feet from the base of each mound. He believed the pits would prove to be the most enduring landmarks, because "the Indians will not allow the posts to stand."[98]

Hutton described the terrain between the lakes as a low flat valley about a mile wide between bluffs sixty feet high. He noted the only trees were a few scattered elms along the river. The land bordering the valley, he proclaimed, was "perfectly worthless high, dry prairie" without timber and water.

Hutton did not mention his trip to the boundary or his return to St. Paul. In all likelihood he moved by wagon along the usual route via Shakopee, Belle Plaine, Henderson, Fort Ridgely and Lac Qui Parle. On August 2, he made the obligatory sworn statement before a St.

Paul notary public that his report was correct and that he had faithfully followed his instructions. His three assistants (two chainman and one rodman) had signed their sworn statements the previous day.

Hutton's report seemed thorough but Joseph S. Wilson, once again commissioner of the General Land Office, refused to accept it as the final word. Consequently, he ordered Emerson to have the Lake Traverse-Big Stone line resurveyed once again.[99]

On August 21, 1860, Emerson employed Frederic Wippermann to conduct the resurvey. Providing Wippermann with a copy of Hutton's field notes, Emerson instructed him to ascertain if the line between the heads of Lake Traverse and Big Stone Lake was straight and correctly measured. Wippermann was also to determine if the line was monumented with mounds, posts and entrenchments as specified in the original Hendricks' instructions to Snow and Hutton.

Emerson agreed to pay Wippermann five dollars a day for the period he was away from St. Paul. For the same time, his assistants were to receive one dollar daily and he was allowed three dollars *per diem* for a team and supplies.

Accompanied by assistants Charles F. Meyer and John McClellan, Wippermann, from August 22 through 31, moved by a mule-drawn wagon from St. Paul to the head of Big Stone Lake via Shakopee, Henderson, Fort Ridgely, Upper Sioux Agency and Lac Qui Parle. They worked two and a half days resurveying the Lake Traverse-Big Stone Lake line before starting their return trip on September 3. They arrived in St. Paul a week later.[100]

In his report to Emerson, Wippermann described the condition of the iron monuments at the heads of Lake Traverse and Big Stone Lake, his resurvey of the line between them and the monuments along the line. He found the iron posts in good condition, although the Lake Traverse one was somewhat inclined because Indians had tried to dig it out. The posts were inscribed as reported by Snow and Hutton. To determine the straight course between the two iron monuments, Wippermann placed signals (probably flags on poles) by each one and then chained the line. He determined the distance between the markers was

348 chains and sixty-eight links, or about forty-five feet shorter than the distance measured by Hutton in his resurvey. Wippermann confirmed that Hutton had erected posts in mounds at the one-, two- and three-mile points and that the posts were inscribed as Hutton had reported.

Although it did not change any markings on the ground, Wippermann noted that determining the head of Big Stone Lake depended on the lake's water levels. On September 1, he reported, the iron monument at the lake's head "was not touched by water . . . but on the 3rd of September after a heavy thunderstorm, Big Stone Lake rose about 12 inches in one night, and the ground on which the monument stands, was covered about six inches with water."

Wippermann's resurvey finally resolved the location of the Lake Traverse-Big Stone line. After four efforts, the General Land Office was satisfied that Emerson could accurately place the line on Minnesota's public land survey maps. The various land office commissioners seemed especially concerned about the short line, because its diagonal northwest-southeast lay meant both Minnesota and Dakota Territory had partial sections abutting that boundary section.

NOTES:

1. Minnesota Territory, *Council Journal, 1849*, 8; William Watts Folwell, *A History of Minnesota*, 1: 352 (St. Paul: Minnesota Historical Society, 1921).
2. Rhoda R. Gilman, *Henry Hastings Sibley: Divided Heart* (St. Paul: Minnesota Historical Society Press, 2004), 117-18; Mary Wheelhouse Berthel, *Horns of Thunder: The Life and Times of James M. Goodhue Including Selections from His Writings* (St. Paul: Minnesota Historical Society, 1948), 201-08.
3. Here and below, Kappler, *Indian Affairs*, 2: 588-93; Lass, *Traverse des Sioux*, 50-55.
4. William E. Lass, *Minnesota: A History* (2d ed.; New York: W. W. Norton, 1998), 112.
5. For detailed coverage of the excursion, see: Charles F. Babcock, "Rails West: The Rock Island Excursion of 1854 as Reported by Charles F.

Babcock," *Minnesota History* 34 (Winter 1954): 133-43; Nancy and Robert Goodman, *Paddlewheels on the Upper Mississippi 1823-1854: How Steamboats Promoted Commerce and Settlement in the West* (Stillwater, MN: Washington County Historical Society, 2003), 1-9; Bertha L. Heilbron, ed., "By Rail and River to Minnesota in 1854," *Minnesota History* 25 (June 1944): 103-16 and Steven J. Keillor, *Grand Excursion: Antebellum America Discovers the Upper Mississippi* (Afton, MN: Afton Historical Society Press, 2004).

6. Here and below, verbatim texts of Gorman's messages in *Pioneer and Democrat* (St. Paul), 10 January 1856, 15 January 1857.

7. *U.S. Statutes at Large* 10: 283; Billington, *Westward Expansion*, 512-14; Robert W. Johannsen, *Stephen A. Douglas* (New York: Oxford University Press, 1973), 439-47.

8. Here and below, George H. Mayer, *The Republican Party 1854-1966* (Second ed.; New York: Oxford University Press, 1967). 25-31; Robert C. Paul, "The Rise of the Republican Party in Minnesota, 1855-1860," Unpublished Master of Science Thesis, Mankato State University, Mankato, Minnesota, 1994, 21.

9. Here and the two paragraphs below: see Paul, "Rise of Republican Party," 30-32 and Charles D. Gilfillan, "The Early Political History of Minnesota," *Collections of the Minnesota Historical Society* 9 (St. Paul, 1901), 171-172.

10. *Pioneer and Democrat*, 10 January 1856.

11. *Ibid.*, 16 February 1856.

12. William Anderson and Albert J. Lobb, *A History of the Constitution of Minnesota with the First Verified Text* (Minneapolis: Univ. of Minnesota Research Publications, Studies in the Social Sciences 15, 1921), 51.

13. *Pioneer and Democrat*, 01 Janurary 1856.

14. *Pioneer and Democrat*, 16, 18 February 1856; *Council Journal, 1856*, 141.

15. On the formation of the Transit Railroad see: Alan R. Woolworth, *The Genesis & Construction of the Winona & St. Peter Railroad,1858-1873* (Marshall MN: Society for the Study of Local & Regional History, Southwest State University, 2000), 2-3.

16. Here and below, *St. Peter Courier,* 01 April 1856 and *Winona Republican,* 25 March 1856.

17. Here and below, *Pioneer and Democrat,* 09 August 1856.

18. Here and below, *Winona Republican,* 16 December 1856.

19. St. Peter Company records, 02 October 1854, positive photographic copy in Nicollet County Historical Society, St. Peter. Originals in Minnesota Historical Society; *St. Peter Courier,* 27 August 1856.

20. *Congressional Globe,* 24 December 1856, 26:201.

21. *St. Peter Courier,* 27 August 1856.

22. *Pioneer and Democrat,* 07 January 1857.

23. *Congressional Globe*, 24 December 1856, 31 January 1857, 26:201, 517-519. Grow obviously did not calculate the size of the reduction, which amounted to about 2,500 square miles.

24. Anderson and Lobb, *Constitution of Minnesota*, 52: W. Turrentine Jackson, *Wagon Roads West: A Study of Federal Road Surveys and Construction in the Trans-Mississippi West, 1846-1869* (Berkeley: University of California Press, 1952), 168-70.

25. Anderson and Lobb, *Constitution of Minnesota*, 52; *Pioneer and Democrat*, 13 January 1857.

26. William E. Lass, "The First Attempt to Organize Dakota Territory," in William L. Lang, ed., *Centennial West: Essays on the Northern Tier States* (Seattle: University of Washington Press, 1991), 145-147.

27. *Daily Minnesotian* (St. Paul) , 16 January 1857; *Pioneer and Democrat*, 09 March 1857. Rice's reported worth of $250,000 would be about $6,137,500 in 2012 dollars. ("Consumer Price Index (Estimate) 1800-," accessed 30 January 2013.

28. *Pioneer and Democrat*, 01 January 1857.

29. *Winona Republican*, 06 January 1857.

30. 21 January 1857.

31. *Pioneer and Democrat*, 21, 23 January 1857.

32. *Ibid.*, 17 March 1857.

33. *Winona Argus*, 26 February 1857.

34. Here and below, *Congressional Globe*, 21 February 1857, 26: 808, 814.

35. *Ibid.*, 613.

36. Stephen L. Hansen, "Shields, James," *American National Biography*, (New York: Oxford University Press, 1999) 19: 838-40; *Biographical Directory of the United States Congress, 1774-2005* (Washington: Government Printing Office, 2005), 1904..

37. Here and below, *U.S. Statutes at Large*, 11:195. Information on acreage of the grants from Folwell, *Minnesota*, vol. 2 (1924), 43n.

38. 07 April 1857.

39. *Pioneer and Democrat*, 21 March 1857; *Winona Argus*, 26 March 1857; *St. Peter Courier*, 08 April 1857.

40. Folwell, *Minnesota*, 2: 41-42.

41. *Pioneer and Democrat*, 6, 14 February 1857; *Council Journal, 1857*, 84.

42. Here and the paragraph below, *Daily Pioneer and Democrat*, 07 February 1857l; Minnesota Attorney General, *Opinion of the Attorney General on the Bill for the Removal of the Seat of Government*, February 16, 1857.

43. Here and the two paragraphs below *Daily Minnesotian* (St. Paul), 10-11, 13, 16-21, 23-24 February 1857; *Pioneer and Democrat*, 10-11, 13, 16-21, 23-24 February 1857; *Shakopee Advocate* as quoted in *Pioneer and Democrat*, 21 February 1857; *Henderson Democrat*, 12 March 1857.

44. Here and below, *Daily Minnesotian*, 26 March 1857; *Daily Pioneer and Democrat*, 01, 11 June 1857; *Winona Argus*, 19 March 1857. The

Minnesota Historical Society has a copy of Dodge's *Address* . . . and it was also published verbatim in the *St. Peter Courier*, 18, 25 March 1857.

45. Holcombe, *Minnesota as a Territory*, 437, 480; *U.S. Statutes at Large*, 11: 166.

46. *Winona Argus*, 19 March 1857.

47. *Daily Minnesotian*, 18 March 1857.

48. Reprint of Brown letter of 20 February 1857 to the *Henderson Democrat* in *Daily Minnesotian*, 07 March 1857.

49. Berry letter of 17 March 1857 to the *Faribault Herald*, reprinted in the *Daily Minnesotian*, 25 March 1857.

50. *Northern Herald*, 11 February 1857, as reported in the *Winona Republican*, 24 February 1857 and the *St. Peter Courier*, 11 March 1857; Sauk Rapids *Frontiersman*, as reported in the *St. Peter Courier*, 18 February 1857.

51. For examples of east-west promotion, see: *St. Peter Courier*, 08 April 1857; *Winona Argus*, 26 February, 19 March 1857.

52. For examples of the north-south case, see: *Daily Minnesotian*, 11 February, 7, 25 March 1857.

53. *Daily Minnesotian*, 05 February 1857.

54. *Pioneer and Democrat*, 18 February 1857.

55. *St. Peter Courier*, 04 February 1857.

56. *Winona Argus*, 26 February 1857.

57. 25 March 1857.

58. Folwell,1:396.

59. *The Debates and Proceedings of the Minnesota Constitutional Convention* (Democratic) (St. Paul: Earle S. Goodrich, territorial printer, Pioneer and Democrat Office, 1857), 3, 99; *Debates and Proceedings: Constitutional Convention for the Territory of Minnesota* (Republican) (St. Paul: George W. Moore, printer, Minnesotian office, 1858), 10.

60. *Debates and Proceedings* (Republican), 25, 37-39.

61. *Ibid.* 68, 88, 221.

62. *Ibid.*, 221-22.

63. *Ibid.*, 223-25, 229.

64. *Ibid*, 227-29.

65. *Ibid.*, 409-10.

66. *Ibid.*, 223-24, 472.

67. *Ibid*, 411-31 *passim*.

68. *Ibid.*, 423, 433.

69. Folwell, *Minnesota*, 1: 387.

70. *Debates and Proceedings* (Republican), 437, 439.

71. *Ibid.*, 467-70.

72. *St. Peter Courier*, 04 May 1857.

73. *Debates and Proceedings* (Democratic), 296.

74. *Ibid.*, 297.

75. *Ibid.*, 302, 305.
76. *Ibid.*, 306.
77. *Ibid.*, 527.
78. *Ibid.*, 529, 532.
79. *Ibid.*, 558.
80. For the county by county tally of the canvassed vote, see *Debates and Proceedings* (Democratic), 677.
81. *U.S. Statutes at Large,* 11:427.
82. Hendricks to Emerson, 25 April 1859 and Joseph S. Wilson, acting commissioner, General Land Office, to Emerson, 10 February 1860, both in U.S. Office of Surveyor General of Minnesota. Letters Received, 1854-1908, in Minnesota Historical Society, St. Paul; Donald Dean Parker, "Surveying the South Dakota-Minnesota Boundary Line," *South Dakota Historical Collections* 32:236 (Pierre, 1964).
83. Here and the two paragraphs below, "Field Notes of the Survey of the Western Boundary of the State of Minnesota," pp. 1-6, 42, 44-45, 47, by C.H. Snow and Henry Hutton, positive photograph copy in Harley R. Schneider Research File on Minnesota Surveys in Minnesota Historical Society. Original in Cartographic Section, NARA, Record Group 49: Field Notes—Case F, Entry 57.
84. *Ibid.*, 6, 27, 33, 42, 49.
85. Here and the two paragraphs below Ibid., 44-49.
86. *Ibid.,*42.
87. On Nicollet's explorations in southwestern Minnesota, see Martha Coleman Bray, *Joseph Nicollet and His Map* (Philadelphia: American Philosophical Society, 1980), 200-21.
88. Snow and Hutton Field Notes, 13, 21-22, 25.
89. *Ibid*, 9, 28, 35; Woolworth, *Winona & St. Peter Railroad.* 5; Jackson, *Wagon Roads West*, 179-90.
90. Snow and Hutton Field Notes, pp. 50-51.
91. Wilson to Emerson, 15 October 1859, in U.S. Office of Surveyor General of Minnesota, Letters Received.
92. Here and the paragraph below, Ehud N. Darling, "Field Notes of the Examination of the Western Boundary of the State of Minnesota . . . " pp. 2-5, 8, positive photographic copy in Schneider Research File. Original in Cartographic Section, NARA, Record Group 49: Field Notes—Case F, Entry 59.
93. Here and the two paragraphs below, *Ibid.*, p. 10-18.
94. Emerson to Smith, 23 December 1859, in U.S. Office of Surveyor General of Minnesota Letters Sent.
95. Parker, "South Dakota-Minnesota Boundary Line," 242.
96. Here and paragraph below, Darling's supplemental report, January 21, 1860, attached to field notes.
97. Smith to Emerson, 04 February 1860, in U. S. Office of the Surveyor General of Minnesota Letters Received.

98. Here and two paragraphs below, Hutton's field notes of Lake Traverse to Big Stone Lake survey, 23 July 1860, in Schneider Research File, MHS. Original in Cartographic Section, NARA, Record Group 49: Field Notes—Case F, Entry 58.
99. Here and the two paragraphs below, Emerson to Frederic Wippermann, 21 August 1860, in U.S. Office of Surveyor General of Minnesota, Letters Sent.
100. Here and the two paragraphs below, Wippermann Field Notes, Cartographic Section, NARA, Record Group 49: Field Notes—Case F, Entry 60.

# CHAPTER FIVE

## MARKING THE NORTHERN BOUNDARY

▬ ▪ ▬ ▪ ▬ ▪ ▬ ▪ ▬ ▪ ▬ ▪ ▬ ▪ ▬

INNESOTA'S NORTHERN BOUNDARY was systematically surveyed and marked under the terms of two agreements between the United States and Great Britain. Negotiations between the two countries in 1870-1871 resulted in the formation of a joint boundary commission to survey and mark the section between the northwest point of Lake of the Woods and the continental divide in the Rocky Mountains. By the Treaty of 1908, the United States and Great Britain agreed to resurvey and either monument or remonument the entire Canada-United States boundary.

When Minnesota's southern, eastern and western boundaries were being formed, its northern boundary, with the lone exception of the point where the Red River crossed the forty-ninth parallel, was of no particular concern. The boundary with Canada had been established diplomatically before the other three boundaries, but the farmer-dominated society that developed in southern Minnesota regarded their north as a barren wilderness. As long as northern Minnesota and bordering portions of Ontario and Manitoba generally remained in the fur-trading realm, the international boundary did not affect many people who sought private land ownership. But once the region attracted farmers, lumbermen and miners, the precise location of the boundary became vitally important.

By the time it negotiated the Convention of 1818 with Great Britain, the United States was already concerned about the international boundary in the Red River valley. In 1811, the Scottish earl Lord Selkirk obtained a massive land grant, Assiniboia, from the Hudson's Bay Company. Assiniboia's southern portion included the entire Red River valley.[1]

By recruiting mainly in Scotland and Switzerland, Selkirk was able to establish settlements in the Red River valley. His first colonists reached the valley in 1812. Their main settlement, which evolved into Fort Garry and then Winnipeg, was established on the Red River's west side just below the mouth of the Assiniboine River. That same year, about 100 colonists from another contingent moved to a site near the mouth of the Pembina River, about sixty-five miles south by land from the first settlement.

While his colonists were establishing themselves at Pembina, Selkirk believed Canada and the United States should be divided by a natural boundary separating the Hudson Bay and Gulf of Mexico watersheds. Such a line would have placed all of Assiniboia north of the border. But when the forty-ninth parallel was decreed by the Convention of 1818, Pembina's location relative to the boundary was uncertain. The Hudson's Bay Company, which had a post at Pembina, was concerned enough to determine the position of the forty-ninth, which it found to be slightly north of its post and the nearby village. Understandably skittish about the possible threat of American customs collectors, the company abandoned its Pembina station in the spring of 1823.[2]

For its part, the United States, although it was experiencing a brief period of relatively good relations with Great Britain, felt threatened by any British activity on its northern flank. Anglophobia dominated American policy when a small army expedition, led by Brevet Major Stephen Harriman Long, explored the Minnesota River-Red River region in 1823. While traveling northward in the Red River valley in early August, Long stopped at Pembina to determine the boundary's location. His astronomer, Captain Joseph Calhoun, Jr., calculated that with the exception of one house, Pembina, on the river's left bank, was south of the forty-ninth parallel. The next day Long had an oak post erected to mark the boundary. Its north side was inscribed with "G.B." and its south side with "U.S." He reported that "our men were then paraded, the Flag hoisted, and a national salute fired under the following declaration viz. 'By authority of the President of the U. States, and in presence of these witnesses I declare the country situat[e]d on Red river above this point to be comprehended within the territory of the U. States.'"[3]

William H. Keating and Long observed that Pembina had a population of about 350 people living in sixty log cabins. At least two-thirds of the male inhabitants were Métis. The remainder were Scotch and Swiss. Although they cultivated some grains and vegetables, their livelihood depended mostly on hunting buffalo. Keating observed that they did not produce enough crops to sustain themselves and had to rely on goods imported by the Hudson's Bay Company via the long route through Hudson Bay and the Nelson and Red rivers.[4]

During the 1820s, the Fort Garry-Pembina area was devastated by a series of natural disasters. Blizzards, floods, prairie fires and infestations of locusts, mice and rats caused several hundred settlers to move into the United States by way of Red River trails leading to Fort Snelling. The largest single group of 243 abandoned the colony after the disastrous 1826 flood. Some took up residency on the fort's reservation but most passed downstream to establish homes in Illinois and Missouri.[5]

Despite this exodus, some several thousand people, dominated by the Métis, remained in the Red River valley. As the Minnesota fur trade declined sharply after the 1837 treaties, Henry H. Sibley, the American Fur Company's factor at Mendota near Fort Snelling, realized the valley's market potential. With Sibley's assistance, young Norman W. Kittson, in 1844, shifted his trading base from Big Stone Lake to Pembina. Kittson's move was the first step in Minnesota's northwestern expansion. Because he competed with the Hudson's Bay Company, Kittson was welcomed by Fort Garry's residents, who resented the company's slow, costly service. Kittson was engaged in a trade war with the Hudson's Bay Company when Minnesota Territory was formed with Sibley as its delegate to Congress.[6]

The territory's formation coincided with the federal government's concern that Hudson's Bay Company agents were crossing the forty-ninth parallel and destroying buffalo. Determined to protect the livelihood of American Indians, the War Department, in 1849, considered establishing an army post at Pembina. But Major Samuel Woods, Fort Snelling's commandant and leader of the Pembina reconnaissance, concluded that such a post was not necessary. However, realizing the significance of Pembina, he wanted its residents to be reminded they were living on American soil. He and his topographical engineer, Captain John Pope, found the old Long post, which had rotted away and been replaced by a stake. Woods replaced the stake with a post inscribed "August 14, 1849."[7]

Despite a memorial from the Minnesota territorial legislature and a plea from Governor Alexander Ramsey, the War Department refused to establish a post at Pembina. After this setback, Minnesota officials found other ways to increase American presence in the borderlands. Using his influence in Congress, Sibley arranged for the establishment of a customs house at Pembina. Around the same time, the territorial legislature, with Ramsey's assistance, created Pembina County. The county's representation in the legislature assured closer links between Pembina and St. Paul. In the meantime, Sibley and Ramsey also worked for the Oibwe Indian cession of the Red River valley. Sibley got a congressional appropriation for the negotiation and Ramsey, only a month after serving as a co-commissioner to negotiate the Dakota treaties in 1851, journeyed to Pembina to treat with the Ojibwe and purchase their Red River valley holdings. But when the Senate investigated alleged irregularities in the Dakota treaties, Sibley had to sacrifice the Ojibwe treaty to gain their acceptance.[8]

Despite this setback, ties between the Red River valley and St. Paul were strengthened in the 1850s. Interest in trans-border trade was piqued by the Reciprocity Treaty of 1854, between Great Britain and the United States. The agreement provided that a long list of commodities could be passed duty free between the Canadian provinces and the United States. The treaty did not apply to the Fort Garry area, however, because it was in Rupert's Land, the holdings of the Hudson's Bay Company. But some St. Paul expansionists, led by James Wickes Taylor, saw it as a vital first step in forming an American-Canadian economic union.[9]

Taylor, who moved from Ohio to St. Paul in 1856, was particularly interested in St. Paul becoming the metropolis for the vast hinterland extending into the plains region west of Fort Garry, an area he identified as Central British America. While serving as Ohio state librarian

James Wickes Taylor. (Courtesy of the Minnesota Historical Society)

for four years, he came to believe St. Paul had a natural destiny to dominate the region as least as far as the Rocky Mountains.[10]

In early 1857, when Minnesotans were debating the shape of their future state, Taylor implicitly endorsed the north-south concept. In a series of articles published in the *St. Paul Advertiser* he stressed that Minnesota's greatest opportunity lay in the Red River valley and beyond.

While St. Paul's acclaimed manifest destiny to dominate the Canadian plains aroused ultra nationalism south of the border, it also had the effect of causing Canadians to become more interested in developing their own west. In 1857, partially in response to American interest, Great Britain and Canada each authorized a reconnaissance of the region between the Red River and the Rockies. The British expedition was led by the John Palliser and the Canadian study was conducted mainly by geologist Henry Youle Hind and surveyor Simon J. Dawson. On the basis of their examinations, both expeditions extolled much of the Canadian prairies as a potentially rich agricultural region.[11]

Interest in the Canadian west was stimulated further in the spring of 1858 by the discovery of gold in the Fraser River canyon area in what would later become British Columbia. The hoopla over this acclaimed new El Dorado caused St. Paul expansionists to organize a Fraser River Convention. Taylor was the key organizer and publicist of the convention's four St. Paul meetings in July 1858. Replete with calls for achieving St. Paul's destiny as the metropolis of the northwest, the convention encouraged development and use of an overland route from Minnesota's capital to far western Canada via the Red and Saskatchewan rivers.[12]

The Fraser River gold rush coincided with a sharp increase in St. Paul's trade with Fort Garry. St. Paul's superiority as the main depot for Red River valley trade was seemingly affirmed by a decision of the Hudson's Bay Company. Reacting to years of frustration with the long, expensive route from England via Hudson Bay, the company, in 1857, experimented with shipping to the valley by way of New York City and St. Paul. Its executives determined that these trial shipments reduced their transportation costs by almost a third. Therefore, in 1859, they began routing their trade with the valley through St. Paul and either Montreal or New York City.

Although this trade was continued and the Fraser River gold rush expanded during the Civil War, Minnesota's wartime interest ebbed because of the crisis precipitated by the Dakota Indian War of 1862. The conflict and its aftermath inhibited Minnesota's frontier expansion.

But after the expulsion of the Dakota Indians and the end of the Civil War, calls for Minnesota expansion were renewed vigorously because of a crisis in Anglo-American relations. Hatred of all things British, inspired by Great Britain's support for the Confederate States of America and protectionist zeal, led the United States, in March 1866, to abrogate the Reciprocity Treaty of 1854.[13]

To Taylor and other Minnesota expansionists, discontinuation of reciprocity doomed a possible American-Canadian economic union. The obvious solution, they believed, was for the United States to annex Canada. After the cancellation of reciprocity, the Treasury Department asked Taylor to prepare a report on trade relations with Canada. Grandly exceeding his mission, Taylor drafted a bill calling for a United States-Canada union. He proposed that the eastern Canadian provinces be made American states and the western areas territories.[14]

Naturally, this proposal elicited much newspaper publicity. But its main effect was to hasten Great Britain's decision to grant Canada virtual independence by the British North America Act of 1867. Significantly, the act authorized the inclusion of Rupert's Land in the newly formed Dominion of Canada. The following year, the Hudson's Bay Company's lands were annexed by the Rupert's Land Act.[15]

Although the Rupert's Land Act facilitated Canada's westward expansion, it did not deter Taylor and his chief political ally—United States Senator Alexander Ramsey of Minnesota. They continued to work for the American annexation of Canada after the presidential inauguration of Ulysses S. Grant on March 4, 1869. They knew Grant and Secretary of State Hamilton Fish personally favored annexation and that Senator Charles Sumner, chairman of the Committee on Foreign Relations, had suggested that Great Britain cede Canada to the United States as compensation for the damages caused by the Confederate battleship *Alabama*, which had been constructed in Great Britain. But the Grant administration could not act on its feelings, because it did not have any justification for pursuing annexation.[16]

To counter the annexationist threat, Canada and Great Britain asserted their authority over the Fort Garry region. To encourage migration, Canada, in the fall of 1868, began building the Dawson Road from Northwest Angle Inlet in Lake of the Woods to St. Boniface, east across the Red River from present-day Winnipeg. The next year land surveyors followed in the wake of the road builders. The local Métis, led by the charismatic Louis Riel, feared the imposition of the English rectangular land survey would strip them of their squatters' claims obtained from the Hudson's Bay Company. Riel's harassment of surveyors escalated into a rebellion in which he and his Métis supporters seized Fort Garry on November 2, 1869. Riel's establishment of a provisional government independent from Canada created an opportunity for more mischief-making by American expansionists. Taylor and his supporters knew there was a pro-annexation faction at Fort Garry, but Riel wanted his own local control. Nonetheless, American annexationists tended to see anything anti-Canadian as pro-American. Therefore Oscar Malmros, United States consul at Fort Garry, and Enos Stutsman, a Pembina customs official, both urged aggressive action to annex the former Rupert's Land.[17]

Canada moved quickly to thwart both Riel and American expansionists. In 1870, it organized the province of Manitoba, which encompassed the Fort Garry area. But even before the act was proclaimed on July 15, a joint British-Canadian military expedition was en route to the troubled region. On August 24, the force occupied Fort Garry.

Taylor and Ramsey persisted in thinking annexation was still possible even after Riel and some of his provisonal government officials fled into the United States. Ramsey arranged for William B. O'Donoghue, ex-treasurer of the Riel government, to meet with President Grant in Washington, D.C. Grant was understandably wary when O'Donoghue related his desire to liberate the Red River area. The president responded that the United States was not interested in annexation unless a decisive majority of the valley's residents called for it.

Understandably, the Riel rebellion and the sharp Canadian reaction raised tensions in Pembina and renewed interest in determining the exact location of the forty-ninth parallel, which was Manitoba's southern boundary. Area residents had good reason to be concerned. By mid-1870, there were five possible international boundary spots near Pembina. The Long-Woods marker was generally accepted, but in 1857, Captain John Palliser and his staff determined the forty-ninth parallel was about 370 yards north of the monument. Rather than provoke a dispute, Palliser chose to accept the Long-Woods site because it was more advantageous to Great Britain. About 1860, some localites marked a third site about a mile north of the Long-Woods post, in order to place a liquor peddler under American jurisdiction. The installers of this so-called "Whiskey post" probably did not bother with astronomical calculations but they did add to the confusion. In 1869, Lieutenant Colonel John S. Dennis and his Canadian surveyors calculated the forty-ninth was 204 feet north of the Long-Woods post. But the next year, American army captain David P. Heap created a crisis when he concluded that the boundary was actually 4,763 feet north of the Long-Woods marker. Heap had to determine the parallel in order to draw reservation boundaries for the newly established Fort Pembina. To underscore the army's intention of controlling trespassers, Heap marked the boundary at one-mile intervals with wooden stakes for thirty-five miles to the west of his original monument.[18]

Seizing on the opportunity presented by Heap's survey, John C. Stoever, the United States collector of customs at Pembina, ordered an inventory of the goods in the Hudson's Bay Company's post located in the strip between the Long-Woods and Heap parallels. However, since he wanted to verify his authority, Stoever asked Secretary of the Treasury George S. Boutwell whether he should treat the Long-Woods or Heap monuments as the international boundary demarcation. Boutwell referred the question to Secretary of State Hamilton Fish, who responded that pending the official determination of the boundary, the United States accepted the Long-Woods site.

Boutwell's inquiry also prompted Fish to notify Edward Thornton, British ambassador to the United States, about Heap's survey and to suggest a joint Anglo-American survey of the entire boundary established by the Convention of 1818. Fish's initiative quickly led to an agreement between Great Britain and the United States to survey the boundary. The Grant administration hoped to launch the survey in 1871, but the House of Representatives refused to appropriate the requested funding. Grant renewed his request in December 1871, and the law authorizing American participation in the joint survey of the boundary from the northwesternmost point of Lake of the Woods to the crest of the Rockies was enacted on March 19, 1872.[19]

In their preliminary planning for the survey, the Americans and British were influenced by their recent joint Oregon boundary survey. Relying on the precedent of the Convention of 1818, Great Britain and the United States agreed on the forty-ninth parallel boundary from the Strait of Georgia eastward to the Rocky Mountains crest in 1846. Only eleven years later, they began surveying the line because some Americans had moved into the Pacific Northwest and some British subjects had established settlements in the present-day areas of Victoria and Vancouver, British Columbia. Surveying and monumenting the over 400-mile boundary was completed in 1861. Because of estranged relations during the Civil War and early Reconstruction years, the two countries did not exchange final reports until 1869.[20]

Like the Oregon survey, the impending determination of the forty-ninth across the northern plains was to be a multi-year task through an isolated area. Consequently, General Andrew A. Humphreys, chief of the United States Corps of Engineers, called for a large, relatively expensive survey party. He estimated that the American complement would be seventy-one men and that its total expenses would amount to about $325,000. Colonel John S. Hawkins, who had served as Great Britain's commissioner on the Oregon survey, prepared the British plan. In principle, he agreed with Humphreys that the expedition should be large and would be quite costly. In particular, he cited the short season for good weather field work and the logistical problems of moving the survey party from Great Britain and eastern Canada.[21]

Staffing the joint commission was easier for the United States, which had complete control of its own mission. Great Britain had to share decision-making with Canada, which had agreed to match Britain's survey costs.

Archibald Campbell was the State Department's choice for commissioner. The fifty-nine-year-old United States Military Academy graduate, a greatly experienced engineer, had served as commissioner on the Oregon boundary survey. The engineer-astronomers, who were to be Campbell's main assistants, were all West Point graduates on active army duty. Francis U. Farquhar was the chief astronomer. William J. Twining and James F. Gregory were respectively named first and second assistant astronomers and Francis V. Greene was appointed as the junior astronomer.[22]

Lord Granville, the British foreign secretary, preferred a commissioner with strong scientific qualifications and boundary surveying experience. Such men as Samuel Anderson or Charles W. Wilson, veterans of the Oregon survey, were logical choices. But Canadian officials had a completely different idea. Their preference was thirty-seven-year-old Donald Cameron, a Royal Artillery officer with no experience in astronomy and surveying. It seemed to Granville and other British officials that Cameron's main qualification was that he was the son-in-law of Dr. Charles Tupper, a cabinet member in Sir John A. Macdonald's Canadian government. But because of Canada's significant financial assistance, British officials felt compelled to compromise and agreed to Cameron's appointment. Other than naming the commissioner, Canadian officials appointed about two dozen other men including the surgeon, veterinarian, commissary officer, surveyors and assistant astronomers.[23]

Again influenced by the Oregon survey, Edward Cardwell, secretary of the British War Office, appointed Royal Engineer officers as the commission's astronomers. Samuel Anderson, who was then teaching at the Chatham Engineering School, was appointed chief astronomer. During his three years on the Oregon survey Anderson had become well-acquainted with Archibald Campbell. Their good relations continued throughout the northern plains survey. Albany Featherstonhaugh, Anderson's Chatham colleague, was named ranking assistant astronomer and William J. Galwey was appointed second assistant astronomer. In addition to the astronomers the British provided a military escort of forty-four Royal Engineers. This detachment's main purpose was to provide security but since many of the men had particular skills such as photography, shoemaking, tailoring and blacksmithing, they facilitated the commission's work.[24]

Cameron and Campbell began planning the survey in Washington, D.C., on July 21, 1872. They agreed to establish their first astronomical station near Pembina before proceeding to survey the boundary from the Red River to the northwesternmost point of Lake of the Woods.[25]

Assembling the joint commission at Pembina required complicated logistics. Anderson led the astronomers and Royal Engineer detachment from England to the Red River valley via trans-Atlantic steamship, a Great Lakes steamboat to Duluth, and the Northern Pacific Railroad to Moorhead. From that newly established depot they moved downstream to Pembina by Red River carts and the steamboat *Dakota*. Meanwhile, Cameron was moving the Canadian contingent from Ottawa. After leaving Lake Superior at Thunder Bay, the group proceeded to Winnipeg, as Fort Garry was then starting to be called, by the Kaministikwia waterway and the Dawson Road. From Winnipeg, Cameron moved his men upstream to near Pembina. Because Cameron planned for the British-Canadian commission to work year-round, he established his permanent base of Dufferin in North Pembina, near the Hudson's Bay Company's post.[26]

Campbell moved the main American party by rail to Breckenridge, the Red River Valley terminus of the St. Paul and Pacific Railroad. With accompanying civilian contractors who were employed to ship supplies purchased in St. Paul, Campbell led the force overland to Fort Pembina. When he arrived on September 5, Campbell found that assistant astronomers Francis Greene and Lewis Boss, who had transported the surveying instruments from New York City, had been there for three weeks. Although they could not do any definitive work, Greene and Boss had determined Pembina's approximate latitude and longitude.[27]

Pending the arrival of the British-Canadian party, Campbell, with a military escort from Fort Pembina, established his camp near the Long-Woods monument. Including the troops and twenty teamsters, Campbell had about 100 men. The British-Canadian contingent included four officers and forty-four enlisted men of the Royal Engineers, forty civilians and some temporary employees.

When Anderson arrived on September 18, Cameron and Campbell held a joint staff meeting to coordinate their season's work. They agreed that five sites were particularly important—the forty-ninth parallel near Pembina, the northwest point of Lake of the Woods, the intersection of the forty-ninth with the lake's west shore, and two astronomical stations between the lake and the Red River. [28]

Determining the boundary near Pembina was routine. The astronomers of both sides made numerous calculations over the course of about two weeks then each side averaged its results. Their difference was only thirty-two feet. Since they had agreed in advance to accept the mean of any divergence of less than fifty feet, they easily positioned the boundary at about the midpoint of the 500 yards between the Long-Woods monument and the Hudson's Bay Company's post. Because their calculations had to be rechecked in their respective offices they deferred marking the site until the entire boundary was monumented. Nonetheless, their field conclusion immediately quieted the anxieties of American and British customs collectors.

Once the Pembina work was done by early October, Cameron and Campbell each organized three parties to determine the boundary from the Red River to the northwest point of Lake of the Woods. They and their leading astronomers, Anderson and Farquhar, went to Angle Inlet to establish the starting point for the due south line to the forty-ninth parallel. Ostensibly, the northwest point should have been easy to determine. Webster and Ashburton had written Tiarks' conclusion into their treaty so fixing the intersection of 49° 23' 55" north latitude and 95° 14' 38" west longitude on the ground would seemingly resolve the matter. However, the British discovered, and the Americans confirmed, that the point where those lines met was not at the head of Angle Inlet but nearly five miles to its west. Anderson and Farquhar agreed that Tiarks's miscalculation was inconsequential, because they obviously had to fix the most northwest point at its actual location. They believed Tiarks had performed well considering the instruments available to him.[29]

Locating the northwest point was complicated even more by a discovery made by A.G. Forrest, head of the first Canadian surveyors to reach Angle Inlet. While surveying the inlet, he found that the mid-water line, specified by the Treaty of 1783, crossed the due south line of the Convention of 1818 in at least two places south of the head of Angle Inlet. This "looped line" meant it was impossible to draw a mid-water line directly to the lake's northwest point.

The Tiarks miscalculation and the looped line gave Cameron a pretext for questioning the validity of using the northwest point as the juncture of the lines specified by the 1783 and 1818 treaties. He was intrigued by the possibility of redrawing the boundary through Lake of the Woods. He preferred the demarcation first proposed by Holland and Auckland in 1807—follow the mid-water line to its intersection with the forty-ninth in the lake and then proceed west along the parallel. Cameron anticipated British support because he knew Granville favored such a line. British and Canadian interest in redrawing the boundary was prompted by their desire to avoid any potential conflicts with the United States over the land where the Dawson Road left Lake of the Woods.

The practically minded Campbell had no patience with Cameron's posturing. He insisted that the survey's mission was to mark the boundary specified in treaties—not to draw a new boundary. Taking the traditional

American position that the northwest point was inviolable, he believed the survey's goal was to locate it on the ground. Farquhar, and more significantly, Anderson, agreed with him. But they all realized it could not be placed at the astronomical point determined by Tiarks.[30]

Consequently, the chief astronomers agreed that they should attempt to locate David Thompson's monument No.1, from which Tiarks had made his first Angle Inlet calculations. After diligent searching with the assistance of local Ojibwe Indians they found parts of two submerged, charred, ax-marked logs that laid at right angles to each other. Since they could not prove these were remnants of Thompson's monument, they dubbed them the "Indian monument." They concluded that even if their discovery was not at the actual site of Thompson's monument, any difference between the two was statistically insignificant.

Cameron refused to accept the Indian monument as the northwest point but conceded that it could be the basis for the meridian line to be drawn due south to the forty-ninth. The savvy Campbell, clearly irked with Cameron, agreed to pay half the expenses for surveying the line over the winter by the British-Canadian party. He correctly assumed that once the line was determined and adjacent timber cleared, it would be very difficult for Cameron to insist on a different starting point.

When the commissioners and head astronomers were at Angle Inlet, other parties led by assistant astronomers were determining the forty-ninth east of the Red River. Greene's crew worked for about five weeks on the thirty-three-mile section from the Red River to the Roseau River. To his east, Featherstonhaugh surveyed through a long, swampy stretch where his men oftentimes had to slog through water four to five feet deep. A joint American-British crew led by Twining and Galwey located the forty-ninth on the west shore of Muskeg Bay in Lake of the Woods. Working from boats they also determined the right angle corner at the eastern end of the forty-ninth and the southern end of the meridian line

Campbell withdrew his men to Pembina in early November. After leaving most of his equipment and animals at either Fort Pembina or Fort Abercrombie, the Americans traveled by rail from Breckenridge to their winter quarters in Detroit, Michigan. Campbell had ruled out St. Paul because he thought it would be too cold and too costly.[31]

Three British-Canadian parties continued surveying during the winter of 1872-1873. Anderson supervised the determination and clearing of the sixteen-mile land portion of the meridian line. Relying on locally hired Indian laborers, he had a narrow trace cut due south from the Indian monument. Anderson hoped the Indian monument would ultimately be accepted as the northwest point so he would not have to clear another line. The eighty-eight and a half-mile forty-ninth parallel boundary between the Red River and Lake of the Woods was surveyed by two crews led respectively by Featherstonhaugh and Galwey. While wintertime work was sometimes challenging, coping with the vast muskeg bogs was much easier when the ground was frozen.

By the conclusion of their work in early April, the British had traced a line along the land boundary east of the Red River, surveyed 500 square miles of land adjacent to the demarcation and established the five astronomical stations at the locations previously agreed upon by Campbell and Cameron. Furthermore, they recorded hundreds of magnetic and astronomical calculations, which were to be rechecked later.

Cameron and Campbell began surveying the forty-ninth parallel west of the Red River in 1873, without having resolved the location of the northwest point and the meridian line due south from it. Although this piece of unfinished business had strained relations between the commissioners, their estrangement was worsened by a disagreement over the method of marking the forty-ninth. When they met at Pembina in early July 1873, Cameron proposed that they measure a latitudinal line exactly parallel to the equator. He called this line, which would curve slightly southward, a mean parallel. Campbell acknowledged that such a line would be theoretically correct, but that fixing it on the ground would require an additional year of field work at considerable expense to both sides. To determine the mean parallel it would be necessary to first establish astronomical stations at approximate twenty-mile intervals along the estimated 800-mile boundary. Then all calculations would have to be rechecked by the astronomers over the winter. Finally, the surveyors would have to resurvey the entire line in order to ascertain the curved line from the stations.[32]

Campbell insisted that the slight territorial gain to Canada did not justify using such a time-consuming, expensive method. He preferred to follow the Oregon boundary practice of connecting astronomical stations with straight lines that at any given point would be slightly north or south of the forty-ninth. Campbell's stance of an astronomical line was supported by Twining, who had replaced Farquhar as chief astronomer, and by Anderson, who was disdainful of Cameron's scientific deficiencies. But Cameron stubbornly held his position. Consequently, the survey was carried westward from the Red River for 408 miles in 1873, without any agreement on how the boundary was to be determined finally.

Over the winter of 1873-1874, Cameron tried to enlist Canadian and British support for his positions on the mean parallel and the northwest point. He first made his case for the mean parallel in meetings with Governor-General Lord Dufferin and other Canadian officials. He stressed there was some urgency in resolving the matter, because of the possibility that American assistant astronomer Greene would cut the permanent boundary trace west of Lake of the Woods. When Campbell disbanded the main American party and sent the astronomers to Detroit, he ordered Greene to survey the Red River-Lake of the Woods stretch to establish that it had been jointly surveyed.[33]

Perhaps with the goal of establishing more of a Canadian presence in the west, a committee of the Dominion Privy Council endorsed the mean parallel method. Once Cameron had this support, he wrote to Lord Granville about the advantages of the curved line. He had no qualms about asking for British support even though he estimated a mean parallel calculation would cost the considerable sum of £50,000.

Cameron may have been unconcerned about the expense, but Granville certainly was. Granville was influenced by Samuel Anderson, who tried to sabotage Cameron's effort. Anderson asked his Royal Engineers comrade Charles Wilson to inform Granville about his opposition to the mean parallel. Anderson thought the proposed survey would be a "most unnecessary waste of public money," which would only move the boundary "a few feet north and south." Demonstrating the tensions between the boundary commission's British and Canadian components, Anderson accused the Canadian government of only wanting to prolong the survey and to get Great Britain to pay for half of it.[34]

Granville never seriously considered supporting Cameron, but for fear of offending the Canadian government, he was reluctant to personally reject the mean parallel. Wanting to make his response seem like a British position, he solicited other opinions. Engineer Charles Wilson opined that the mean parallel would be "of no practical value" and terribly expensive. The Earl of Carnarvon, the colonial secretary, believed the boundary should be the astronomical line favored by Campbell and the American and British astronomers. Sensing an advantage in making a decision based on science rather than politics, he suggested Granville consult with George Airy, the royal astronomer.

Everyone involved knew where Airy stood. Before the start of the survey he had recommended the astronomical line method. Nonetheless, to respond to the question at hand, he interpreted the intent of the Convention of 1818. Its signers, he adjudged, meant "parallel" as drawn in ordinary maps where slight discrepancies would not be shown. He recommended that the boundary be determined by establishing astronomical stations and letting the commissioners choose either straight or curved connecting lines. He favored straight lines, but conceded that curved lines would be slightly more accurate. Airy seemed puzzled by the fuss over a slight amount of land. He noted that the difference between Cameron's pure mean line and Campbell's astronomical one would "be for the most part less than the breadth of a London square."

Airy's opinion was the last word. By the time he rendered it, because of a change in British government ministries, Granville had been replaced by the Earl of Derby. Derby, like his predecessor, believed the boundary should be determined as expeditiously and as inexpensively as possible. Although Cameron peevishly claimed that his only motive in seeking the mean line was greater accuracy, he was bluntly informed by the Foreign Office to adhere to Airy's method.

When he raised the mean line issue, Cameron also broached the question of establishing the northwest point with the Foreign Office. He insisted that the point where the mid-water line touched the latitude specified in the Webster-Ashburton Treaty should be accepted as the northwest point instead of the Indian monument. But he did not even have the support of his chief astronomer. Anderson noted that accepting Cameron's point would shift the meridian line only 106 feet west of the line already cleared south from the Indian monument. Furthermore, he pointed out, moving the line slightly west would not solve the problem of the looped line and would further aggravate the matter of relocating the Dawson Road docks.[35]

The Foreign Office invited Major Charles Wilson to submit his expert opinion. Wilson, who seems to have shared Anderson's disdain for Cameron, thought the meridian line should be based on the Indian monument. He was particularly critical of the idea of expending more time and effort to clear another meridian line, which would have no advantage. As for the looped line, he suggested eliminating it by shifting the northwest point to the southernmost intersection of the mid-water and meridian lines. Accepting Wilson's reasoning, Derby promptly ordered Cameron to accept the Indian monument as the northwest point. The looped line feature, he admonished, had resulted from treaty provisions and thus could only be adjusted by another treaty.

Before the start of field work in 1874, Cameron had been ordered to make an agreement with Campbell about the parallel determination and the northwest point. But Cameron did not broach the subjects with Campbell until mid-August, when they were encamped on the Milk River along the Montana-Canadian boundary. Cameron offered to accept the Indian monument as the northwest point and a forty-ninth parallel line based on astronomical stations, provided the lines between them "shall follow a course having the uniform curvature of a parallel of 49th North Latitude." Recognizing that Cameron was determined to salvage some of his pride, Campbell accepted the offer.

After they resolved their differences, the commissioners addressed the matter of monumenting the boundary. In their judgment, the area west of the southwest corner of Manitoba lay beyond the pale of agriculture and would not be settled for years, if ever. Therefore, they agreed to make a distinction between the sections west and east of the southwest corner of Manitoba. The more desolate western part was to be marked by stone cairns and earthen mounds, and iron monuments were to be placed from the southwest corner of Manitoba to the northwest point of Lake of the Woods.[36]

Cameron and Campbell agreed that monumenting the boundary would be done jointly but that the two sides would work separately. When the commissions parted ways at the eastern foot of the Rockies at the end of the 1874 season, the Americans returned east by first moving southeastward to Fort Benton on the Missouri River. Cameron's party, which moved to Dufferin along the forty-ninth, adjusted the boundary between astronomical stations, completed the mound construction west Manitoba's southwestern corner and erected alternate iron monuments east of that point.[37]

Cameron and Campbell had agreed to place iron monuments at approximate one-mile intervals. The markers were to be of the same specifications as those used on the Maine-New Brunswick boundary. On average, the hollow cast iron monuments, which were filled with seasoned cedar poles, weighed 285 pounds. They were eight feet tall with equal portions placed above and below ground. Each monument was topped by a pyramidal cap, which was set upon a truncated pyramid eight inches square at its base and four inches square at its top. For some reason, the monuments did not bear the names of the countries but dealt only with the authority for the boundary. With two-inch high raised letters, the side facing Canada was inscribed "Convention of London" and the opposite side "October 20, 1818." The other two sides were left blank.

During the fall and winter of 1874-1875, Cameron coordinated the work of three small crews that placed alternate monuments on the 169 miles from the southwest corner of Manitoba to Lake of the Woods. Working from the west, they had no difficulty placing iron monuments approximately every two miles. But in the marshy section, which they reached fifty-five miles west of Lake of the Woods, they generally had to use earth and timber mounds. Cameron and Campbell had agreed that the iron monuments in the sixteen-mile meridian strip would be at two-mile intervals. Work on this section was supervised by D'Arcy East, the chief British surveyor. East's crew also widened the vista strip and at the forty-ninth parallel on the west shore of Lake of the Woods built a substantial stone cairn seven and half feet high and eight feet in diameter.

James F. Gregory supervised the American share of the monumenting in late summer and early fall, 1875. He organized a small party in St. Paul and supplemented it near the boundary with more men, teams and wagons and a military escort from Fort Pembina. Meanwhile, he had the American consignment of iron monuments sent by rail from Detroit, where they were manufactured, to Moorhead. Over a five-week period, Gregory's crew set forty-three monuments to the west of Pembina and seventeen to the east. They were placed midway between those erected by the British.[38]

As a contribution to the commission's final report, Gregory also compiled two lists of monuments for the surveyed boundary. The first, numbered one to seven, identified the meridian line south from Angle Inlet. The second list showed the sites of the 382 monuments from Lake of the Woods to the crest of the Rockies. Seventy of these (numbers one through seventy) were located between the lake and the Red River astronomical station. Gregory recorded the monuments by location and number, but no numbers were placed on them. Consequently, they were not readily distinguishable on the ground.

The northwest angle is one of the quirkiest boundary features in the world. But if Great Britain had prevailed, it would have been eliminated in 1875. By the time the commissions entered their monumenting phase, the Foreign Office had approached the United States about ceding the angle. Canadian officials had persuaded Lord Derby about the benefits of adding the angle to their country.[39]

Lord Dufferin and the Dominion Privy Council had been influenced by Cameron. The commissioner believed Canadian acquisition of the angle would make the boundary in that section a more natural line, would eliminate a likely sanctuary for smugglers and would facilitate planning transportation routes west of Lake of the Woods. Cameron's favorite idea was for a boundary that followed the Lake of the Woods shore between the mouth of the Rainy River and the forty-ninth parallel. If this was not attainable, he suggested the mid-water line be followed to its intersection with the forty-ninth in the lake.

Lord Derby ordered Edward Thornton, the British ambassador to the United States, to approach Secretary of State Hamilton Fish about the angle matter. Thornton was to try to convince Fish that the United States should give up the angle as an "international convenience." If this failed, then he was authorized to raise the possibility of buying it. Derby and Thornton both knew that the Dominion Privy Council had decided to pay as much as $25,000 for the angle.[40]

Thornton met with Fish twice in February 1875. In their first meeting, Fish refused to consider shifting the boundary to the shore of Lake of the Woods. Contending that the northwest point had already been marked, he also would not consider moving it to the southernmost intersection of the mid-water and meridian lines. When they met again a week later, Thornton offered to buy the angle. Fish's blunt response was, "nothing that Her Majesty's Government would be prepared to offer would be accepted by the United States."[41]

In their haste to bring the boundary survey to a close, Great Britain and the United States neglected to consider one eminently practical idea. Cameron, fearing boundary monuments would be obliterated by natural phenomena over time or vandalized, suggested markers be inspected every five years and repaired as necessary. In this respect, he proved to be years ahead of his time.[42]

Throughout their history of surveying and marking the American-Canadian boundary, the United States and Great Britain responded to local crises. The boundary in an unsettled region was of no concern to either country but as Americans and Canadians expanded on their respective frontiers, the inevitable land disputes in the region abutting the unmarked boundary had to be resolved. Although frontier movement in both Canada and the United States was toward the Pacific, it did not shift gradually westward. Consequently, because the Pacific coastal region attracted settlers before the Great Plains, establishing the international boundary in the Oregon country was done before any part of the Minnesota-Canada boundary was marked. With respect to Minnesota's international boundary, its westernmost section was marked first because of the boundary dispute near Pembina.

During the 1870s survey, there was no need to resurvey and mark the boundary in the unsettled region from Lake Superior to the northwesternmost point of Lake of the Woods. But frontier expansion on both sides of the boundary over the next three decades made resurveying and monumenting imperative.

Because of the need to stimulate its westward movement, Canada took the lead in promoting settlement of the borderlands west of Lake Superior. Canada's interest in Manitoba caused it to develop the Dawson Road from Lake Superior to Winnipeg. The route, initially surveyed by Isaac J. Dawson in 1858, was not improved until the joint British-Canadian military force moved from Prince Arthur's Landing (renamed Port Arthur in 1883) near Fort William to Winnipeg in 1870. From Lake Superior to the boat landing in Angle Inlet, the route followed the Kaministikwia waterway and then the boundary lakes and the Rainy River to Lake of the Woods. The portion west of Lake of the Woods was a wagon road.[43]

Although the Dawson Road facilitated some movement to Manitoba, it proved to be short-lived. In 1871, when British Columbia became a province, the Canadian government made a commitment to construct the Canadian Pacific Railway. The completion of the section from Fort William to Winnipeg in 1882 made the Dawson Road obsolete. Because the railroad's route from Lake Superior to Winnipeg via Kenora lay well north of the white pine and red pine stands needed for ties, trestles, bridges and other structures, its agents were the first lumbermen in northern Minnesota. They obviously did not know precisely where the boundary lay through such a waterway as Rainy Lake, but they certainly knew that any cutting south of the lake was being done in the United States. Nonetheless, thousands of board feet of illegally cut logs were floated to Fort Frances mills or towed to other mills on Lake of the Woods.[44]

As Fort William and Port Arthur were benefitting from their railroad connections and nearby silver strikes, the discovery or iron ore on the Vermilion Range caused the rapid development of northeastern Minnesota. The first ore was exported by railroad from Tower in 1884. Three years later the town of Ely was founded when a major iron ore strike was made there. These initial successes caused prospectors to fan out both south and north of the range. Some of them discovered ore on the Minnesota side of Gunflint Lake. This development caused a mining company to build a short, privately owned railroad line.[45]

Meanwhile, the prospects of discovering iron ore and silver southwest of Thunder Bay caused Fort William and Port Arthur promoters to build the Port Arthur, Duluth and Western Railway. Their original intention was to link Thunder Bay and Duluth but in 1892, when the line was finished, for about eighty-five miles from Thunder Bay it met the Minnesota mining company's line at the border. From that point, it was extended westward over the next nine years to Fort Frances. The railroad was extremely important in providing access for lumbermen to lands near the international boundary.

As the Canadian line was being built toward Fort Frances, Minnesota experienced the Rainy Lake gold rush. In July 1893, gold was discovered on the lake's Little American Island. This find precipitated a rush of several hundred prospectors who founded Rainy Lake City on the east side of the strait connecting Rainy Lake and Black Bay (also known as Rat Root Lake). Although the rush did not lead to significant discoveries, it attracted land claimants to the borderlands.[46]

As Rainy Lake City declined, American lumbermen and fishermen were drawn to the site of Rainy Lake's outlet, where the village of Koochiching sprang up. Koochiching (renamed International Falls in 1909) became an important shipping point for the small steamboats that hauled logs and lumber down the Rainy River and through Lake of the Woods to Kenora.

The Americans and Canadians who moved to the borderlands obviously knew they were near an international boundary. But unless they were on opposite sides of a large body of water such as Rainy Lake they could not visualize the boundary. Consequently, they were generally unaware of the nationality of islands and the precise course of the boundary through lakes. This ignorance extended to the surveyors of the Canadian Department of Crown Lands and the United States General Land Office. These surveyors did not have access to the boundary maps prepared by the Article Seven commission and apparently were not aware that the boundary through the lakes had to be a mid-water line. Consequently, they surveyed islands that were not even in their own country. Once the survey was made and the land claimed, county officials routinely registered the claim.[47]

The boundary's impreciseness was first exposed by the controversy over Frank Gardner's claim to a portion of Coleman Island in Lac la Croix. In 1882 and 1883, when he purchased his interest in the island, Gardner naturally assumed that because it had been surveyed by the United States General Land Office it was in St. Louis County. Accordingly, he registered his claim with the county and paid county property taxes on it for about a decade. But when he decided to cut some timber on it, he was blocked by Ontario officials, because a Canadian survey had placed his land on their side of the boundary.[48]

Gardner did not take rejection lightly. He first appealed to the United States General Land Office, whose acting commissioner opined that since the dispute "appears to be international in its character," Gardner should direct his complaint to the State Department. The determined Gardner not only wrote to the State Department but also sought assistance from Congressman Charles A. Towne of Duluth. Towne seized on the Gardner complaint to champion his own belief that the boundary should be adjusted to the most continuous water line rather than the one specified in the Webster-Ashburton Treaty.

As the Gardner matter was being considered, some local residents were confused about the boundary near Oak Island in Lake of the Woods. Oak Island, which had been identified as Island No. 1 by the Article

Seven surveyors, was on the American side of the mid-water line but steamboat captains usually navigated around its south and west sides. Some nearby Canadians, assuming that the boat channel was the boundary, wanted their government to secure the island. Somehow this request evolved into the rumor that Canada was about to claim Oak Island. After he received this bit of misinformation in the fall of 1895, Secretary of State Richard Olney notified Sir Julian Pauncefote, the British ambassador to the United States, that Oak Island was the same as Island No. 1. Olney reminded Pauncefote that the island had been placed in the United States by the Webster-Ashburton Treaty, which specified the boundary through Lake of the Woods was to be as decided by the Article Seven commissioners. Pauncefote agreed and assured Olney that Canada had only investigated the claims of some of its concerned citizens. Although the Oak Island question was easily resolved, it gave Towne another reason for calling for a boundary survey and marking.[49]

In large part because of Towne's zeal, the House of Representatives, in early 1896, passed resolutions calling for a boundary survey and the shifting of the international line to the north side of Hunter Island. Recognizing that the Webster-Ashburton Treaty had fixed the boundary, the State Department concluded that the mere existence of a continuous water passage to the north side of Hunter Island was immaterial. The United States, which was then seeking improved relations with Great Britain, refused to be drawn into Towne's desire to add a small piece of land to the United States. The State Department was evidently satisfied that Great Britain and Canada wanted to settle boundary issues amicably, because Ontario had withdrawn its objection to Gardner's claim.

Towne's criticism of the State Department decision prompted Canada to launch its own investigation of the boundary near Hunter Island. In the summer of 1896, dominion astronomer William F. King ordered surveyor A.J. "Jack" Brabazon to inspect most of the Minnesota-Ontario boundary. Brabazon and his crew, equipped with the maps prepared by the Article Seven commission, surveyed the mid-water line and adjacent islands for about 210 miles. Brabazon's work confirmed the need to carefully survey and mark the boundary. He found the 1820s survey had misplaced a number of islands and failed to make a record of others. Nonetheless, because he had easily followed the general mid-water line specified in the Webster-Ashburton Treaty, he concluded that the United States had no valid claim to Hunter Island. The Brabazon survey assured Canada that a resurvey of the Minnesota-Canada boundary could only make it more accurate, but could not change it to the most continuous waterway.[50]

Although the need to accurately survey and mark the Minnesota-Ontario boundary was evident by 1896, the problems there paled in comparison to the controversial Alaska Panhandle boundary. The settlement of the Alaska Panhandle boundary by an Anglo-American tribunal in 1903 created a willingness to resolve issues on the entire Canada-United States boundary. From 1903 to 1908, William F. King, Canada's astronomer, and Otto H. Tittman, director of the United States Coast and Geodetic Survey, headed a joint commission that opened work on three projects—surveying and marking the Alaska Panhandle boundary, surveying and marking the Alaska-Canada meridian boundary and resurveying and remonumenting the boundary between the Rockies crest and the Gulf of Georgia.[51]

Meanwhile, there were continuing complaints about boundary problems in other sections. Rather than approach them piecemeal, the United States and Great Britain, by the Treaty of 1908, agreed to resurvey the entire transcontinental Canada-United States boundary. An article of the treaty specified that the ongoing survey from the Gulf of Georgia eastward to the crest of the Rockies would be continued. Other articles mandated a resurvey of those boundary sections established by the Treaty of Paris of 1783 and the Convention of 1818. This meant that the work on the Minnesota-Canada boundary would have two discrete sections, with the northwesternmost point of Lake of the Woods as their dividing point.[52]

Soon after the treaty's ratification, the United States and Great Britain respectively named Tittman and King as commissioners for all Canada-United States boundary surveys and resurveys. Until 1925, they and their successors worked under the mandates of the Alaska tribunal award of 1903, the Alaska Boundary Treaty of 1906, and the Treaty of 1908.[53]

King and Tittman were each assisted by approximately twenty full-time employees. The commissioners coordinated the field work by assigning a designated boundary section to either an American or Canadian crew.

In contrast to the 1870s survey, the resurvey of the Convention of 1818 section was done from west to east. In 1912-1913, an American crew resurveyed and remonumented the boundary from the Red River to the northwesternmost point of Lake of the Woods. Taking advantage of the frozen ground, they used horse-drawn sleighs to distribute cast iron monuments along the forty-ninth parallel in February and March of 1912. From the spring thaw through most of the summer they erected the monuments east to Lake of the Woods. That fall they began surveying the Angle Inlet area and the following winter hauled monuments to the appropriate sites on the meridian strip. They placed these markers soon after the spring thaw.[54]

The cast iron monuments set in 1912-1913 generally resembled those used in the 1870s. Like their predecessors, they were eight feet high but had a five-foot shaft above ground with a three-foot base set in concrete. The shaft of each marker was eight inches square at the bottom and four inches square to the point just below they pyramidal cap. It was imperative that the monuments be perfectly straight, because the boundary connected the points of the pyramidal caps. The replacement monuments weighed about ninety-five pounds more than the original ones. Their cast iron shell was thicker and they were filled with concrete rather than wood.

The inscriptions on the new markers provided more information than the originals. A small brass plate on the flange of each marker provided such details as the elevation and all sides of each shaft were inscribed with raised letters. The monuments along the forty-ninth parallel were inscribed with "CANADA" on the north, "UNITED STATES" on the south, "CONVENTION OF 1818" on the east and "TREATY OF 1908" on the west. Along the meridian line "CANADA" faced west and "UNITED STATES" east.

The remonumenting of the Convention of 1818 line was completed in 1914, when a three-man American crew numbered the monuments. The commissioners decided to use one series of numbers from Port

Roberts on the Gulf of Georgia to the northwesternmost point of Lake of the Woods. Numbers zero through 271 were already done when E.R. Martin and his men started working on Number 272 at the Rockies crest. From June 6 to December 14, they worked their way to Monument 925, on the south shore of Angle Inlet. On each monument they etched the identifying number horizontally between the "CONVENTION OF 1818" inscription and the pyramidal cap.

Surveying and monumenting the boundary between Lake Superior and the northwesternmost point of Lake of the Woods proved to be arduous and time-consuming. Significant field work was done during eleven consecutive years, beginning with 1908.

Starting with the initial meeting between King and Tittman in December 1908, the boundary commissioners, over a period of time, established certain principles in surveying and monumenting the demarcation. To facilitate surveying and where necessary, resurveying, they agreed that the boundary would be a series of straight lines, which were to be as close as possible to the slightly curved lines on the maps prepared by the Article Seven surveyors. Further, they reaffirmed the Article Seven precedent that the boundary through the lakes and rivers should not intersect islands.[55]

During 1908-1911, all of the surveying of the old Article Seven line west of Lake Superior was done by American crews of ten to fourteen men led by W.B. Fairfield. Working westward from the mouth of the Pigeon River, by the end of their fourth season they had completed a triangulation survey to Gneiss Lake. As they proceeded they recorded all of their calculations and placed temporary markers at designated reference points on both sides of the boundary. They marked the boundary over portages by clearing a twenty-foot wide vista strip.[56]

In 1912, King and Tittman decided to survey the boundary from Lake Superior to the northwesternmost point of Lake of the Woods from both the east and the west. James J. McArthur, a Canadian surveyor who had completed his assignment west of the Red River, was sent to Lake of the Woods. By the end of the season McArthur's crew had surveyed and monumented the boundary as far as Oak Island

Reference marker 34 on Oak Island in Lake of the Woods. This is typical of the markers flanking the boundary in Lake of the Woods. (Photo by William E. Lass.)

Meanwhile, Fairfield had advanced to the west end of Knife Lake.

Most of the northwesternmost point-Lake Superior section was surveyed and monumented in 1913 and 1914. Working eastward, McArthur's party and two American crews surveyed and monumented alternate areas between Oak Island and Lac La Croix. During the same time, Fairfield's crew completed the survey west to Crooked Lake, only about twenty miles from Lac La Croix. In 1915, an American and a Canadian crew completed the survey.

Completing the monumenting of the boundary took several more years. An American party set permanent markers on a section east of Crooked Lake in 1916 but monumenting the easternmost boundary section along the Pigeon River was not completed until 1918. This work was delayed by the need to recheck turning points in some narrow waterways.

Monumenting the 426-mile boundary from the northwesternmost point to Lake Superior entailed placing a series of 1,373 reference markers on lake shores, islands and stream banks and another series of nine monuments on the three portages. Both series were numbered from west to east with the even numbers on the American side and the odd numbers on the Canadian side.[57]

The reference markers from which the turning points in water could be determined were of four types—large cast iron monuments similar to those set on the meridian line, wrought iron posts two inches square and about a foot above ground, manganese-bronze posts two inches square and eight inches above ground and bronze disks two inches in diameter. Reference marks one and two on Angle Inlet were the only cast iron monuments. The foot-long iron wrought iron posts (Numbers three through eight-six) were set in rock from Angle Inlet to the lower Rainy River. The short manganese-bronze posts, whose shanks were drilled into rock, were the most common markers from the lower Rainy to Lake Superior, but in some places they were supplemented by bronze disks. All of the posts from the northwest point of Lake of the Woods to Lake Superior bore an identifying number made with drill holes spaced about a quarter-inch apart.

The nine monuments placed on the land portion of the boundary were equally divided among Swamp Portage between Swamp and Cypress lakes, Height-of-Land Portage from North Lake to South Lake and Watab Portage connecting Watab and Mountain lakes. The portage monuments, set in concrete bases, were of two types—short conical posts made of

Easternmost boundary marker on Height-of-Land Portage between North Lake and South Lake. Identical markers were placed at the west end and midpoint of the portage. (Photo by William E. Lass.)

bronze or bronze-aluminum and bronze obelisks that stood five feet above ground level.

With the completion of the monumenting along the Pigeon River in 1918, the entire Minnesota-Canada boundary was easily identifiable for the first time. The boundary's main land portions—the section between the Red River and Lake of the Woods and the short meridian line south of Angle Inlet—were marked by obelisks at approximate one-mile intervals. With the exception of three portages, the boundary from the northwesternmost point of Lake of the Woods to Lake Superior was a mid-water line referenced by on-shore monuments. By triangulation from these markers, turning points could be determined along the mid-water line. The actual boundary was a series of straight-line courses connecting the turning points.[58]

Vista strip at Height-of-Land Portage. (Photo by William E. Lass)

Reference marker 1124 at the outlet of Little Gunflint Lake. This is typical of the markers on both sides of the water boundary from the mouth of the Rainy River to Lake Superior. (Photo by William E. Lass)

## Notes:

1. Here and below, W.L. Morton, *Manitoba: A History* (2d ed.; Toronto: University of Toronto Press, 1967), 45-48; James A. Jackson, *The Centennial History of Manitoba* (Winnipeg: Manitoba Historical Society, 1970, 39-40; John Morgan Gray, *Lord Selkirk of Red River* (Toronto: The Macmillan Company of Canada, 1963), 73.

2. Manning, ed., *Diplomatic Correspondence*, vol. 1, 589-91; William H. Keating, *Narrative of an Expedition to the Source of St. Peter's River, Lake Winnepeek, Lake of the Woods, etc. Performed in the Year 1823* (Reprint ed.; Minneapolis: Ross & Haines, 1959), 2: 38.

3. Kane, Holmquist and Gilman, eds, *Northern Expeditions*, 183; Heitman, *Historical Register*, 1: 640.

4. Keating, *Narrative of an Expedition*, 39-42; Kane, Holmquist and Gilman, eds., *Northern Expeditions*, 182.

5. Morton, *Manitoba*, 66; Jackson, *History of Manitoba*, 63-65; G. A. Belcourt, "Department of Hudson's Bay," *Collections of the Minnesota Historical Society*, vol. 1 (St. Paul, 1872): 220-21; Folwell, *Minnesota*, 1: 215-17.

6. Clarence W. Rife, "Norman W. Kittson: A Fur Trader at Pembina," *Minnesota History* 6 (September, 1925): 225-29, 249-51.

7. *Report of Major Wood, relative to his expedition to Pembina Settlement, and the condition of affairs on the North-Western frontier of the Territory of Minnesota.* 31 Congress, 1 session, House Executive Documents 51, p. 19 (serial 577).

8. Alvin C. Gluek, Jr., *Minnesota and Manifest Destiny of the Canadian Northwest: A Study in Canadian-American Relations* (Toronto: University of Toronto Press, 1965), 107, 110-11; Rife, in *Minnesota History*, 6:245; Folwell, *Minnesota*, 1: 288-291; Willoughby M. Babcock, "With Ramsey to Pembina: A Treaty-Making Trip in 1851," *Minnesota History*, 38 (March, 1962): 1-10.

9. Gluek, *Minnesota and Manifest Destiny*, 183-84; For the text of the Receiprocity Treaty see Bevans, *Treaties*, 12: 116-20.

10. Here and below, Gluek, *Minnesota and Manifest Destiny*, 132-33.

11. Morton, *Manitoba*, 94-100; John Palliser, *Papers Relative to the Exploration . . . of British North America* (London: G. E. Eyre and W. Spottiswoode , 1859); Henry Youle Hind, *North-West Territory, Reports of Progress* (Toronto: J. Lovell, 1859).

12. Here and the paragraph below, Gluek, *Minnesota and Manifest Destiny*, 134-135, 142-143.

13. Bailey, *Diplomatic History*, 373-77.

14. Theordore C. Blegen, "A Plan for the Union of British North America and the United States, 1866," *Mississippi Valley Historical Review* 4 (March, 1918): 472-75.

15. United Kingdom, *The British North America Act, 1867*, 30-31 Victoria, c. 3 and *Rupert's Land Act, 1868*, 31-32 Victoria, c. 105.

16. Donald F. Warner, *The Idea of Continental Union: Agitation for the Annexation of Canada to the United States 1849-1893*, (Lexington: University of Kentucky Press, 1960), 94-98, 106; Lester B. Shippee, *Canadian-American Relations 1849-1874*, (New Haven: Yale University Press, 1939), 204.

17. Here and the two paragraphs below, Morton, *Manitoba*, 118-145; Gluek, *Minnesota and Manifest Destiny*, 249, 251, 262-294; Ruth E. Sanborn, "The United States and the British Northwest, 1865-1870," *North Dakota Historical Quarterly* 6 (October 1931): 36; Canada, *Manitoba Act, 1870*, 33 Victoria, c. 3.

18. Here and below, Stafford Northcote, Hudson's Bay Company, to Sir F. Rogers, 15 November 1870, in FO/5, vol. 1475, pp. 90-93; Irene M. Spry, ed., *The Papers of the Palliser Expedition, 1857-1860*, (Toronto: Champlain Society, 1968), cxxiv, 98-101; Thornton to [J. C. B.} Davis, 04 November 1870; Heap to Hancock, 09 July 1870; Stoever to secretary of the treasury, 23 June 1870, in *Papers Relating to the Foreign Relations of the United States, 1870*, (Washington, D.C.: Government Printing Office, 1870), 400-403.

19. Boutwell to Fish, 19 July 1870; J.C.B. Davis to "Mr. Richardson,"13 August 1870, in *Foreign Relations of the United States, 1870*, 401;

Thornton to Sir John Young, governor-general of Canada, 21 July 1870, to Lord Granville, secretary of state for foreign affairs, 01 August 1870, Archibald to secretary of state for the provinces, 29 September 1870, in FO/5, vol. 1475, pp. 1-6, 66-68; Survey of Boundary from Lake of the Woods to Summit of Rocky Mountains Act, U.S., *Statutes at Large* (1872), vol. 17, p. 43.

20. John E. Parsons, *West on the 49th Parallel: Red River to the Rockies, 1872-1876*, (New York: William Morrow and Co., 1963), 7-12; H. George Classen, *Thrust and Counterthrust: The Genesis of the Canada-United States Boundary*, 210-283 (Chicago: Rand McNally & Co., 1965), 210-83.

21. Humphreys to W.W. Belknap, secretary of war, 23 November 1870, in *Foreign Relations of the United States, 1870*, 406; Hawkins' report in FO/5, vol. 1475, p. 171.

22. George W. Cullum, *Biographical Register of the Officers and Graduates of the U. S. Military Academy*, (3rd ed., Boston, 1891), 1: 610, 2: 812, 868, 3: 38, 143; Heitman, *Historical Register*, 1: 276, 414, 474, 477, 976.

23. Foreign Office to Colonial Office, 04 May 1871, H. Holland , undersecretary of state for colonial affairs, to E. Hammond, undersecretary of state for foreign affairs, 23 October 1871, both in FO/5, vol. 1475, pp. 189-191, 199-201; [Sir James] Lindsay to [Granville?], 22 April 1871, in FO/5, vol. 1475, p. 185; Holland to Cameron, 23 February 1872, in FO/5, vol. 1476, p. 43.

24. Parsons, *West on the 49th Parallel*, 19, 21, 30, 36; Cameron to Granville, 30 March 1872; Featherstonhaugh to Granville, 27 April 1872, Foreign Office to War Office, 27 April 1872, War Office to undersecretary of state, 14 May 1872 – all in FO/5, vol. 1476, pp. 55-57, 77-80, 103-105.

25. Cameron to Granville, 25 July, 05 August 1872, both in FO/5, vol. 1476, pp. 232-234, 250-263.

26. Anderson to E. Hammond, 19 August 1872, in FO/5, vol. 1476, p. 246; S[amuel] Anderson, "The North-American Boundary from the Lake of the Woods to the Rocky Mountains," *Journal of the Royal Geographical Society*, 46 (1877): 230; [Albany] Featherstonhaugh, *Narrative of the Operations of the British North American Boundary Commission, 1872-1876*, 26 (Reprint ed., Woolwich, England, 1876); Cameron final report, 08 February 1876, in FO/5, vol. 1667, pp. 35-36.

27. Here and the paragraph below Campbell to Fish, 24 June , 24 August 1872, to Charles Hale, U.S. acting secretary of state, 26 June , 06 July 1872, to Brig. Gen. M.C. Meigs, quartermaster general U.S. Army—all in Letters Sent by the U.S. Commissioner, NB/NARA RG 76; Hale to Campbell, 25 June 1872, Fish to Campbell, 16 July 1872, both in Letters Received by the U.S. Commissioner, NB/NARA RG 76; U.S. Dept. of State, *Reports upon the Survey of the Boundary between the Territory of the United States and the Possessions of Great Britain from the Lake of the Woods to the Summit of the Rocky Mountains*, 332 (Washington, D. C., 1878).

28. Cameron to Granville, 23 September 1872; in FO/5, vol. 1476, pp. 299-301; Campbell to Fish, 22 September 1872, to Cameron, 12 April 1873, both in Letters Sent by the U.S. Commissioner, NB/NARA RG 76; Anderson, in *Journal of the Royal Geographical Society*, 46: 231.

29. Here and the two paragraphs below, Cameron to Granville, 23 September 1872, Cameron's final report, 08 February 1876, both in FO/5, vol. 1476, pp. 294-298, vol. 1667, p. 32, 35; Granville to Cameron, 28 June 1872, in FO/5, vol. 1476, pp. 179-181.

30. Here and the three paragraphs below, Cameron to Campbell, 08 November 1872, Farquhar to Campbell, 14 December 1872, both in Letters Received by the U.S. Commissioner, NB/NARA RG 76; U.S. Dept. of State, *Reports upon the Survey of the Boundary*, 305-307; Gregory, 1872 journal, in Survey Journals, 1872-74, NB/NARA RG 76; Featherstonhaugh, *Narrative of the British North American Boundary Commission*, 31.

31. Here and the two paragraphs below, Campbell to Fish, 22 September, 06, 10 October, 13 November i872, in Letters Sent by the U.S. Commissioner, in NB/NARA RG 76; Anderson, "Report of Operations during the Winter of 1872-73," 31 May 1873, in FO/5, vol. 1670, pp. 25, 28-34.

32. Here and below, Cameron to Campbell, 04 July, 29 August, 14 September 1873, in Letters Received by the U.S. Commissioner, in NB/NARA RG 76; U.S. Dept. of State, *Reports upon the Survey of the Boundary*, 69; Campbell to Cameron, 29 August 1873, in Letters Sent by the U.S. Commissioner, NB/NARA RG 76; Cameron, "Confidential memorandum for the information of the Government of the Dominion of Canada relative to the Location of the international boundary line," 19 November 1873, Cameron to Granville, 04 February 1874, both in FO/5, vol. 1505, pp. 123-129, 197-200.

33. Here and below, Cameron, "Confidential memoradum . . . relative to the location of the international boundary line," 19 November 1873, and "Memorandum of a verbal statement referring to the demarcation of the international boundary line," 29 November 1873; Cameron to Col. Fletcher, secretary to the governor-general, December 14, 1873; Cameron to Granville, 04, 25 February 1874, all in FO/5, vol. 1505, pp. 108, 129, 197-204.

34. Here and the three paragraphs below, Anderson to Wilson, 07 February 1874 and Wilson to Lord Tenterden, 05 March 1874, both in FO/5, vol. 1505, pp. 105, 108; Foreign Office to Cameron, 17 April 1874, Airy, report of 02 April 1874, in Vernon Lushington, Lords Commissioners of the Admirallty, to undersecretary of state for foreign affairs, 10 April 1874, both in FO/5, vol. 1506, pp. 17, 35.

35. Here and the two paragraphs below, Anderson to Cameron, 31 January, 1874, Cameron to Granville, 04 February 1874, both in FO/5, vol. 1505, pp. 137-154, 161-164; Wilson, report, enclosed in undersecretary of war to undersecretary of state, 17 April 1874, in FO/5,

vol. 1506, p. 40; Cameron to Derby, 23 May, 03 November 1874, in FO/5, vol. 1506, pp. 108-111, 260-264.

36. Cameron to Campbell, 08 November 1874, Twining to Campbell, 01 December 1874, both in Letters Received by the U.S. Commissioner, NB/NARA RG 76. The southwest corner of Manitoba at that time was at the intersection of the forty-ninth line of latitude and the ninety-ninth degree of longitude west. This point is only a few miles from present-day Sarles, North Dakota. (Manitoba Act, 1870, 33 Victoria, c. 3 (Canada).

37. Here and the two paragraphs below, U.S. Dept. of State, *Reports upon the Survey of the Boundary*, 37, 40, 285; Cameron to Campbell, 04 April 1874, in Letters Received by the U.S. Commissioner; Campbell to Cameron, 16 April 1874, in Letters Sent by the U.S. Commissioner, both in NB/NARA RG 76; D'Arcy East, report, 04 February 1875, in Interior Department, North American Boundary Records, Record Group 15, Public Archives of Canada; Cameron, final report, 08 February 1876, FO/5, vol. 1532, pp. 173-175. The cairn erected by East's crew has disappeared. The shoreline near its site is reveted by numerous granite rocks, which suggests that at some point the cairn was disassembled by local property owners. (William E. Lass, Tour of Lake of the Woods organized by David G. Malaher, Kenora, Ontario, Canada, 20 July 2010.)

38. Here and below, U.S. Dept. of State, *Reports upon the Survey of the Boundary*, 35, 285-287, 309.

39. Here and below, Carnarvon to undersecretary of state for foreign affairs, 05 September 1874, Laird memorandum, 03 July 1874, report of the Privy Council of Canada, 18 July 1874, all in FO/5, vol. 1506, pp 234-236, 239, 246.

40. Colonial Office to undersecretary of state for foreign affairs, 07 January 1875, Derby to Thornton, 13, 16 January 1875, all in FO/5, vol. 1532, pp. 12, 15-19.

41. Thornton to Derby, 15 February 1875, in FO/5, vol. 1532, p. 137.

42. Cameron to Derby, 10 June 1875, in FO/5, vol. 1532, pp. 173-175.

43. Lyn Harrington, "The Dawson Route," in *Canadian Geographical Journal*, 43 (September, 1951): 136-43.

44. *Historic Fort William: Canada's Diamond Jubilee. 1867-1927*, 10 (Fort William, Ontario: Times-Journal Presses, 1927); Elizabeth Arthur, ed., *Thunder Bay District 1821-1892: A Collection of Documents*, (Toronto: Champlain Society, 1973), 128; Grace Lee Nute, *Rainy River Country: A Brief History of the Region Bordering Minnesota and Ontario*, (St. Paul: Minnesota Historical Society, 1950) 51-56.

45. Here and below, David A. Walker, *Iron Frontier: The Discovery and Early Development of Minnesota's Three Ranges*, (St. Paul,: Minnesota Historical Society Press, 1979), 49-72; *Historic Fort William*, 12; Nute, *Rainy River Country*, 83.

46. Here and below, Nute, *Rainy River Country*, 50-83.

47. *Foreign Relations of the United States, 1895*, 1: 724.

48. Here and below, *Boundary Line Between the United States and Canada*, in 54 Congress, 1 session, House Reports no. 1310, 7, 9, 12-15 (serial 3461)

49. Here and below, *Foreign Relations of the United States, 1895*, 1:724; 54 Congress, 1 session, House Reports, no. 1310, pp. 2, 5, 16.

50. Brabazon, report to King, 01 February 1897, pp. 1, 6-14, in Report on the Minnesota-Ontario Border, 1903, NB/NARG 76.

51. Classen, *Thrust and Counterthrust*, 284-351; *Joint Report upon the Survey and Demarcation of the International Boundary between the United States and Canada along the 141st Meridian from the Arctic Ocean to Mount St. Elias*, 15-109 (Washington, D.C.: Government Printing Office, 1918); *Joint Report upon the Survey and Demarcation of the Boundary between the United States and Canada from the Gulf of Georgia to the Northwesternmost Point of Lake of the Woods*, 34-93 (Washington, D.C.: Government Printing Office, 1937) hereafter cited as IBC, *Report of Boundary from Gulf of Georgia to Lake of the Woods.*

52. Bevans, *Treaties*, 12: 297-310.

53. Here and below, Tittman to Secretary of State William Jennings Bryan, 30 August 1913; E. C. Barnard to Secretary of State Robert Lansing, 14 September 1916, both in State Dept. Decimal File, 1910-1929, file no. 711.42151, items no. 303, 323, NARA RG 59; International Boundary Commission, *Joint Report upon the Survey and Demarcation of the Boundary Between the United States and Canada from the Northwesternmost Points of Lake of the Woods to Lake Superior* (Washington: Government Printing Office, 1931), 32 (Hereafter cited as IBC, *Report of Boundary from the Northwesternmost Point of Lake of the Woods to Lake Superior).*

54. Here and the three paragraphs below, IBC, *Report of Boundary from Gulf of Georgia to Lake of the Woods*, 100-103, 118, 140.

55. IBC, *Report of Boundary from the Northwesternmost Point of Lake of the Woods to Lake Superior.*, 23-24.

56. Here and the three paragraphs below, *Ibid.*, 31-76.

57. Here and the two paragraphs below, *Ibid.*, 88-93, 357-481

58. IBC, *Report of Boundary from Gulf of Georgia to Lake of the Woods*, 156-159; IBC, *Report of Boundary from the Northwesternmost Point of Lake of the Woods to Lake Superior*, 474-479. Appendix V (pp.228-356) of this publication is a listing of the "Geographic Positions and Descriptions of Triangulation and Traverse Stations.

# CHAPTER SIX

## BOUNDARY ADJUSTMENTS AND MAINTENANCE

SINCE THE ADVENT OF STATEHOOD, Minnesota's boundaries have undergone some adjustment and clarification. The northern boundary in Lake of the Woods was changed slightly by the Treaty of 1925 between the United States and Canada. The eastern boundary has been affected by two events—a United States Supreme Court decision about the Minnesota-Wisconsin demarcation in the lower St. Louis River and an agreement by Minnesota, Michigan and Wisconsin to define their shared boundaries in Lake Superior. Because of the meandering Red River, a minor adjustment in the Minnesota-North Dakota boundary was made near Fargo-Moorhead. The state's northern boundary, the only one that is systematically monumented, has been maintained since 1925 by the joint United States-Canada International Boundary Commission.

During the late stages of monumenting from Lake Superior to the northwesternmost point of Lake of the Woods, American commissioner Edward C. Barnard and his Canadian counterpart, James J. McArthur, discussed the need for another treaty to resolve outstanding boundary matters. They were particularly concerned with eliminating the overlapping between the 1783 and 1818 treaty lines in Angle Inlet, superseding Cameron's curved line method on the forty-ninth parallel boundary west of Lake of the Woods and establishing a permanent joint Canada-United States international boundary commission to maintain their Atlantic to Pacific and Alaska boundaries.[1]

In August 1917, Barnard broached the possibility of a new boundary treaty with Secretary of State Robert Lansing, who delayed acting on the matter because of American, Canadian and British pre-occupation with World War I. In 1920, two years after the end of the war's military stage, Barnard reminded the State Department about the unresolved boundary issues. Although the department had asked Barnard to write a treaty draft, it did not act promptly, because of its reluctance to ask Congress to add to the federal bureaucracy by creating a permanent international boundary commission.

By 1925, the State Department was ready to negotiate a boundary treaty with Canada. Its acceptance of the need for the agreement was influenced by John W. Davis, who had served as the American ambassador to Great Britain in the years 1918-1921. In his article "The Unguarded Boundary," Davis reviewed the history of the Canada-United States boundary and emphasized that cooperation, rather than antagonism, dominated its development. To Davis, the genesis of the "unguarded boundary" was the prelude to a new era of American-Canadian goodwill. Davis' emphasis struck exactly the right tone in the post-World War I years. In part because of its substantial participation in the allied cause during World War I, Canada had achieved unprecedented recognition and gratitude from Great Britain. Recognizing that Canada helped save Great Britain, the British government was receptive to the idea that the Dominion of Canada should assume control of its own foreign affairs. Consequently, the British did not object when Canada made its first treaty in 1924. This precedent setting-document with the United States dealt with the suppression of smuggling. Because of it, the way for opened for Canada and the United States to negotiate their first boundary treaty.[2]

The Treaty of 1925 was a landmark in the history of Canada-United States boundary history. It was a tacit acknowledgment that both nations had matured into post-frontier societies in which their shared boundary had reached a new zenith of stability. Therefore, they accepted the premise that henceforth their emphasis should be on the maintenance of an established boundary.

Several articles in the Treaty of 1925 affected the Minnesota-Canada boundary. In order to eliminate the awkward crossing of the 1783 and 1818 lines in Lake of the Woods, the first article moved the northwesternmost point due south for nearly a mile. Because of this shift the United States and Minnesota lost two and a half acres of water area to Canada. The second article specified that the monuments from Lake of the Woods to the crest of the Rockies were to be connected by straight lines. This abandonment of Cameron's slightly curved lines was done to enable future surveyors to locate the exact boundary conveniently. The change involved very little territory. As noted in the treaty, the average distance between the curved and straight lines was only four inches, with the greatest difference being only one and four-fifths feet. The fourth article specified that the joint boundary commissioners authorized by the Treaty of 1908 would be continued and:

> empowered and directed: to inspect the various sections of the boundary line between the United States and the Dominion of Canada and between Alaska and the Dominion of Canada at such times as they shall deem necessary; to repair all damaged monuments and buoys; to relocate and rebuild monuments that have been destroyed; to keep the boundary vistas open; to move boundary markers to new sites and establish such additional monuments and buoys as they shall deem desirable; to maintain at all times an effective boundary line ... and to determine the location of any point of the boundary line which may become necessary in the settlement of any question that may arise between the two governments.[3]

Rainy River at the mouth of Rapid River near Clementson, Minnesota. The Rainy River is the longest river on the Minnesota-Canada boundary. (Photo by William E. Lass)

In dedicating themselves to systematic boundary maintenance under the Treaty of 1925, the United States and Canada made the International Boundary Commission established under the Treaty of 1908 permanent.

The commission observed its centennial with commemorative celebrations in 2008. In June of that year, a plaque was unveiled in the Peace Arch Park at the Blaine, Washington-Pacific Highway crossing. It was inscribed: " 'Maintaining a peaceful boundary for more than a century.'" Furthermore, Michael Wilson, Canada's ambassador to the United States, hosted a reception at the Canadian embassy in Washington, D.C., to recognize Canadian-American cooperation in maintaining their boundaries.[4]

Since 1925, the Canada-Minnesota boundary has not been altered. However, such activities as highway, pipeline and building construction have changed land adjacent to the boundary. These activities, as well as natural phenomena such as deterioration, frost heaves, ice breakups and stream erosion and manmade threats, including snowmobile damage to

Boundary monument 852 near U.S. Highway 59 crossing north of Lancaster, Minnesota. This is an example of the standard markers placed along the 49th parallel and the meridian strip between the Northwest Angle Inlet and Buffalo Bay in Lake of the Woods. (Photo by William E. Lass)

Monument 924 on meridian line just south of Northwest Angle Inlet. Harl A. Dalstrom is on the left and David G. Malaher is on the right. (Photo by William E. Lass, 2010)

monuments, have challenged the International Boundary Commission in fulfilling its mission to maintain a clearly marked visible demarcation.

Along the boundary's land portion, the commission operates on the premise that any given monument must be visible from adjacent monuments. This requirement has entailed placing special monuments at major highway crossings and keeping the vista strip cleared in timbered areas. The vista strip mentioned in the 1925 treaty was an outgrowth of earlier openings cut through forested lands along the Canada-United States boundary. Under the current maintenance system the vista strip must be twenty feet wide at skyline level—ten feet on each side of the boundary. But in many sections, including the meridian line from Angle Inlet to Buffalo Bay and the forty-ninth parallel between Lake of the Woods and the Red River, it is considerably wider. Because it would be virtually impossible to cut a strip precisely twenty feet wide at skyline level, International Boundary Commission maintenance crews routinely cut all trees whose trunks are within ten feet of the boundary. This practice and the use of the vista by maintenance crew vehicles has the effect of creating a lane that is sometimes as much as fifty to sixty feet

Boundary monument 833B at Highway U.S. 75 crossing Emerson, Minnesota. This is typical of the decorative monuments placed at major highway crossings along the 49th parallel. (Photo by William E. Lass)

wide. From certain points in Buffalo Bay of Lake of the Woods, boaters can easily see the north-south and east-west vista strips from miles away.[5]

In timbered areas the vista strip is the boundary's most distinctive feature, which has led some to assume that the strip is the boundary. But the boundary itself is the meeting place of adjacent jurisdictions. Although often called the boundary line, the Canada-United States boundary and all other boundaries do not have the dimension of width. Boundaries, however, do have length and height (as in the air space above them) dimensions.

Keeping vistas open requires periodic maintenance. Many of the trees along the vista strips in northwestern Minnesota are fast-growing aspen. Aspen shoots and brush can obscure sight lines from monument to monument in only a few years after a strip has been cleared.

From 1925 to 1978, the commission informally followed a plan calling for an inspection of all sections on the Canada-United States boundary at least once every ten years. The commissioners shifted to a

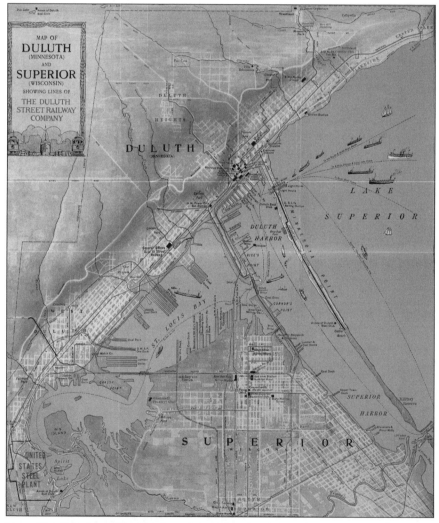

Map of Duluth harbor, 1917. (Courtesy of the University of Minnesota Duluth Library Archives)

more formal maintenance system in 1978 when they adopted a fifteen-year schedule.[6]

Under the current fifteen-year schedule, the American and Canadian commissioners have projected a maintenance schedule through 2019. In 2009, International Boundary Commission crews did some maintenance work on the Ontario-Minnesota between Lake of the Woods and Lake Superior as well as along the forty-ninth parallel boundary west of Lake of the Woods. On the Ontario-Minnesota section they inspected twenty-one monuments and repaired one. The forty-ninth parallel work, which entailed inspecting 775 monuments, repairing seven monuments and clearing seventy-two miles of the vista strip, was carried westward to the continental divide.[7]

During the navigation seasons of 2010, 2011 and 2012, an IBC crew that traveled by canoe and camped along the way continued the maintenance project on the Minnesota-Ontario boundary between Lake of the Woods and Lake Superior. This work entailed inspecting markers, recovering lost monuments and sometimes cleaning and re-painting monuments. In 2013, the IBC plans to clear about fifty-five miles of the vista strip along the forty-ninth west of Lake of the Woods and to restore and repair monuments in the same sector.[8]

Although it has an extensive mission, the joint boundary commission is a relatively small organization. Both the American and Canadian sections are headed by a commissioner and they meet twice a year to plan and coordinate maintenance activities. In 2011, the United States section had eight fulltime employees including the commissioner, deputy commissioner, administrative assistant and three regional field office supervisors. The commissioner is a political appointee, but the deputy commissioner has to be a professional surveyor. In any given year the commission employs ten to twenty-five temporary workers for field work who are hired and supervised by the regional field office directors. The eastern, central and western regional offices, respectively located in Houlton, Maine; Thief River Falls, Minnesota; and Great Falls, Montana, are each headed by an "engineering technician." The two sections continue the practice used in the nineteenth century surveys of equally sharing expenses. For the fiscal year April 1, 2008-March 31, 2009, the American expenditures including compensation for fulltime and temporary staff were $14,127,533.34. The Canadian equivalent in Canadian dollars was $17,237,111.77.[9]

Concerning Minnesota's boundaries with other states, its eastern boundary with Wisconsin and Michigan has been the most contentious. In the twentieth century this boundary was clarified in two sections—Duluth harbor and Lake Superior.

The roots of the Duluth harbor boundary controversy between Minnesota and Wisconsin lay in the vague wording of Wisconsin's Enabling Act. The measure specified that a portion of Wisconsin's northwestern boundary was to run "through the centre of Lake Superior to the mouth of the St. Louis River; thence up the main channel of said river to the first rapids in the same, above the Indian village, according to Nicollet's map; thence due south to the main channel of the River St. Croix. . . ."[10]

Nicollet's map, which showed a well-defined St. Louis River flowing into Lake Superior, made it appear that such a boundary could be easily determined. But drawn on a scale of about twenty miles to an inch, the map did not portray the complicated nature of the lower St. Louis River.[11]

The first systematic survey of the lower St. Louis River where the twin ports of Duluth and Superior, Wisconsin later developed was done in 1861, by Captain George G. Meade of the United States Army's Corps of Topographical Engineers. Approaching the river from Lake Superior, Meade found water entering the lake at the narrow opening between Minnesota Point and Wisconsin Point. From that spot, later designated "The Entry," Superior Bay ran northwestward toward Duluth. About two-thirds of the way to the Duluth shore an opening between Rice's Point on the Minnesota side and Connor's Point on the Wisconsin side led into Lower St. Louis Bay. The bay, which extended southwestward for about three miles to Grassy Point, was approximately a mile and a half wide. From The Entry to the west side of Grassy Point there was no obvious current. The water passage around Grassy Point connected with Upper St. Louis Bay, roughly half the size of the lower bay. In this bay a discernible current ran along the west side of Grassy Point and then close to the Minnesota shore as far as Big Island.

Big Island, in the southwestern end of the upper bay, was an important demarcation. Below it the St. Louis River consisted mainly of three relatively broad bays, which looked more like lakes than a river course. But above Big Island the St. Louis River had the standard river features of a relatively narrow channel, sharply eroded banks and an easily discernible current.

Meade's survey showed the prevailing water depth from The Entry through most the three bays to Big Island was about eight feet, sufficient for the boats used at that time. Some places along the current in the upper bay had as much as ten to fifteen feet.

But during the last three decades of the nineteenth century, as Duluth and Superior were transformed into major ports, the large ships used in Great Lakes commerce required much deeper channels. Congress authorized the dredging of thirteen-foot channels in 1873, and appropriated funds for sixteen-foot channels eight years later. After 1892, when the first Mesabi Iron Range ore was exported from Duluth-Superior, ships needed yet deeper passageways. By 1902, the Duluth-Superior harbor had seventeen miles of shipping channels dredged to twenty feet. This level was increased to twenty-two feet within another two decades. The channel system consisted of two branches through Lower St. Louis Bay, a channel above there around Grassy Point and through the upper bay, and the St. Louis River upstream to Fond du Lac above Big Island.[12]

During the various channelization projects, everyone involved, including officials from Duluth and Superior, evidently assumed that the state boundary line ran through the approximate center of the lower and upper bays. Consequently, until 1910, there was no disagreement about the presumed boundary through the lower St. Louis River.

But in that year the long-standing *status quo* was upset by a decision rendered by the United States Court of Appeals in St. Louis. Ruling on a suit brought by a private party, who contended that Big Island was in Minnesota, the court decided the island was in Wisconsin. The justices concluded that the state boundary followed the long, natural channel around the island's west side rather than the shorter course to its east.[13]

The decision was limited to the Big Island dispute. However, City of Superior officials interpreted it to mean that the state boundary below Big Island followed the center of the river's natural channel. Consequently, they started levying Wisconsin property taxes on the portion of ship docks that had been extended from the Minnesota shore over the newly claimed state boundary.

As calculated by the Superior assessor, 600 to 700 feet of the Zenith Furnace Company's dock in the upper bay was in Wisconsin. Duluth officials maintained that all of the dock was in Minnesota because the boundary ran through the dredged channel near the center of the bay. As a result, from 1910 to 1920, Superior collected property taxes on a portion of the dock and Duluth taxed the entire dock that extended approximately half a mile into the bay. Superior's 1919 collection was $8,500. William Tiedeman, the city's assessor, estimated the total collections on the property over the decade at $40,000 to $50,000.

Objecting to Superior's action, Duluth's dock owners filed a suit in 1916, with the intention of carrying the controversy to the United States Supreme Court. Acting on a request from two Duluth attorneys, Lyndon A. Smith, Minnesota's attorney general, agreed to pursue the case in the name of the State of Minnesota versus the State of Wisconsin.

The heart of Minnesota's suit was about the boundary through Upper St. Louis Bay. Minnesota contended that the demarcation was in the exact middle of the bay but Wisconsin insisted the dividing line followed the sinuous course near the Minnesota shore. In such places, a line crossed and re-crossed the border claimed by Minnesota and intersected some docks built out from the Minnesota shore. While refusing to accept Minnesota's middle line principle in the lower bay, Wisconsin's preference was not greatly different. The two parties did not extend their disagreement to Superior Bay, because it was a moot issue for navigation purposes. In 1871, the City of Duluth completed dredging a ship canal through the northwestern end of Minnesota Point. After that, commerce flowed through the canal and across Superior Bay to the passage between Rice's Point and Connor's Point. To support its preferred upper bay boundary, Minnesota claimed the St. Louis River ended at the point where it entered Upper St. Louis Bay. Wisconsin maintained that the stream ran all the way to its juncture with Lake Superior at The Entry.[14]

In September 1916, the Supreme Court agreed to hear the case. Over the course of eight months a court-appointed commissioner obtained testimony from many persons, including ship captains, geographers, historians and old settlers.[15]

The case of *State of Minnesota v. State of Wisconsin* was argued before the justices on October 16-17, 1919. The court's decision was read by Justice James C. McReynolds on March 8, 1920.[16]

Although the court did not literally accept Minnesota's claimed boundary in the upper bay, Minnesota and Duluth were pleased with the outcome. Rejecting Wisconsin's claim that the boundary followed the "narrow winding channel near the Minnesota shore," the court held the line should be the "shorter and more direct course westward to the deeper channel, about seven-eighths of a mile northeast of Big Island." Wisconsin salvaged a bit of pride when the court also ruled that the St. Louis River extended through the three lake-like bays all the way to the Entry.

Most of the court's decision was an explanation of its rationale for deciding on a boundary quite close to Minnesota's preference through the upper and lower bays. The court's guiding principle was that the boundary had to be determined on the prevailing conditions of 1846, when Congress approved the Wisconsin Enabling Act. Meade's Chart, the justices held, was the first accurate portrayal of the 1846 water levels. The court found no evidence that the lower St. Louis River had been changed from 1846 to 1861.

With specific reference to Lower St. Louis Bay, the justices concluded that since the advent of commerce, vessels regularly plied along an approximate mid-water line. In the upper bay, ships followed a direct course from south of Grassy Point to near Big Island rather than the winding channel. The court observed that "for many years officers and representatives" of both states "regarded the boundary as on or near" the middle of both bays.

As the court explained, its ruling in favor of a boundary adhering to the traditional commercial route was in keeping with a modification of the well-established precedent of thalweg. Literally, thalweg, which originated in European common law, meant a line connecting the deepest points of a river. But as McReynolds noted, the strict application of thalweg to the Duluth harbor would deprive Minnesota of equal navigation rights because such a line would follow the narrow, winding channel close to the Minnesota shore in the upper bay. Observing that "deepest water and the principal navigation channel are not necessarily the same," McReynolds opined that the boundary should be along the middle of the main navigation channel through the lower and upper bay. The court cited several cases involving river boundary disputes between states where it had established the precedent that thalweg was the center of the principal navigation channel "as opposed to the physical middle line."[17]

The court's opinion made it clear that thalweg applied only to navigable portions of waterways. Citing a previous Supreme Court case involving Louisiana and Mississippi, the justices observed that the boundary separating states in waters that lacked a navigation track had to be a midway line.

In concluding its opinion the court announced that:

> A decree will be entered, declaring and adjudging as follows: That the boundary line between the two states must be ascertained upon a consideration of the situation existing in 1846 and accurately disclosed by the Meade Chart. That when traced on this chart the boundary runs midway between Rice's Point and Connor's Point, and through the middle of Lower St. Louis Bay to and with the deep channel leading into Upper St. Louis Bay, and to a point therein immediately south of Grassy Point; thence westward along the most direct course, through water not less than 8 feet deep, eastward of Fisherman's Island and as indicated by the red trace 'A, B, C,' on Minnesota's Exhibit No. 1, approximately one mile, to the deep channel and immediately west of the bar therein; thence with such channel north and west of Big Island up stream [sic] to the falls.

The court included these specifications verbatim in its decree issued on October 11, 1920. The order also designated a three-man commission consisting of Samuel S. Gannett of Washington, D.C., William B. Patton of Duluth and John G. D. Mack of Madison, Wisconsin, to survey and mark the boundary. The commissioners were to "proceed with all convenient dispatch to discharge their duties" and to submit their final report no later than May 1, 1921.[18]

At their first meeting, held in Duluth on October 29, 1920, the commissioners elected Gannett chairman of the survey project. During the period until the field work was started in early January 1921, Gannett, Mack and Patton developed a plan. This involved drawing the court-dictated boundary on a tracing of the Meade map. To establish appropriate reference points for this water line the commissioners decided to use on-shore triangulation points previously located and marked by army engineers. They also decided that their first reference point, designated "Station No. 0," would be fixed midway between Rice's Point and Connor's Point. This station point proved to be the center of the pivot point on the "Inter-State Bridge" connecting Rice's and Conner's points. From Station 0 to the start of the meridian line they decided to mark the boundary in a series of straight line courses. In the unnavigable section above the village of Fond du Lac the boundary line was to be the river's center line.[19]

During this preliminary stage the commissioners organized their eleven-man survey crew, which consisted of three consulting engineers, a transit man, two chainmen, three rodmen and two draftsmen. These men worked for about two and a half months before completing the survey on March 19, 1921. The commissioners decided to conduct the work in the winter with the expectation that working on the ice would expedite the survey but the project was prolonged because the winter was mild and fragile ice oftentimes made the tasks dangerous and difficult.[20]

The survey resulted in the establishment of eighty-five stations from Station Nos. 0 to 84 at the upper end of the line in the St. Louis River. The surveyors connected the stations with eighty-four straight line courses on the eighteen and two-fifths-mile boundary. The length of the courses ranged from 206.38 to 6,452.20 feet. The longest segments were in Lower St. Louis Bay, where the boundary was an approximate center line and the shortest were in the most sinuous part of the river above Big Island. With two exceptions, the boundary was a water line. When the surveyors calculated the courses through the upper bay they found that the court-ordered boundary, which had to adhere to the conditions existing in 1846, ran across portions of two docks. The effect of these determinations was to place about twenty acres total at the ends of the docks that had been built out from the Minnesota shore in Wisconsin. The commissioners also reported the azimuths and distances from stations to on-shore triangulation points.[21]

The second phase of the survey, which consisted of monumenting the boundary at approximately three dozen triangulation and reference points, was done from late April to late June of 1921. The surveyors wanted to start earlier but had to wait for the ground to thaw completely. The commissioners found that most of the triangulation points originally established by army engineers had each been marked with iron pipes two inches in diameter and four feet tall. Each of these was capped by a bronze tablet inscribed "Corps of Engineers, U.S. Army. Do not move without authority of the United States Engineer Office, Duluth, Minn." After obtaining consent, the surveyors removed these pipes and replaced them with more substantial concrete monuments.[22]

The standard monuments each weighed about two tons. The four-foot high underground portion was four feet square at its base and tapered to two feet square at ground level. The above-ground portion was a post two feet tall and fifteen inches square capped by a sloping flat-topped piece four inches high. The below-ground part of each monument was reinforced with five iron rods.

Each of the standard monuments was marked in two ways. The tablet removed from the army engineers' triangulation markers was cemented in the top. On the side facing the boundary the commissioners cemented in a bronze tablet three and nine-tenths inches in diameter. It was inscribed: "Minnesota-Wisconsin Boundary Line. 250 Dollars

Fine for Disturbing This Point. Set in 1921 Under Orders of he Supreme Court of the United States. Reference Point No. __."

Generally, the monuments were set only at sites such as those on Big Island and the St. Louis River banks above, where they would not obstruct traffic. Where the triangulation points were located on public streets or docks, the surveyors erected modified monuments with tops at ground level. Each of these monuments was identified by a Corps of Engineers bronze tablet cemented in the concrete floor.

In their final report filed with the clerk of the Supreme Court on August 5, 1921, the commissioners showed the total cost of surveying and marking the boundary was $15,626.06, which was shared equally by Minnesota and Wisconsin.[23]

The boundary through the lower St. Louis River did not become official until the Supreme Court issued its final decree on February 27, 1922. After they received copies of the survey report, the states of Minnesota and Wisconsin approved the boundary as determined by the commissioners. Both states then requested a final decree from the Supreme Court. Most of the decree was a résumé of the commissioners' report but it also included the information that the states had to equally bear the $2,790 cost of printing the case record and commissioners' report.[24]

Unlike the Minnesota-Wisconsin boundary in the lower St. Louis River, the Minnesota-Wisconsin and Minnesota-Michigan boundaries in Lake Superior were resolved without litigation by a 1947 tri-state compact. The Lake Superior boundaries originated in the enabling acts of the three states. When it became a state in 1837, Michigan was assigned the single largest portion of Lake Superior. A portion of its northernmost boundary followed the international demarcation, which generally angled northwestward from the lake's southeastern tip to the "point where the said line last touches Lake Superior." From that location the prescribed boundary was southwestward "thence in a direct line through Lake Superior, to the mouth of the Montreal river [sic]." In 1848, when Wisconsin was admitted to statehood, its boundary in Lake Superior started at the mouth of the main channel of the Montreal River. From there it ran "to the middle" of the lake, which became the starting point for a line "through the centre [sic] of Lake Superior to the mouth of the St. Louis River." Ten years later when Minnesota was added as the thirty-second state its northeastern boundary, as specified in its 1857 enabling act, ran down the St. Louis River "to and through Lake Superior, on the boundary line of Wisconsin and Michigan, until it intersects the dividing line between the United States and the British possessions; then up Pigeon River. . . ."[25]

Traditionally, the state boundaries in Lake Superior were not shown on maps, which left the impression that the states ended at the lake shore. Thus, Minnesota's northeastern part between Ontario and the lake became popularly identified as the Arrowhead. However, beginning in 1906, three federal agencies—the Census Bureau, Geological Survey and Land Office in the Interior Department—cooperatively calculated the approximate Lake Superior area of each state, but did not include them in the official state area calculations. At that time any area determinations had to be made by interpreting the rather imprecise specifications of the enabling acts.[26]

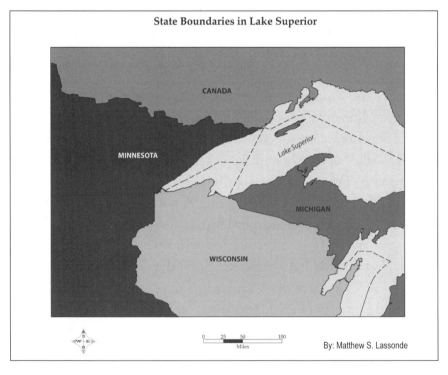

**State Boundaries in Lake Superior**

By: Matthew S. Lassonde

The need to identify specific boundaries in Lake Superior arose out of two Supreme Court cases about a boundary dispute between Michigan and Wisconsin. The cases (1923-26 and 1932-36) involved the boundary from the mouth of the Montreal River to the center of Lake Michigan. Finally, in 1936, the Supreme Court decided on the course of the line, whose eastern end was the middle of Lake Michigan, a point specified in Michigan's enabling act.[27]

After this decision Michigan and Wisconsin officials were prompted to define their boundary line through the middle of Lake Michigan as well as their demarcation in Lake Superior. Because Minnesota bordered both Michigan and Wisconsin in Lake Superior it was included in the 1947 compact.

The second section of the compact dealt with the Minnesota-Michigan and Minnesota-Wisconsin boundaries in Lake Superior. With respect to the Minnesota-Michigan line, officials recognized that the boundary specified in Michigan's enabling act was an impossibility, because it was to run through the lake from the mouth of the Pigeon River to the mouth of the Montreal River. With imperfect geographic information in 1837, Congress assumed the two river points could be connected by an all-water line. But officials in 1947 knew the Pigeon River flowed into Pigeon Bay. On the bay's south side Pigeon Point, a very narrow peninsula, jutted out eastwardly about four miles into Lake Superior. Thus a direct line running from the mouth of the Pigeon River to the mouth of the Montreal River could not have been entirely in the lake. Consequently, the compact adjusted Michigan's northwesternmost terminus to "the point where a line drawn through the most easterly point of Pigeon Point and the most southerly point of Pine Point intersects the international boundary." Once that site had been established it was possible to draw a direct water line to it from the point where the Michigan-Wisconsin boundary line "through the middle of the main channel of the Montreal River enters Lake Superior." As specified in the compact, the length of Michigan's western boundary in Lake Superior was 108.86 miles.[28]

The parties to the compact furthermore agreed that the middle of the lake stipulation in Wisconsin's enabling act meant the midpoint of the 108.86 mile boundary, which Michigan shared equally with Minnesota to the northeast and Wisconsin to the southwest. This midpoint, designated Point A in the compact, marked the beginning of the Minnesota-Wisconsin boundary that was to run through the center of the lake to the St. Louis River. Its coordinates were 47° 17' 30" north latitude and 89° 57' 00" west longitude.

The compact's framers decided the most practical way of establishing a line through the center of this portion of the lake was to draw a series of three straight line courses whose turning points B and C and terminal Point D would be equidistant from specified points on the Minnesota and Wisconsin shores. The respective distances of lines A-B, B-C and C-D were 33.15 , 49.60 and 26.43 miles. Point B at 47° 18' 35" north latitude and 90° 39' 15" west longitude was equidistant on a direct line from "the mouth of Cross River, Minnesota and the Lighthouse [sic] on Outer Island in Wisconsin." Point C, with coordinates of 46° 54' 10" and 91° 31' 25" was the midpoint on a direct line from the lighthouse "on shore at Two Harbors, Minnesota and the light at the lakeward end of the government east pier at Port Wing, Wisconsin." Point D at 46° 42' 39.875" and 92° 00' 24.571 was "the midpoint in a direct line at right angles to the central axis of the Superior entry between the tops of the eastern ends of the pierheads at the lakeward ends of the United States government breakwaters at the Superior entry to Duluth Superior [sic] harbor."

The compact provided that it was to become operative immediately upon ratification by the respective states legislatures. Minnesota acted first, with its legislature approving the compact on April 26, 1947. By the end of June, the Wisconsin and Michigan legislatures ratified the boundary settlement. On June 30, 1948, Congress by a joint resolution consented to the compact.[29]

After the compact it became possible to determine the precise areas of Minnesota, Michigan and Wisconsin in Lake Superior. In the 1990 census, the Census Bureau recalculated the area of all states. The greatest changes were in the Great Lakes states and those along oceans where their bordering water areas were included as part of their official areas. In Minnesota's case its area of 86,943 square miles included 2,546 in Lake Superior.[30]

Since the 1990 Census Bureau's decision, there has been an increasing awareness of Minnesota's boundary with Michigan and Wisconsin in Lake Superior. Consequently, some recent maps have shown the correct location of Minnesota's northeastern boundary.

Compared to its northern and eastern boundaries, Minnesota's western and southern boundaries have been of scant concern since statehood. However, two minor changes were made in the Fargo-Moorhead section of the Minnesota-North Dakota boundary in 1961. A United States Army Corps of Engineers flood control project resulted in the re-routing of the Red River, which left some 22.54 acres of land that had been in Minnesota on the North Dakota side of the

Tri-State Marker at the junction of Minnesota, Iowa, and South Dakota (looking north). (Photo by William E. Lass)

The refurbished Lee Monument, New Albin, Iowa (looking northwesterly into Minnesota). (Photo by William E. Lass)

Lee Monument Marker. (Photo by William E. Lass)

river. Rather than perpetuate this awkward situation, Minnesota and North Dakota agreed the tracts should be transferred from Clay County, Minnesota to Cass County, North Dakota.[31]

Since the transfers changed the boundaries specified in the enabling acts of the two states, Congress had to agree to the changes. On August 25, 1961, Congress granted its consent to the agreement that had been approved by the North Dakota legislature on February 4, 1961, and the Minnesota legislature on April 10, 1961.

The only monumenting of Minnesota's western boundary was done by Snow and Hutton in 1859. The mounds they erected on the meridian line from the outlet of Big Stone Lake to Iowa's northern boundary were obliterated by such things as water and wind erosion, cultivation and road construction. But the only monuments the United States General Land Office ever assumed would be permanent were the iron posts the surveyors placed at the head of Lake Traverse, the head and foot of Big Stone Lake, and the point where the meridian line intersected Iowa's northern boundary. Of these, the one at the juncture of the meridian line and 43° 30" north latitude has been the most enduring. Because it marks the spot where Minnesota, Iowa and South Dakota meet, it is now locally identified as the "Tri-State Marker."

The marker has had a rather remarkable history. In the early twentieth century it was removed after partial destruction by vandals. In 1938, it was repaired and reset by the adjacent counties at the original site, under direction of the Department of the Interior. It was broken from its base by vehicle traffic in 1979. But the next year the county governments and historical societies of Lyon County, Iowa, Rock County, Minnesota and Minnehaha County, South Dakota restored and relocated it. When it was dedicated at a ceremony held on October 26, 1980, its restorers were concerned that its location at the northwest corner of a road junction would probably result in more vehicle damage. Consequently, the post was placed fifteen feet west-northwest of the actual spot where the meridian line meets Iowa's northern boundary. The point determined by Snow and Hutton in 1859 is marked by a small tablet flush with the ground.[32]

In 1964, Will G. Robinson, superintendent of the South Dakota State Historical Society, attempted to locate the iron monuments Snow and Hutton placed at Lake Traverse and Big Stone Lake. He reported that the two at the ends of Big Stone Lake "are not to be found now." With respect to the Lake Traverse monument, he found that it was essentially obscured by road construction. After the highway connecting Browns Valley, Minnesota, and Sisseton, South Dakota, was graded, the monument was left at the side of the road about eight feet below grade level. An effort to preserve the monument was made by enclosing it in a section of vertical culvert topped by a manhole. Robinson found that after removing the cover, the top six inches of the post was visible. The monument was mostly buried by gravel and debris.[33]

The Lee monument at the north edge of New Albin, Iowa, is the only remaining marker of the Iowa-Minnesota boundary survey. As such it is of considerable local interest. It stands in a small well-maintained park and has been refurbished by the Allamakee County, Iowa Historical Society.[34]

The Lee monument, the tri-state marker and the hundreds of monuments defining the Minnesota-Canada boundary serve as reminders of the age when the North Star State was shaped.

## NOTES:

1. Here and below, Barnard to Lansing, August 10, 14, 1917, January 5, 1920; memorandum on "Boundary between the United States and Canada east of the summit of the Rocky Mountains," November 9, 1917;memorandum on "Demarcation of boundary," November 12, 1920—all in State Dept. Decimal File, 1910-1929, file no. 711.42151, items no. 324, 333, file no. 711.42152 items no. 70, NARA, RG 59.
2. William H. Harbaugh, "Davis, John William," *American National Biography*, 6: 209-10 (New York: Oxford University Press, 1991); John W. Davis, "The Unguarded Boundary," *Geographical Review* 12 (1922): 585-601.
3. Here and the paragraph below, Bevans, *Treaties*, 6: 12 (Washington, D. C., 1971).

4. International Boundary Commission, *Annual Joint Report, 2008*, 6.

5. Here and the paragraph below, Peter Sullivan, David Bernhardt and Brian Ballantyne, "The Canada-United States Boundary: The Next Century"; William E. Lass, Tour of Lake of the Woods organized by David G. Malaher, Kenora, Ontario, Canada, 19-21 July 2010.

6. International Boundary Commission, *Annual Joint Report, 1978*, 24.

7. IBC, *Annual Joint Report, 2009*, 8.Accessed 15 December 2010.

8. IBC, *Annual Joint Report, 2010*, 6; Kyle K. Hipsley, acting commissioner, U.S. Section, IBC, email message to William E. Lass, 13 March 2013.

9. Author's telephone interview with Kyle K. Hipsley, deputy commissioner, United States Section, 06 January 2011; IBC, *Annual Joint Report, 2009*, 11.

10. *U.S. Statutes at Large*, 9:56.

11. Here and the three paragraphs below, "STATE OF MINNSEOTA v. STATE OF WISCONSIN," *Supreme Court Reporter* (1921), vol. 40, pp. 315, 318.

12. "History of the Lower St. Louis River," online source accessed 16 March 2013; *Supreme Court Reporter*, 40: 318.

13. Here and the three paragraphs below, "State Retains Three Miles of Dock Frontage," *Duluth News-Tribune*, March 9, 1920, p.1.

14. *Supreme Court Reporter*, 40: 314, Holmquist and Brookins, *Major Historic Sites*, 167-69.

15. *Duluth News-Tribune*, Maarch 9, 1920, p. 4.

16. Here and the three paragraphs below, *Supreme Court Reporter*, 40: 313-15.

17. Here and the two paragraphs below, *Ibid.* , 318-19.

18. *Supreme Court Reporter* (1922), vol. 41 p. 10.

19. "Report of Commissioners Appointed to Run, Locate and Designate Boundary Line between the States of Minnesota and Wisconsin, August 5, 1921, in Supreme Court of the United States Records, Federal Judicial Records, NARA, RG 267, Box 162, pp. 2-5. Hereafter cited as "Report of Commissioners."; "Tracing of Parts of Original Map of St. Louis Bay and St. Louis River Made under Direction of Capt. George G. Meade T. E. Showing Boundary Line between Minnesota and Wisconsin," Exhibit No. 01, *Minnesota v. Wisconsin*, Supreme Court of the United States, October Term 1920, RG 267, in Cartographic Section, NARA.

20. "Report of Commissioners," 5-6. 31-32.

21. *Ibid.*, 6-11; "Map Showing Boundary Line between Minnesota and Wisconsin through St. Louis Bay and up St. Louis River to Falls," Exhibit No.. 02, *Minnesota v. Wisconsin*, Supreme Court of the United States, October Term 1920, RG 267, in Cartographic Section, NARA.

22. Here and the three paragraphs below, "Report of Commissioners," 12-30; Map showing boundary line, Exhibit No. 02.

23. "Report of Commissioners," 44-46; The estimated 2012 worth of one 1921 dollar is $12.83. "Consumer Price Index (Estimate) 1800-."

24. *Supreme Court Reporter* (1923), vol. 42, pp. 591-93; "Decree Sought in St. Louis Bay Boundary," *Duluth News-Tribune,* 29 January 1922, p. 2.

25. *U.S. Statutes at Large,* 5:49 (1837); 9:56 (1848) and 11: 166 (1857).

26. William E. Lass, "Enlarging Minnesota," *Minnesota History* 61 (Fall 2009): 308.

27. *Ibid.,* 309, 311; *Wisconsin v. Michigan,* 297 U. S. 547 (1936).

28. Here and the two paragraphs below, Copy of compact, Minnesota, *Session Laws, 1947,* ch. 589.

29. *U.S. Statutes at Large,* 62, pt. 1, pp. 1152-55

30. Lass, "Enlarging Minnesota," 310.

31. Here and the paragraph below, Minnesota, *Session Laws 1961,* ch. 236; *U.S. Statutes at Large,* vol. 75, p. 399. (The two tracts were described in the Minnesota law as: "That portion of Government Lot 2 in the northeast quarter (NE ¼) of Section 29, Township 140 North, Range 48 West of the Fifth Principal Meridian, Clay County, Minnesota, bounded by the thread of the Red River of the North, as it existed prior to January 1, 1959, and the new thread of the Red River of the North as established by the United States Army Corps of Engineers . . . containing 9.78 acres more or less; and that portion of Government Lot 2 in the northeast quarter (NE ¼) of Section 7, Township 139 North, Range 48 West of the Fifth Principal Meridian, Clay County, Minnesota, bounded by the thread of the Red River of the North as it existed prior to January 1, 1959, and the new thread of the Red River of the North as established by the United States Army Corps of Engineers . . . containing 12.76 acres more or less.")

32. Inscription on tri-state marker, inspected by William E. Lass, 29 June 2009.

33. Will G. Robinson "South Dakota Boundaries," *South Dakota Historical Society Collections,* vol. 32 (Pierre, 1964), 259.

34. Lass inspection, 03 November 2009.

# BIBLIOGRAPHY

---

## ARCHIVAL AND MANUSCRIPT SOURCES

Brown, Joseph R. and Samuel J. Brown. Papers. Minnesota Historical Society.

Canada. Interior Department. North American Boundary Records. Record Group 15, Public Archives of Canada, Ottawa.

Folsom, W.H.C. and family. Papers, 1836-1944. Minnesota Historical Society.

Great Britain. Foreign Office Records, series 5, vols. 54, 187, 200, 215,, 378, 380, 1475, 1476, 1505, 1506. 1532, 1667, 1670 Microfilm copy in Public Archives of Canada, Ottawa. Originals in Public Record Office, London.

Porter, Peter B. Papers. Originals and microfilm copy owned by Buffalo and Erie County Historical Society, Buffalo, New York.

Rapp, Burleigh Keith. "The Life of George R. Stuntz." Minnesota Historical Society.

St. Peter Company, Records. Copy in Nicollet County Historical Society, St. Peter. Originals in Minnesota Historical Society.

Schneider, Harley R. Research File on Minnesota Surveys. Minnesota Historical Society.

Sibley, Henry Hastings. Papers, 1815-1891. Microfilm copy in Memorial Library, Minnesota State University, Mankato. Originals in Minnesota Historical Society.

Stuntz, George. Papers. Northeast Minnesota Historical Center, University of Minnesota, Duluth.

Thompson, David. Papers. Minnesota Historical Society, St. Paul.

Tweedy, John Hubbard. Papers. State Historical Society of Wisconsin. Madison.

U.S. National Archives and Records Service. "Territorial Papers of the United States Senate, 1789-1873." Microfilm roll 14.

U.S. Northern Boundary, Records Relating to International Boundaries, Record Group 76. National Archives and Records Administration (NARA). Washington, D.C.

_____. Letters Received, 1859-60. Minnesota Historical Society.

U.S. Office of the Surveyor General of Minnesota. Letters Sent, 1859-60.

U.S. Supreme Court Records. Record Group 267, NARA.

U.S. State Department. Decimal File, 1910-1929. Record Group 59, NARA.

Wippermann, Frederic. Field Notes. Case F, Entry 60. Record Group 49, Cartographic Section, NARA.

## GOVERNMENT DOCUMENTS

*American State Papers: Foreign Relations*, vols. 2, 3, 4.

Canada. *Manitoba Act, 1870.* 33 Victoria, c. 3.

*Congressional Globe,* 1842, 1845-48, 1856-57.

International Boundary Commission. *Annual Joint Report,* 1978, 2008, 2009, 2010.

_____. *Joint Report upon the Survey and Demarcation of the Boundary Between the United States and Canada Along the 141st Meridian from the Arctic Ocean to Mount St. Elias.* Washington: Government Printing Office, 1918.

_____. *Joint Report upon the Survey and Demarcation of the Boundary Between the United States and Canada from the Gulf of Georgia to the Northwesternmost Point of Lake of the Woods.* Washington: Government Printing Office, 1937.

_____. *Joint Report upon the Survey and Demarcation of the Boundary Between the United States and Canada from the Northwesternmost Point of Lake of the Woods to Lake Superior.* Washington: Government Printing Office, 1931.

Minnesota Attorney General, *Opinion of the Attorney General on the Bill for the Removal of the Seat of Government,* February 16, 1857.

Minnesota. *Session Laws,* 1947, 1961.

Minnesota Territory. *Council Journal,* 1849, 1856-57.

*Papers Relating to the Foreign Relations of the United States, 1870, 1895.* Washington: Government Printing Office, 1870, 1895.

United Kingdom. *The British North America Act, 1867.* 30-31 Victoria, c. 3.

_____. *Rupert's Land Act, 1868.* 31-32 Victoria, c. 105.

U.S. Congress. House. *Boundary Line Between the United States and Canada.* 54 Cong., 1 sess. House Reports 310. Serial 3461.

_____. *Iowa's Northern Boundary.* 32 Cong., 1 sess. House Ex. Doc. 66. Serial 641.

_____. Nicollet, Joseph Nicholas. *Report Intended to Illustrate a Map of the Hydrographical Basin of the Upper Mississippi River.* 28 Cong., 2 sess. House Doc. 52. Serial 464.

_____. *Report of Major Wood, relative to his expedition to Pembina Settlement, and the condition of affairs on the North-Western frontier of the Territory of Minnesota.* 31 Cong., 1 sess. House Ex. Doc. 51. Serial 577.

U.S. Congress. Senate. *Documents from State Department.* 27th Cong., 3 sess. Sen. Doc. 1, Serial Set 413.

_____. *Memorial of Citizens of the United States Residing within the Limits of the Territory of Minnisota* [sic] . . . 30 Cong., 1 sess., Sen. Misc. Doc. 98. Serial Set 511.

*Report of the Secretary of the Interior Relative to Iowa's Northern Boundary Survey,* December 27.1953. 33 Cong., 1 sess. Senate Ex. Doc. 10. Serial Set 694.

U.S. Department of State. *Reports upon the Survey of the Boundary between the Territory of the United States and the Possessions of Great Britain from the Lake of the Woods to the Summit of the Rocky Mountains.* Washington, D. C., 1878.

*U.S. Statutes at Large,* vols. 3, 5, 9-11, 17, 62, 75.

U.S. *Supreme Court Reporter,* vols. 40, 41, 42.

*Wisconsin v. Michigan,* 297 U. S. 547 (1936).

NEWSPAPERS

*Daily Minnesotian* (St. Paul).1857.

*Duluth News-Tribune,* 1920, 1922.

*Henderson Democrat*, 1857.
*Madison Express* (Wisconsin Territory), 1846.
*Pioneer and Democrat* (St. Paul), 1856-57.
*St. Peter Courier*, 1856-57.
*Winona Argus*, 1857.
*Winona Republican*, 1856-57.
*Wisconsin Herald* (Lancaster), 1848.


ARTICLES AND CHAPTERS


Anderson, S[amuel]. "The North-American Boundary from the Lake of the Woods to the Rocky Mountains." *Journal of the Royal Geographical Society* 46 (1877): 228-62.

Babcock, Charles F. "Rails West: The Rock Island Excursion of 1854 as Reported by Charles F. Babcock." *Minnesota History* 34 (Winter 1954): 133-43.

Babcock, Willoughby M. "With Ramsey to Pembina: A Treaty-Making Trip in 1851." *Minnesota History* 38 (March 1962): 1-10.

Baldwin, J.R. "The Webster-Ashburton Settlement." *Canadian Historical Association Report, 1938.* (Toronto, 1938): 121-33.

Barrows, Harold K. "Whistler, George Washington." *Dictionary of American Biography.* New York: Charles Scribner's Sons, 1936.

Baxter, Maurice G. "Webster, Daniel." *American National Biography.* New York: Oxford University Press, 1999.

Belcourt, G.A. "Department of Hudson's Bay." *Collections of the Minnesota Historical Society,* vol. 1. (St. Paul, 1872): 207-44.

Bemis, Samuel Flagg. "Jay's Treaty and the Northwest Boundary Gap." *American Historical Review* 27 (April 1922): 465-84.

Blegen, Theodore C. "A Plan for the Union of British North America and the United States, 1866." *Mississippi Valley Historical Review* 4 (March 1918): 470-83.

Courtney, William Prideaux. "Baring, Alexander." *Dictionary of National Biography,* vol. 1. Reprint ed. London: Oxford University Press, 1921.

Davis, John W. "The Unguarded Boundary." *Geographical Review* 12 (1922); 585-601.

"Ferguson, James." *Appleton's Cyclopedia of American Biography.* New York: D. Appleton, 1888.

Folsom, William H. C. "History of Lumbering in the St. Croix Valley, with Biographic Sketches." *Collections of the Minnesota Historical Society,* vol. 9. (St. Paul, 1901): 291-324.

Fredriksen, John C. "Porter, Peter Buell." *American National Biography.* New York: Oxford University Press, 1999.

Gilfillan, Charles D. "The Early Political History of Minnesota." *Collections of the Minnesota Historical Society,* vol. 9. (St. Paul, 1901): 167-80.

Hansen, Stephen L. "Shields, James." *American National Biography.* New York: Oxford University Press, 1999.

Harbaugh, William H. "David, John William." *American National Biography.* New York: Oxford University Press, 1999.

Harrington, Lyn. "The Dawson Route." *Canadian Geographical Journal* 43 (September 1951): 136-43.

Heilbron, Bertha L., ed. "By Rail and River to Minnesota in 1854." *Minnesota History* 25 (June 1944): 103-16.

Jefferson, Thomas. "The Limits and Bounds of Louisiana." *Documents Relating to the Purchase & Exploration of Louisiana.* Boston: Houghton Mifflin, 1904.

"John Mitchell's Map of the British and French Dominions in America, compiled and edited by Walter W. Ristow from various published works of Lawrence Martin." Ristow, Walter W. , comp. *Ala Carte: Selected Papers on Maps and Atlases.* Washington: Library of Congress, 1972.

Jones, Wilbur D. "Lord Ashburton and the Maine Boundary Negotiations." *Mississippi Valley Historical Review* 40 (December 1953): 477-90.

Kilpatrick, Mrs. Andrew E. "William Holcombe." *Collections of the Minnesota Historical Society,* vol. 10, pt. 2 (St. Paul, 1905): 857-61.

Knauth, Otto. "Reporter Tells Story of Iowa-Minnesota Boundary Survey." *DisClosures* (Fall 1989; Winter 1990): 16-19, 34-36.

Krueger, William R. "Parvin, Theodore Sutton." *The Biographical Dictionary of Iowa.* Edited by David Hudson, Marvin Bergman and Loren Horton. Iowa City: University of Iowa Press, 2008.

Larson, Edward J. "Mitchell, John." *American National Biography.* New York: Oxford University Press, 1999.

Lass, William E. "The Birth of Minnesota." *Minnesota History* 55 (Summer 1997): 267-79.

_____. "Enlarging Minnesota." *Minnesota History* 61 (Fall 2009): 306-11.

_____. "The First Attempt to Organize Dakota Territory." William L. Lang, ed. *Centennial West: Essays on the Northern Tier States.* Seattle: University of Washington Press, 1991.

_____. "How the Forty-Ninth Parallel Became the International Boundary." *Minnesota History* 44 (Summer 1975): 209-19.

_____. "Minnesota's Separation from Wisconsin: Boundary Making on the Upper Mississippi Frontier." *Minnesota History* 50 (Winter 1987): 309-20.

Le Duc, Thomas. "The Maine Frontier and the Northeastern Boundary Controversy." *American Historical Review* 53 (October 1947): 30-41.

Marshall, William R. "Reminiscences of Wisconsin—1842 to 1848." *Magazine of Western History* 7 (January 1888).

Parker, Donald Dean. "Surveying the South Dakota-Minnesota Boundary Line." *South Dakota Historical Collections,* vol. 32. (Pierre, 1964): 236-45.

Pratt, Joseph Hyde. "American Prime Meridians." *Geographical Review* 32 (April 1932): 233-44.

Randak, Leigh Ann. "Lucas, Robert." *The Biographical Dictionary of Iowa.* Edited by David Hudson, Marvin Bergman and Loren Horton. Iowa City: University of Iowa Press, 2008.

Reynolds, Terry S. and Barry C. James. "Burt, William Austin." *American National Biography.* New York: Oxford University Press, 1999.

Rife, Clarence W. "Norman W. Kittson: A Fur Trader at Pembina." *Minnesota History* 6 (September 1925): 225-52.

Robinson, Will G. "South Dakota Boundaries." *South Dakota Historical Collections,* vol. 32 (Pierre, 1964): 232-35, 245-59.

Rohrbough, Malcolm J. "Lucas, Robert." *American National Biography.* New York:

Oxford University Press, 1999.

Sanborn, Ruth E. "The United States and the British Northwest, 1865-1870." *North Dakota Historical Quarterly* 6 (October 1931): 5-41.

Smith, Alice E. "Caleb Cushing's Investments in the St. Croix Valley." *Wisconsin Magazine of History* 28 (September 1944): 7-19.

"Survey of the Iowa-Minnesota Boundary Line." *Annals of Iowa* 16 (January 1929): 483-503.

"Talcott, Andrew." *Appleton's Cyclopedia of American Biography.* New York: D. Appleton, 1889.

"Thompson, David." *Dictionary of Canadian Biography Online.* Accessed 10 December 2010.

Tiarks, J[ohann] L. "N. W. Point of Lake of the Woods." *American Journal of Science and the Arts (Silliman's Journal).* 1829.

Thwaites, Reuben G. "The Boundaries of Wisconsin." *Collections of the State Historical Society of Wisconsin,* vol. 11. Madison, 1888): 451-401.

Walker, David A. "Chambers, John." *The Biographical Dictionary of Iowa.* Edited by David Hudson, Marvin Bergman and Loren Horton. Iowa City: University of Iowa Press, 2008.

Watkins, Albert. "Three Military Heroes of Nebraska." *Nebraska History and Record of Pioneer Days* 2 (October-December 1919): 3-5.

## BOOKS

Anderson, William and Albert J. Lobb. *A History of the Constitution of Minnesota with the First Verified Text.* Minneapolis: Univ. of Minnesota Research Publications, Studies in the Social Sciences 15, 1921.

Arthur, Elizabeth, ed. *Thunder Bay District 1821-1892: A Collection of Documents.* Toronto: Champlain Society, 1973.

Bailey, Thomas A. *A Diplomatic History of the American People,* 8th ed. New York: Appleton-Century-Crofts, 1969.

Bemis, Samuel Flagg. *The Diplomacy of the American Revolution,* rev. ed. Bloomington: Indiana University Press, 1957.

Berkeley, Edmund and Dorothy Smith Berkeley. *Dr. John Mitchell: The Man Who Made the Map of North America.* Chapel Hill: University of North Carolina Press, 1974.

Berthel, Mary Wheelhouse. *Horns of Thunder: The Life and Times of James M. Goodhue Including Seclections from His Writings.* St. Paul: Minnesota Historical Society, 1948.

Bevans, Charles I., comp. *Treaties and other International Agreements of the United States of America,* vol. 7, 12. Washington: Government Printing Office, 1971, 1974. (Chap. 1, note 6, 15)

Billington, Ray Allen. *Westward Expansion: A History of the American Frontier,* 4th ed. New York: Macmilllan Publishing Co., 1974.

*Biographical Directory of the United States Congress 1774-2005.* Washington: Government Printing Office, 2005.

Bird, William A. *The Boundary Line Between the British Provinces and the United States.* Buffalo, N.Y., 1864.

Bloom, John Porter, comp. and ed. *The Territorial Papers of the United States,* vol.28: *The Territory of Wisconsin 1839-1848 .* Washington: National Archives and

Records Service, 1975.

Bray, Martha Coleman. *Joseph Nicollet and His Map*. Philadelphia: American Philosophical Society, 1980.

Burt, Alfred L. *The Old Province of Quebec*. Reprint, New York: Russell and Russell, 1970.

_____ *The United States Great Britain and British North America: From the Revolution to the Establishment of Peace after the War of 1812*. Reprint, New York: Russell and Russell, 1961.

Chalmers, George. *A Collection of Treaties Between Great Britain and Other Powers*, vol. 1. London: J. Stockdale, 1790.

Clark, Charles E. *Maine: A Bicentennial History*. New York: W. W. Norton, 1977.

Classen, H. George. *Thrust and Counterthrust: The Genesis of the Canada-United States Boundary*. Chicago: Rand McNally & Co., 1965.

Commager, Henry Steele, ed. *Documents of American History, vol. 1: To 1898*, 7th ed. New York: Appleton-Century-Crofts, 1963.

Cullum, George W. *Biographical Register of the Officers and Graduates of the U. S. Military Academy . . .*, 3rd ed. Boston: Houghton, Mifflin, 1891.

Davidson, Gordon Charles. *The North West Company*. Berkeley: University of California, 1918.

*Debates and Proceedings: Constitutional Convention for the Territory of Minnesota* (Republican). St. Paul: George W. Moore, printer, Minnesotian office, 1858.

*The Debates and Proceedings of the Minnesota Constitutional Convention* (Democratic). St. Paul: Earle S. Goodrich, territorial printer, Pioneer and Democrat Office, 1857.

[Delafield, Joseph]. *The Unfortified Boundary: A Diary of the Survey of the Canadian Boundary Line from St. Regis to the Lake of the Woods. . . .* Edited by Robert McElroy and Thomas Riggs. New York: Privately printed.1943.

Dodds, J.S., ed. *et al. Original Instructions Governing the Public Land Surveys of Iowa: A Guide to Their Use in Resurveys of Public Lands*. Ames: Iowa Engineering Society, 1943.

Dunn, James Taylor. *Marine on St. Croix: From Lumber Village to Summer Haven 1838-1968*.

_____ *Marine on St. Croix*: Marine Historical Society, 1968.

Engelman, Fred L. *The Peace of Christmas Eve*. London: Rupert Hart-Davis, 1962.

Featherstonhaugh, [Albany]. *Narrative of the Operations of the British North American Boundary Commission, 1872-1876*. Woolwich, England,: A.W. & J.P. Jackson, 1876.

Folsom, W.H.C. *Fifty Years in the Northwest*. [St. Paul]: Pioneer Press Co., 1888.

Folwell, William Watts. *A History of Minnesota*, vols. 1-2. St. Paul: Minnesota Historical Society, 1921, 1924.

Gilman, Rhoda R. *Henry Hastings Sibley: Divided Heart*. St. Paul: Minnesota Historical Society Press, 2004.

Gluek, Alvin C. Jr. *Minnesota and the Manifest Destiny of the Canadian Northwest: A Study in Canadian-American Relations*. Toronto: University of Toronto Press, 1965.

Goodman, Nancy and Robert. *Joseph R. Brown Adventurer on the Minnesota Frontier 1820-1849*. Rochester, MN: Lone Oak Press, 1996.

_____. *Paddlewheels on the Upper Mississippi 1823-1854: How Steamboats Promoted Commerce and Settlement in the West*. Stillwater, MN: Washington County

Historical Society, 2003.

Goodman, Nancy, ed. *Minnesota Beginnings: Records of St. Croix County, Wisconsin Territory 1840-1849.* Stillwater, MN: Washington County Historical Society, 1999.

Gray, John Morgan. *Lord Selkirk of Red River.* Toronto: The Macmillan Company of Canada, 1963.

Gue, Benjamin F. *History of Iowa: From the Earliest Times to the Beginning of the Twentieth Century,* 4 vols. New York: The Century History Co., 1903.

Heitman, Francis B. *Historical Register and Dictionary of the United States Army,* 2 vols. Washington: Government Printing Office, 1903.

Hind, Henry Youle. *Northwest Territory, Reports of Progress.* Toronto: J. Lovell, 1859.

*Historic Fort William: Canada's Diamond Jubilee, 1867-1927.* Fort William, Ontario: Times-Journal Presses, 1927.

Holcombe, Return I. *Early History—Minnesota as a Territory.* Vol. 2 of Lucius F. Hubbard, *et al., Minnesota in Three Centuries 1655-1908.* New York: Publishing Society of Minnesota, 1908.

Holmquist, June Drenning and Jean A. Brookins. *Minnesota's Major Historic Sites: A Guide,* 2d ed. St. Paul: Minnesota Historical Society, 1972.

Horsman, Reginald. *The Causes of the War of 1812.* New York: Octagon Books, 1975.

Jackson, W. Turrentine. *Wagon Roads West: A Study of Federal Road Surveys and Construction in the Trans-Mississippi West, 1846-1869.* Berkeley: University of California Press, 1952.

Jackson, James A. *The Centennial History of Manitoba.* Winnipeg: Manitoba Historical Society, 1970.

Johannsen, Robert W. *Stephen A. Douglas.* New York: Oxford University Press, 1973.

Johnson, Hildegard Binder. *Order Upon the Land: The U.S. Rectangular Land Survey and the Upper Mississippi Country.* New York: Oxford University Press, 1976.

Jones, Howard. *To the Webster-Ashburton Treaty: A Study in Anglo-American Relations, 1783-1843.* Chapel Hill: University of North Carolina Press, 1977.

Kane, Lucile M., June D. Holmquist and Carolyn Gilman, eds. *The Northern Expeditions of Stephen H. Long: The Journals of 1817 and 1823 and Related Documents.* St. Paul: Minnesota Historical Society Press, 978.

Kane, Lucile M. *The Waterfall That Built a City: The Falls of St. Anthony in Minneapolis.* St. Paul: Minnesota Historical Society, 1966.

Kappler, Charles J. *Indian Affairs: Laws and Treaties,* vol. 2. Washington: Government Printing Office, 1904.

Keating, William H. *Narrative of an Expedition to the Source of St. Peter's River, Lake Winnepeek, Lake of the Woods, etc. Performed in the Year 1823,* reprint ed. Minneapois: Ross & Haines, 1959.

Keillor, Steven J. *Grand Excursion: Antebellum America Discovers the Upper Mississippi.* Afton, MN: Afton Historical Society Press, 2004.

Kellogg, Louise Phelps. *The British Régime in Wisconsin and the Northwest.* Madison: State Historical Society of Wisconsin, 1935.

Lass, William E. *Minnesota: A History,* 2d ed. New York: W. W. Norton, 1998.

_____. *Minnesota's Boundary with Canada: Its Evolution since 1783*. St. Paul: Minnesota Historical Society Press, 1980.

_____. *The Treaty of Traverse des Sioux*. St. Peter, MN: Nicollet County Historical Society Press, 2011.

Lavender, David. *The Fist in the Wilderness*. Garden City, NY: Doubleday & Co., 1964.

Mackenzie, Alexander. *Voyages from Montreal on the St. Laurence, Through the Continent of North America, to the Frozen and Pacific Oceans; In the Years 1789 and 1793*. London: T. Cadill, Jr. and W. Davis, 1801.

Manning, William R., ed. *Diplomatic Correspondence of the United States: Canadian Relations 1784-1860*, vol. 1. Washington: Carnegie Endowment for International Peace, 1940.

Mayer, George H. *The Republican Party 1854-1966*, 2d ed. New York: Oxford University Press, 1967.

Meyer, Roy W. *History of the Santee Sioux: United States Indian Policy on Trial*. Lincoln: University of Nebraska Press, 1967.

Miller, Hunter, ed. *Treaties and other International Acts of the United States of America*, vol. 3. Washington: Government Printing Office, 1931.

Morris, Richard B. *The Peacemakers: The Great Powers and American Independence*. New York: Harper & Row, 1965.

Moore, John Bassett. *History and Digest of the International Arbitrations to Which the United States Has Been a Party*, vol. 1. Washington: Government Printing Office, 1898.

Morton, W. L. *Manitoba: A History*, 2d ed. Toronto: University of Toronto Press, 1967.

Nute, Grace Lee. *Rainy River Country: A Brief History of the Region Bordering Minnesota and Ontario*. St. Paul: Minnesota Historical Society, 1950.

Palliser, John. *Papers Relative to Exploration . . . of British North America*. London: G.E. Eyre and W. Spottiswoode, 1859.

Parsons, John E. *West on the 49th Parallel: Red River to the Rockies, 1872-1876*. New York: William Morrow and Co.,1963.

Pelzer, Louis. *Augustus Caesar Dodge*. Iowa City: State Historical Society of Iowa, 1908.

Perkins, Bradford. *Prologue to War: England and the United States, 1805-1812*. Berkeley: University of California Press, 1961.

Phillips, Paul Chrisler. *The West in the Diplomacy of the American Revolution*. Reprint, New York: Russell and Russell, 1967.

Powell, J[ohn] H. *Richard Rush, Republican Diplomat 1780-1859*. Philadelphia: University of Pennsylvania Press, 1942.

Pratt, Julius W. *A History of United States Foreign Policy*, 3rd ed. Englewood Cliffs, N. J.: Prentice-Hall, 1972.

Quaife, Milo M., ed. *The Attainment of Statehood. Collections of the State Historical Society of Wisconsin*, vol. 29. (Madison, 1928).

_____. *The Convention of 1846. Collections of the State Historical Society of Wisconsin*, vol. 27. (Madison, 1919).

_____. *The Struggle Over Ratification 1846-1847. Collections of the State Historical Society of Wisconsin*, vol. 28. (Madison, 1920).

Raney, William Francis. *Wisconsin: A Story of Progress*. New York: Prentice-Hall, 1940.

*Report of the First Annual Meeting of the Iowa State Bar Association, Held at Des Moines, Iowa, June 27 and 28, 1895.* Davenport, IA: Egbert, Fidlar & Chambers, 1895.

Robertson, James A. *Louisiana under the Rule of Spain, France, and the United States 1785-1807.* Cleveland: Arthur H. Clark, 1911.

Royce, Charles C. *Indian Land Cessions in the United States,* reprint ed. New York: Arno Press and the New York Times, 1971.

Rush, Richard. *Memoranda of a Residence at the Court of London.* Philadelphis: Crey, Lea & Blanchard, 1833.

Sage, Leland L. *A History of Iowa.* Ames: Iowa State University Press, 1974.

*Secret Journals of the Acts and Proceedings of Congress.* Boston: Thomas B. Wait, 1820.

Shambaugh, Benj.[amin] F. *The Constitutions of Iowa.* Iowa City: State Historical Society of Iowa, 1934.

Shambaugh, Benjamin F. , comp. and ed. *Fragments of the Debates of the Iowa Constitutional Conventions of 1844 and 1846 Along with Press Comments and Other Materials on the Constitutions of 1844 and 1846.* Iowa City: State Historical Society of Iowa, 1900.

Shippee, Lester B. *Canadian-American Relations 1849-1874.* New Haven; Yale University Press, 1939.

Smith, Alice E. *The History of Wisconsin,* vol. 1: *From Exploration to Statehood.* Madison: State Historical Society of Wisconsin, 1973.

_____. *James Duane Doty: Frontier Promoter.* Madison: State Historical Society of Wisconsin, 1954.

Spry, Irene M., ed. *The Papers of the Palliser Expedition, 1857-1860.* Toronto: Champlain Society, 1968.

Strong, Moses M. *History of the Territory of Wisconsin from 1836 to 1848.* Madison: Democrat Printing Co., 1885.

Tenney, H[orace] A. and David Atwood. *Memorial Record of the Fathers of Wisconsin.* Madison: D. Atwood, 1880.

Walker, David A. *Iron Frontier: The Discovery and Early Development of Minnesota's Three Ranges.* St. Paul: Minnesota Historical Society Press, 1979.

Warner, Donald F. *The Idea of Continental Union: Agitation for the Annexation of Canada to the United States 1849-1893.* Lexington: University of Kentucky Press, 1960.

Williams, J. Fletcher. *A History of the City of Saint Paul, and of the County of Ramsey, Minnnesota. Collections of the Minnesota Historical Society,* vol. 4 (St. Paul 1876).

Woodbridge, Dwight E. and John S. Pardee, eds. *History of Duluth and St. Louis County,* 2 vols. Chicago: C. F. Cooper & Co., 1910.

Woolworth, Alan R. *The Genesis & Construction of the Winona & St. Peter Railroad, 1858-1873.* Marshall, MN: Society for the Study of Local & Regional History, Southwest State University, 2000.

## OTHER

"Consumer Price Index (Estimate) 1800-" Online.

[Dodge, William C.] *Address of the Majority Members of the Legislature to the People of Minnesota* [1857].

Hipsley, Kyle K. (acting commissioner, United States Section, IBC) Email message to William E. Lass, 13 March 2013.

"The History of Lower St. Louis River." Online, accessed 18 December 2010.

Lass, William E. Inspection of Lee monument. New Albin, Iowa, 03 November 2009.

_____. Inspection of tri-state marker, 29 June 2009.

_____. Telephone interview with Kyle Hipsley, deputy commissioner, United States Section, IBC. 06 January 1911.

_____. Tour of Lake of the Woods organized by David G. Malaher, Kenora, Ontario, Canada, 19-21 July 2010.

Nicollet, J[oseph] N. Map of the "Hydrographical Basin of the Upper Mississippi River." 1843.

Paul, Robert C. "The Rise of the Republican Party in Minnesota, 1855-1860." Unpublished Master of Science Thesis. Mankato State University, Mankato, Minnesota, 1994.

Sullivan, Peter, David Bernhart and Brian Ballantyne. "The Canada-United States Boundary: The Next Century." Online.

Treaty of San Ildefonso, The Avalon Project, *Documents in Law, History and Diplomacy*, Yale Law School. Online.

Wolf, Trevor (Winnebago County, Iowa, assistant engineer). Letter to William E. Lass, 29 December 2010.

# INDEX